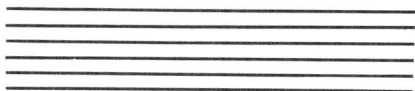

READING AND REASONING

JUDITH RESNICK
RHEA PAGE

MACMILLAN PUBLISHING COMPANY
NEW YORK

Collier Macmillan Publishers
London

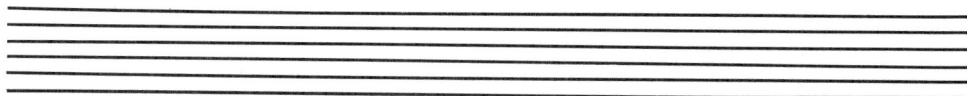

TO OUR FAMILIES
J. R.
R. P.

Copyright © 1984, Macmillan Publishing Company, a division of Macmillan, Inc.

Printed in the United States of America

Macmillan Publishing Company
866 Third Avenue, New York, New York 10022

Collier Macmillan Canada, Inc.

Library of Congress Cataloging in Publication Data

Resnick, Judith.
　Reading and reasoning.

　Includes index.
　1. College readers.　I. Page, Rhea.　II. Title.
PE1122.R45　1984　　　　428.6　　　　83-11980
ISBN　0-02-399320-0

Printing: 1 2 3 4 5 6 7 8　　　Year: 4 5 6 7 8 9 0 1 2

ISBN　0-02-399320-0

CREDITS AND ACKNOWLEDGMENTS

CHAPTER 1

Christopher Irby. "How Observant are You?" From *Cosmopolitan* (August 1981), p. 182. Reprinted by permission of Christopher Irby.

Elizabeth Loftus. *Eyewitness Testimony*. Cambridge, MA: Harvard University Press, 1979. Copyright © 1979 by the President and Fellows of Harvard University. Reprinted by permission.

A. Daniel Yarmey. *The Psychology of Eyewitness Testimony*. Adapted with permission of Macmillan Publishing Co., Inc. Copyright © 1979 by the Free Press, a division of Macmillan Publishing Co., Inc.

Stephen A. Saltzburg. *Introduction to American Criminal Procedure*. Adapted by permission. Copyright © 1980 by West Publishing Company. All rights reserved.

Elizabeth Loftus and Geoffrey Loftus. *Human Memory: The Processing of Information*. Hillsdale, NJ: Lawrence Erlbaum Associates, Inc., copyright © 1976. Reprinted with permission.

CHAPTER 2

Elisabeth Kübler-Ross. *On Death and Dying*. Reprinted with permission of Macmillan Publishing Co., Inc. Copyright © 1969 by Elisabeth Kübler-Ross.

Susan Jacoby. "Last Rights." From *McCall's* (June 1980), p. 170. Reprinted by permission of the author. Copyright © 1980 by Susan Jacoby.

Anonymous. *Death in the First Person*. Copyright © 1970, American Journal of Nursing Company. Reproduced with permission from the *American Journal of Nursing* (February 1970), Vol. 70, No. 2.

Michael Bayles. "The Value of Life—By What Standard?" From the *American Journal of Nursing* (December 1980), p. 2226.

Arthur J. Dyck. "The Value of Life: Two Contending Policies." From *Harvard Magazine* (January 1976). Copyright © 1976 *Harvard Magazine*. Reprinted by permission.

David Hendon. *Death as a Fact of Life*. New York: W. W. Norton & Co., Inc., 1973. Reprinted by permission.

American Friends Service Committee. *Who Shall Live? Man's Control Over Birth and Death*. New York: Hill and Wang, 1970.

Concern for Dying. "A Living Will." Reprinted with the permission of Concern for Dying, 250 West 57th Street, New York, NY 10107.

Elizabeth Ogg. "The Right to Die with Dignity." Public Affairs Pamphlet No. 587. Reprinted with permission of Public Affairs Committee, Inc., 381 Park Avenue South, New York, NY 10013.

Patrick Young. "What's Right?" From *The National Observer* (Sept. 27, 1975).

Anonymous. "I Had to Play God." From *Medical Economics* (Nov. 27, 1978). Copyright © 1978 and published by Medical Economics Company, Inc. at Oradell, NJ 07649. Reprinted by permission.

CHAPTER 3

Don Atyeo. *Blood and Guts: Violence in Sports.* New York: Paddington Press, 1979.

Jack R. Nation and Arnold D. Leunes. "Semi-Tough and Supernormal." From *Psychology Today* (Sept. 1981). Reprinted from *Psychology Today* magazine. Copyright © 1981 Ziff-Davis Publishing Company.

Lou Lipsitz. "To a Fighter Killed in the Ring." From *Cold Water*. Middletown, CT: Wesleyan University Press, 1963. Copyright © 1963 by Lou Lipsitz. Reprinted from *Cold Water* by permission of Wesleyan University Press. This poem first appeared in *San Francisco Review Annual*.

Eldon E. Snyder and Elmer Spreitzer. *Social Aspects of Sports*. Englewood Cliffs, NJ: Prentice-Hall, 1978. Copyright © 1978. Reprinted by permission of Prentice-Hall, Inc., Englewood Cliffs, NJ.

Skills for Learning (Foundation Series). Surrey, England: Thomas Nelson and Sons, Ltd.

G. Kenyon (ed.). *Contemporary Psychology of Sport*. Adapted from J. P. Scott. "Sport and Aggression." From *Contemporary Psychology of Sport*, edited by G. Kenyon. Copyright © 1970. Reprinted by permission of Athletic Institute, N. Palm Beach, Florida.

Jay J. Cookley. *Sports in Society: Issues and Controversies*. New York: C. V. Mosby Co., 1978.

Grantland Rice. © 1955 by A. S. Barnes & Co.

CHAPTER 4

T. Berry Brazelton. "What it Means to Adopt a Baby." From *Redbook* (April 1979). Reprinted by permission.

Margaret Mead and Rhoda Metraux. *Aspects of the Present*. From pp. 298–300, 303–304, "Adoption: Adopting Parents, Adopted Children—A Real Family?—September 1978" in *Aspects of the Present* by Margaret Mead and Rhoda Metraux. Copyright © 1980 by Mary Catherine Bateson Kassarjian and Rhoda Metraux. By permission of William Morrow and Company.

Annette Baran, Arthur Sorosky, and Reuben Pannor. "The Dilemma of Our Adoptees." From *Psychology Today* (December 1975). Reprinted from *Psychology Today* magazine. Copyright © 1975 Ziff-Davis Publishing Company.

Henry Ehrilch. *A Time to Search*. New York: Paddington Press, 1977.

Eda LeShan. "Should Adoptees Search for Their Real Parents." From *Woman's Day* (March 8, 1977).

Arthur D. Sorosky, Annette Baran, and Reuben Pannor. *The Adoption Triangle*. Copyright © 1978 by Arthur D. Sorosky, Annette Baran, and Reuben Pannor. Reprinted by permission of Doubleday and Company, Inc.

Shirley Cochrane. "Letters to the Other Mother." From *McCall's* (September 1980). Reprinted with permission.

Jill Krementz. *Blessed arc the Children*. New York: Knopf, 1982. Copyright © 1982 by Jill Krements. Reprinted by permission of Alfred A. Knopf, Inc.

Mary Howard. "I Take After Somebody; I Have Real Relatives; I Possess a Real Name." From *Psychology Today* (December 1975). Reprinted from *Psychology Today* magazine. Copyright © 1975 Ziff-Davis Publishing Company.

CHAPTER 5

"Are You a Drug Quiz Whiz?" U.S. Department of Health and Human Services Publication No. 81-1082.

Cartoon. From *The Wall Street Journal*. Reprinted with the permission of Cartoon Features Syndicate.

Jeremy Larner. *The Addict in the Street*. Reprinted by permission of Grove Press, Inc. Copyright © 1964 by Grove Press, Inc.

William Novak. *High Culture: Marijuana in the Lives of Americans*. New York: Random House, 1980. Copyright © 1980 by William Novak. Reprinted by permission of Alfred A. Knopf, Inc.

Joseph Brenner, M. D., Robert Coles, M. D., and Dermot Meagher. *Drugs and Youth: Medical, Psychiatric, and Legal Facts*. Reprinted by permission of Liveright Publishing Corporation. Copyright © 1970 by Liveright Publishing Corporation.

Barbara Millbauer. *Drug Abuse and Addiction*. Copyright © 1970 by Barbara Millbauer. Reprinted with permission of Crown Publishers.

Daniel A. Girdano and Dorothy Dusek-Girdano. *Drug Education: Content and Method*. Copyright © 1972 Addison-Wesley, Reading, MA, pp. 68, 73, 76–77. Reprinted with permission.

"For Parents Only: What You Need to Know About Marijuana." U.S. Department of Health and Human Services Publication No. 81-909.

Margaret O. Hyde. *Mind Drugs*. Copyright © 1981. Used with the permission of McGraw-Hill Book Company.

"Drug Abuse Prevention for Your Family." U.S. Department of Health and Human Services Publication No. 78-584.

Spencer Rathus. *Psychology*. New York: Holt, Rinehart & Winston, 1981.

Whitney North Seymour. *The Young Die Quietly*. New York: Wm. Morrow & Co., 1971.

The Congressional Digest. "Controversy Over Policy Controlling Marijuana Use—Pros and Cons" (February 1979). Congressional Digest Corporation, Washington, D.C. Reprinted by permission.

Milton Mezzrow and Bernard Wolfe. *Really the Blues*. Copyright © 1946 by Milton Mezzrow and Bernard Wolfe, copyright renewed 1974. Reprinted by the permission of the Harold Matson Co., Inc.

CHAPTER 6

Ken Auletta. *The Underclass*. Copyright © 1982. Reprinted with the permission of Random House, Inc. Originally published in *The New Yorker* (November 23, 1981).

Kathleen Kroll. "American Pie, in Some Sky." From *The New York Times* (March 15, 1981). Copyright © 1981 by The New York Times Company. Reprinted by permission.

CHAPTER 7

Frederick Brown. "The Weapon." Reprinted by permission of the author and the author's agents, Scott Meredith Literary Agency, Inc., 845 Third Avenue, New York, New York 10022.

Children of Hiroshima. Copyright © 1980 Publishing Committee for "Children of Hiroshima." Reprinted with permission of publisher.

CHAPTER 8

Robert J. Sternberg. "Who's Intelligent?" From *Psychology Today* (April 1982).

Dennis Coon. *Introduction to Psychology: Exploration and Application*. Reprinted by permission. Copyright © 1977 by West Publishing Company. All rights reserved.

Gail K. Gaines. *Brain Power: Understanding Human Intelligence*. New York: Franklin Watts, 1979.

Reader's Guide to Periodical Literature. Copyright © 1983 by the H. W. Wilson Company. Material reproduced by permission of the publisher.

Evelyn Sharp. *The I.Q. Cult*. New York: Coward, McCann, and Geoghegan, 1972.

N. J. Block and Gerald Dworkin. *The I.Q. Controversy*. New York: Pantheon, 1976.

Benjamin Fine. *Stranglehold of the I.Q.* Copyright © 1975 by Benjamin Fine. Reprinted by permission of Doubleday and Company, Inc.

Erma Bombeck. "Geniuses' Sperm Bank a Dumb Idea."

Paul R. Erlich and S. Shirley Feldman. *The Race Bomb*. New York: Quandrangle/N.Y. Times Book Co., 1977.

Arthur Whimbey, with Linda Shaw Whimbey. *Intelligence Can Be Taught*. New York: Dutton, 1975.

H. J. Eysenck and Leon Kamin. *The Intelligence Controversy*. New York: Wiley, 1981.

Daniel Cohen. *Intelligence—What is It?* Copyright © 1974 by Daniel Cohen. Reprinted by permission of the publisher, M. Evans and Co., Inc., New York, NY 10017.

David C. McClelland. From remarks given at the Educational Testing Service in Princeton, NJ, on January 4, 1971. In *Contrast and Controversy in Modern Psychology* (Daniel P. Kimble, Ed.) Goodyear Publishing Co., Inc. Reprinted with the permission of David C. McClelland.

Dr. Paul Jacobs. *Up the I.Q.—How to Raise Your Child's I.Q.* New York: Wyden Books, 1977.

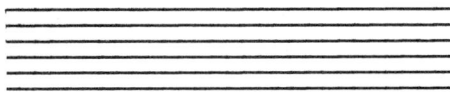

PREFACE

This book is based on the premise that, for meaningful learning to take place, material must be relevant to students. Therefore we have organized the book around eight topics which we have found to be of great interest to young adults. Once students begin reading the material, they quickly become involved in exploring the ideas presented. Students are introduced to each of these topics through a series of questions which tap their own related knowledge and experiences. These introductory questions are designed to lead students to discover that they already know something about each topic. Reading then becomes an active process—an interaction between the reader and the author.

Rather than using the usual approach of introducing skills in isolation, with disconnected practice readings, we have integrated the important reading skills with the material of each chapter. A Skills Chart which follows lists each skill, indicating where it is first introduced and where it is practiced in subsequent chapters. We believe that this approach of introducing skills in a meaningful context makes sense to students and is therefore more effective.

In each chapter a variety of viewpoints is presented and students are led to analyze, compare, and reflect upon the merits of the various arguments. In effect, each student will explore the assumptions that form his or her own opinions. Only when facts are separated from assumptions can the student begin to develop critical reading skills.

In the area of vocabulary development, students are asked to make individual choices, learning those words that he or she needs. Tear-out sheets are provided at the back of the book for recording these words and their definitions.

Extended readings and a bibliography are included at the close of each chapter to encourage students to read further in particular areas of individual interest.

We would like to thank the many reviewers who offered their time and expertise in reading and commenting on the manuscript: Robert Tierney of the Center for the Study of Reading at the University of Illinois; John Readance of the University of Georgia; Martha Berry of Vincennes University; Barbara Schwom of Northwestern University; Deborah Blake of DePaul

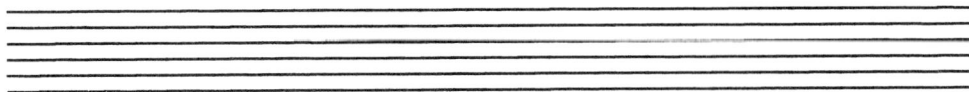

University; Myrna Charry of Queensborough Community College; Rose Ortiz of the College of Staten Island; Miriam Chaplin of Rutgers University (Camden Campus); and Miriam Goldberg of Teacher's College at Columbia University. We also wish to express our gratitude to our editor, Susan Didriksen. Her support and enthusiasm during the writing of this book is greatly appreciated.

Judith Resnick
Rhea Page

SKILLS

Chapter	Previewing	Headings	Italics	Prereading Questions	Signal Words	Outline using Headings	Mnemonics	Comparison	Main Idea	Inferences	Examples	Underlining	Categorizing	Points of View	Cause-Effect	Fact-Opinion	Definitions	Hypothetical Thinking	Library Skills—Research	Test-Taking Strategies	Graphs	Taking Notes
1	*	*	*	*	*	*	*	*														
2	✓	✓		✓				✓	*				✓									
3	✓	✓	✓			✓			✓	*	*	*	✓									
4					✓				✓	✓	✓	✓		*								
5	✓	✓			✓			✓	✓	✓	✓	✓	✓	✓	*		✓					
6								✓		✓	✓		✓	✓		*						
7								✓		✓	✓	✓	✓	✓	✓		*	*				
8	✓	✓		✓				✓	✓	✓		✓	✓	✓	✓		✓		*	*	*	*

*First introduced.

TO THE STUDENT

One of the most important skills you need to be a successful student is the ability to figure out the meaning of unfamiliar words. *Using the dictionary* is one method you have probably used many times as a means of learning new words. In your experience, what are some of the advantages and disadvantages of this method?

Advantages	*Disadvantages*

A second method, perhaps the simplest and most direct, is to *recognize a definition when provided by the author*. In this case, you do not need to refer to another source such as the dictionary in order to find the meaning.

Textbooks frequently provide the meanings for technical terms that pertain to the subject. It is important to master these terms if you are to understand the subject. Sometimes the definitions are printed in the margins of the book, at other times they are given in a glossary (a kind of minidictionary), and sometimes they appear in the text itself. Once an author of a textbook has decided how he or she wants to present these terms to the reader, the approach is usually the same throughout the book. Therefore, when you begin reading a textbook, you should determine the method used.

Using context clues is a third way to get at the meaning of unknown words. You have used this technique most of your life, although you might not have been aware of it. The following examples will help you understand how context clues enable you to understand unfamiliar words.

1. She was in a *quandary*.

If you do not know the meaning of the italicized word, can you define it from the sentence above? _____ Explain. _____

_____

_____

2. She was in a *quandary* about whether to enroll in a math or science course.

Can you define the italicized word from the sentence above? _____ What do you think the word *quandary* means? _____

_____

You used context clues in sentence 2 to get the meaning of the word *quandary*. Try another one.

1. He was *vulnerable*.

Can you define the underlined word? _____

2. He was *vulnerable* after his divorce and, for a long time, was afraid to date women.

Can you define the italicized word? _____ Why? _____

_____

The context provided in the second sentence gives you a better idea of the meaning of the word than does the first sentence. You still may not be absolutely certain of the meaning. The more often you hear and read a word in context, the clearer the meaning becomes. If you feel the need, you can refer to a dictionary to check out your guess.

What do you think *context clues* means? _____

_____

_____

As you read this book, there will be many words that you do not know. These will be different from the words other students in your class do not know. At the end of the book, you will find tear-out sheets for *your* words and their meanings. Here are some suggestions as to how you can use them.

- As you read, underline the words you do not know. It is not necessary to interrupt your reading to look up words in a dictionary. This would only interfere with your involvement in the material.
- Try to determine the meaning of words from the context (the sentence in which the word appears).
- When you have finished reading a selection, write the words you have underlined on one of the tear-out sheets. Use the dictionary to find the meaning of the words.

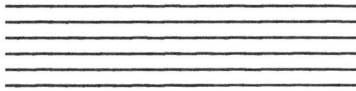

CONTENTS

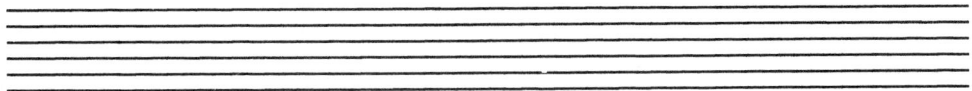

He who decides a case without hearing the other side . . . though he decides justly, cannot be considered just.

—*Seneca*

CHAPTER 1

Photo Researchers, Inc.

Of all liars, the smoothest and
most convincing is memory.
—John Ehrlichman

EYEWITNESS TESTIMONY

This chapter explores the topics of memory and eyewitness testimony. First you will engage in several activities which will show you how well your *own* memory works. Then you will read three selections that describe the ways in which one's memory actually functions and why the testimony of eyewitnesses is not always completely reliable.

In addition, you will discover some techniques for following an author's writing. This should be of help to you in reading other school textbooks. These techniques include previewing, asking yourself questions before reading, and being aware of special words an author uses to help you follow his or her ideas.

Finally, this chapter includes a section on mnemonics—memory tricks you can use when studying for exams.

Now let's see how well your own memory works!

How Observant Are You?

The red half of a Campbell's soup label is on the . . .
    a. Top
    b. Bottom

From memory, draw the shape of the "head" of your front-door key in the space below .

Which faucet do you normally turn to get hot water?

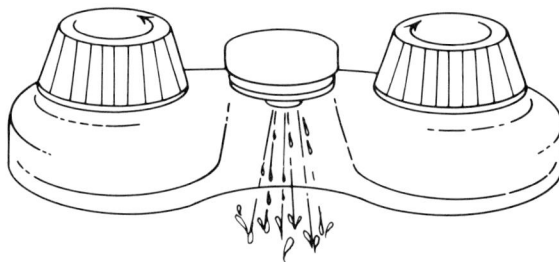

How many digits are in your Social Security number?
    a. 7
    b. 8
    c. 9
    d. 10

Bananas, of course, aren't round. How many sides do they usually have?
    a. 3
    b. 4
    c. 5
    d. 6

[Christopher Irby]

Look at the following picture. When your instructor calls time, turn the page.

Photo Researchers, Inc.

List as many details of the picture as you can recall. Do not refer back to the picture.

_____

_____

_____

_____

_____

_____

_____

Now look back at the picture and check the number of items you have listed correctly.

Look at picture 2 carefully for 30 seconds. You will be asked to recall some of the details in it.

Photo Researchers, Inc.

The following eight statements are about the picture on the preceding page. Indicate in the blank space next to each statement whether each is true or false. Do not look back at the picture.

_____ 1. The produce truck comes from Atlanta, Georgia.

_____ 2. Both of the children in the picture are wearing shorts.

_____ 3. There is a soda bottle resting on a crate.

_____ 4. All of the vegetables are in square wooden crates.

_____ 5. The woman selling produce is wearing glasses.

_____ 6. There are only two scales in the picture.

_____ 7. Some of the fruits and vegetables are protected from the sun by large umbrellas.

_____ 8. There are four men in the picture.

_____ 9. Tomatoes are being sold at 5 lbs for $1.

_____ 10. The woman is carrying a straw bag.

Now refer back to the picture to see how many items you recalled correctly.

You probably have some correct answers as well as some incorrect ones. Those items which you identified correctly are not necessarily the same ones which the student seated next to you recalled.

Look again at each of the pictures and try to explain why some things were overlooked and others remembered incorrectly.

Picture 1

1. How many items did you remember correctly? _____

2. How many items did you remember incorrectly? _____

3. List some of the reasons which you think caused you to remember incor-

   rectly. _____

   _____

   _____

_____

_____

_____

_____

Picture 2

1. How many of your answers were correct? _____

2. Can you think of some reasons for your mistakes? _____

_____

_____

_____

_____

_____

Your recall of the details of the pictures is similar to your recall of an actual event. The memory "tests" you just completed give you some idea of how effectively (or ineffectively) your memory works.

If you were an eyewitness to an accident or crime, your recall of the event could be crucial. An eyewitness to an actual event might not remember all the important details, or might remember them inaccurately, for the same reasons you listed in the previous exercise. Such inaccuracy could lead to the imprisonment of an innocent person.

PREVIEWING

Do you look through a magazine at the newstand before deciding whether or not you want to buy it? What you are doing is *previewing* the magazine. You look at it in order to decide if it contains material you want to read.

Do you ever look at the TV listings in a newspaper to plan the programs you will watch that evening? Looking at the entire list helps you organize your time. If you decide to watch a movie that runs for two hours, you know that you will not be able to watch some other program during that time. You preview the TV listings in order to organize your time.

Previewing a section in a textbook can also be helpful. By looking at the material *before* you begin reading, you get a sense of how it is organized. When you do begin reading, you know what to expect. You will also notice some aids the author includes to help you follow the organization of the material.

Look at Selection 1 and notice the different methods the author uses to help you understand the material.

- One is the use of headings. What makes the headings in this selection identifiable? _They are in bold print_

  How many headings are there in this selection? _4_

- Printing certain words in *italics* is another technique used by the author. Why do you think she has used this kind of print?

  to emphisize the word for understanding

Most authors of college textbooks use headings and italics to help you organize and understand the information. You could think of a textbook chapter as a jigsaw puzzle. When putting together a puzzle, most people begin by constructing the outside edges or frame. It is then easier to fit the pieces together. The headings of a textbook chapter are similar to the outside frame of a puzzle. If you organize these headings into some meaningful arrangement—either in a list or diagram—the information presented will make sense to you.

PREREADING QUESTIONS

There are probably many times when you ask yourself questions about an experience before it happens. For instance, did you have any questions in your mind before the first class of this course?

What questions did you have? _How can I improve my reading skills._

Before looking at the daily newspaper, what questions do you ask yourself? _I ask myself which articles interest me, what the importance of the event is._

Formulating questions before any new experience is common to most people. It is an attempt to make sense out of the unknown. By asking questions first, you are actually trying to predict what will happen.

Reading a textbook is similar to any other new experience. You are faced with the task of making sense out of material that is usually unfamiliar to you. If you create questions before you begin reading, you will provide yourself with a reason to read—that is, to find the answers to your own questions. This will help you concentrate on the material.

Look at Selection 1 on page 9. Write the name of each stage of memory on the line provided. Then write a few questions which you would like answered about each stage.

Stage 1: _Acquisition - how do I pull information out of a article_
retention - how can I put it in my memory
retrieval - whats the easiest way to recall

Stage 2: _retention - how can I put it in my memory_

Stage 3: _Retrieval - whats the easiest way to recall information_

SELECTION 1

Overview

When we experience an important event, we do not simply record that event in memory as a videotape recorder would. The situation is much more complex. Nearly all of the theoretical analyses of the process divide it into three stages. . . . First, there is the *acquisition* stage—the perception of the original event—in which information is encoded, laid down, or entered into a person's memory system. Second, there is the *retention* stage, the period of time that passes between the event and the eventual recollection of a particular piece of information. Third, there is the *retrieval* stage during which a person recalls stored information. This three-stage analysis is so central to the concept of the human memory that it is virtually universally accepted among psychologists.

Acquisition

When a complex event is experienced, some of the features of that experience are extracted first to be stored and later to be utilized in arriving at action decisions. Early on, in the acquisition stage, the observer must decide to which aspects of the visual stimulus he should attend. Our visual environment typically contains a vast amount of information, and the proportion of information that is actually perceived is very small. The process of deciding what to attend to can be broken down into an even finer series of decisions, each corresponding to where a person will make his next eye fixation.

Retention

Once the information associated with an event has been encoded or stored in memory, some of it may remain there unchanged while some may not. Many things can happen to a witness during this crucial retention stage. The witness may engage in conversations about the event, or overhear conversations, or read a newspaper story—all of these can bring about powerful and unexpected changes in the witness's memory.

Retrieval

Finally, at any time after an event a witness may be asked questions about it. At this point the witness must recreate from long-term memory that portion of the event needed to answer a specific question. This recreation may be based both on information acquired during the original experience and on information acquired subsequently. In other words, both the acquisition and the retention stages are crucial to what happens during retrieval. The answer that a person gives is based on this recreation.

[Elizabeth Loftus, *Eyewitness Testimony*]

Check each of the following statements which you believe is correct according to the information given in the preceding selection. Explain your choices on the lines provided.

_____ 1. In general, people do not notice many things in their environment.

_____

_____

_____

✓ 2. Talking with someone about a past event may alter one's memory of that event. _Recalling an event with someone can alter the persons memory of it_

_____

✓ 3. Both acquiring and storing information affect the eventual recall of an event. _the better you aquire and then store information the better you Remember it_

_____

10   **Reading and Reasoning**

_F_ 4. Memories remain unchanged. _Memories can_
change if a person discusses
a memory

_____ 5. Seeing is believing. _____

SIGNAL WORDS

You have already read about the importance of previewing and self-questioning as aids to following an author's writing. Another aid often included in textbooks, and one you can use to help follow an author's writing, is *signal words*. These are words that let you know what to expect as you read.

Lists

One common group of signal words acts as a clue to a series or list of items. Notice how the words *first*, *second*, and *finally* indicate the three stages of memory in the following paragraph.

> First, the witness must have been able to see the event. Second memory itself has considerable psychological importance with respect to eyewitness testimony. Finally, a third factor of psychological importance is the communication process itself.

In the following paragraph, the words *one* and *the other* are signals to items in a list.

> A popular theory of forgetting is called the interference theory, which states that you forget because other information gets in the way of retrieving the desired information. There are two types of interference. One is called proactive interference (information already stored in memory interferes with the remembering of new material). The other type is called retroactive interference (the learning of new information affects the retention of previously learned information).

Other words that signal a list or series of items include:

next	also	in addition to
last	furthermore	moreover
then	and	likewise

Comparison

Some signal words let you know that two ideas are being compared. In the next example, the phrase *on the other hand* clues you to such a comparison.

> When early learning makes later learning easier, it is called positive transfer of training. . . . It may take you several weeks to learn to ride a bicycle, but once you have mastered it, you can learn to ride a three-speed or a ten-speed or even perhaps a motorcycle in a much shorter time, thanks to positive transfer. On the other hand, if you learn to ride a bicycle with foot brakes and then switch to one with hand brakes, you may find yourself frantically pedalling backward at first every time you want to slow down: This is negative transfer.
>
> [James Geiwitz, *Looking at Ourselves*]

Here's another paragraph which contains a signal word, *but*, to indicate a comparison. This time the comparison is between the past and present attitude of psychologists toward memory "tricks."

> There are several "tricks" that allow one to memorize large amounts of information with relative ease. Psychologists have typically viewed these tricks as irrelevant to "real" psychology, but lately scientists have become extremely interested in what they call "mnemonic devices."
>
> [James Geiwitz, *Looking at Ourselves*]

Other words that signal a comparison or contrast are:

however	in spite of	despite
yet	instead	nevertheless
although	in contrast	on the contrary
but	similarly	notwithstanding

Examples

Another group of signal words lets you know that an example is being given. Notice the phrase *to illustrate* in the following excerpt.

> To illustrate the psychological processes just discussed, suppose that our witness is asked by an attorney to state the color of the face of the person he saw commit a shooting.

In the next sample paragraph, underline the words that introduce the example.

In retrograde amnesia, shock or some other source of trauma prevents recently learned material from being recalled, suggesting that memories must be allowed to rest undisturbed for a while if they are to enter long-term memory. For instance, a football player who is knocked unconscious, or a victim of an automobile accident, may be unable to recall events occurring a few minutes prior to the accident.

[Spencer A. Rathus, *Psychology*]

Here are some other words that signal an example:

for example   such as   like   to demonstrate

Cause-Effect

The following two sentences express a cause–effect relationship. Can you combine them using the word *because*?

The football player was knocked unconscious.
He suffered retrograde amnesia.

_____

_____

Here's another example.

As a result of knowing how to ride a bicycle, you can learn how to ride a motorcycle in a much shorter time.

Some other words that signal cause-effect relationships are:

therefore	as a result	since
consequently	thus	so

Signal words let you know when you should slow down and when you can move ahead quickly. Understanding them will help you to be a more efficient reader.

Here is another author's description of the memory process of an eyewitness. There are no headings as there were in the previous selection. The author uses signal words to help you follow the organization of the writing and to identify the three stages of memory. Underline the three signal words used to introduce each stage.

SELECTION 2

When a witness is called to testify in court that he saw "Mr. Brown shoot Mr. Jones," a large number of psychological factors influence his report. In order for the witness to testify meaningfully, we must assume the following conditions.

First, the witness must have been able to see the event. Remembered information is based upon observation, but in everyday experience observations are not planned and deliberate. In other words, they are not intentionally studied and stored for subsequent testing and questioning. How complete and accurate the observations were is questionable. Since his perceptual experiences are private events which are dependent upon the capabilities of his sensory and motor systems, we can never share the experience itself. We can, however, learn about his observations through what he reports. Unfortunately, the report may or may not be accurate.

The second factor having considerable psychological importance with respect to eyewitness testimony is memory. The witness must be able to recall the events. However, the long delay between the time of observing the critical incident and testifying in court can only interfere with remembering. At one time psychologists thought of memory as the records of sensory experiences etched onto the mind. These memory traces were thought to be more or less permanent. Psychologists no longer believe this. Instead, memory is now explained by some as a system of structures through which information sequentially passes. As information moves through these structures, it is constantly being changed by later information. Moreover, the traces of these encodings are susceptible to all forms of interference and decay. According to this theory, a witness is continually being subjected to conditions which have a high likelihood of influencing his memory. Being asked questions by the police, reading accounts of the crime in the daily newspaper, engaging in discussions with friends and acquaintances, and all of the everyday experiences of living which normally affect memory are possible sources of bias, distortion, and forgetting. Once the witness is in the courthouse and takes the stand, a new set of events will act to confuse his recall. The testimony that the witness gives is subject to cross-examination, which is intended to determine the reliability of his reports and to separate truth from error. However, the questions of cross-examination also may act to distort memory.

Finally, a third factor of psychological importance is the communications process itself. The witness must be able to tell the court in his own words what he saw and heard. Witnesses must be able to find the correct phrases and sentences which convey most accurately the meanings of their experiences. Memory and language obviously overlap a great deal, and some psychologists are convinced that what we see in the world and what we think about these experiences are dependent upon the language of our culture. In order for the judge and the jury to understand the witness, the words that he chooses must be free of double or multiple meanings. This problem may appear to be simple, but the consequences of different interpretations given to witnesses' statements are profound. Again, the cross-examination will influence the reports of the witness. A good lawyer wants to destroy the credibility of the opposing witness. He wants to show that the knowledge of the witness is doubtful or wrong and therefore untrustworthy.

To illustrate the psychological processes just discussed, suppose that our witness is asked by an attorney to state the color of the face of the person he saw commit a shooting. Most people would agree that the response "Black" is simple, direct, and easily understood. Nevertheless, the reliability of this statement is debatable. . . . Further questioning of the witness may reveal that even his answer "Black" is suspicious. How good is his eyesight? How much light was available in the area of the crime? What distance was he from the crime? How many other persons were present when the crime was committed? Were they black, or were there whites also in the general vicinity? What physical features of faces determine whether or not a face is considered black, brown, swarthy, or white? And finally, what are the attitudes of the witness toward blacks, and how familiar in his everyday experiences is he with blacks? The answers to questions such as these help to establish the credibility of witnesses, and courts judge the truth or validity of witnesses' perceptions, memory and accuracy of communication on the basis of them.

[A. Daniel Yarmey, *The Psychology of Eyewitness Testimony*]

Check each of the following statements which you believe is correct according to the information given in the preceding selection. Explain your choices on the lines provided.

_____ 1. An event must be seen before it can be remembered.

_____ 2. Seeing is a personal experience.

_____ 3. Time distorts memory.

_____ 4. Cross-examination of a witness may cause his/her recall to become distorted.

_____ 5. What we see is influenced by what we think.

_____ 6. A statement may mean different things to different people.

_____ 7. The personal prejudices of a witness may affect his/her recall of an event.

You have read two different explanations of the memory process. The authors have used different terms for each of three separate stages. It is often advantageous to read several sources on a given topic you are studying. By doing this you gain familiarity with the material. At times you will find one author's discussion more understandable than another's.

But it is not enough merely to read the material. It is important to see the similarities and differences in the information offered. By comparing them you will be thinking critically, which, in turn, improves your understanding.

Compare the three stages of memory discussed in the two selections you have just read by listing the terms each author uses to describe the three stages of memory.

Selection 1   *Selection 2*

Stage 1: _____   _____ _____

Stage 2: _____   _____

Stage 3: _____   _____

Are the three stages of memory basically the same in each? _____

Which of the two selections did you find more understandable? _____

Why? _____

_____

_____

_____

_____

Psychologists have investigated the ways in which memory functions with respect to the reliability of eyewitness testimony. The following selection deals with some of the influences which can change the way a person perceives an event.

SELECTION 3

[Years ago psychologists] assumed that the human brain operated more or less as a mechanical recording device. [They believed that] a person saw everything and recorded this information on a memory "tape." When necessary to describe a past event, the person simply selected the appropriate memory tape and played it back, producing a faithful recounting of the original perception.

Over the past half-century, however, psychological research emphatically has demonstrated the invalidity of this conception and has revealed that the "videotape recorder" analogy is misleading in three respects.... First, perception is not a mere passive recording of an event. Instead, it is a constructive process by which people choose consciously and unconsciously to attend selectively to only a few environmental stimuli. Second, over time, the representation of an event stored in memory undergoes constant change; some details are added or altered unconsciously, while others simply are forgotten. Finally, the way in which information is remembered is almost always distorted.

[Stephen A. Saltzburg, *Introduction to American Criminal Procedure*]

Signal words are used in the paragraph above, as they were in the previous selection. Again, circle each of the signal words and underline each main point. Does the information in the paragraph seem familiar to you? If it does, explain why.

_____ No _____

Look at the remainder of this selection. How can you tell the difference between the headings and subheadings? List all the techniques the author has used to help you differentiate between them.

_____

_____

_____

_____

Before reading, use the headings and subheadings to make an outline of the text.

I. _____

    A. _____

    B. _____

    C. _____

    D. _____

    E. _____

    F. _____

II. _____

    A. _____

    B. _____

III. _____

    A. _____

    B. _____

C. _____

D. _____

Your instructor will now organize the class into groups. Each group will be responsible for reading one part of the text and explaining the contents of that section to the rest of the class.

1. Perception of the Original Event

Perceptual Selectivity. People can perceive only a limited number of simultaneous events in the environment at any time; the number of these that can be encoded in memory is even smaller. In order to cope with these limitations, an observer develops unconscious strategies to aid in the selectivity of perceptual processes and to concentrate attention on the most necessary and useful details. In short, a human must "learn" how to perceive efficiently.

Unfortunately, the resulting perceptual shortcuts and strategies, although generally effective in daily life, often lead to inaccurate perceptions when the eye must make the fine distinctions necessary to observe and recognize faces accurately. Furthermore, witnesses generally are unaware of the distortions produced by these perceptual strategies. . . .

The major problem this poses is the failure to observe the details of an event, especially those that are at first unimportant but later assume great significance. The ability to perceive and recall such details plays a crucial role in eyewitness identifications, yet numerous studies have confirmed that even trained observers find it difficult to describe such obvious physical characteristics as height, weight, and age.

Time Perception. Humans also find it especially difficult to perceive time accurately, that is, to estimate either the duration of an event or the interval between successive events. Studies have shown that people tend to judge time by the amount of activity occurring; during sudden, action-packed events such as crimes, people almost always overestimate the length of time involved because the flurry of activity leads them to conclude that a significant amount of time has passed. Time is also perceived to pass more slowly when the observer is caught in an anxiety-producing situation; the desire to "escape" makes it seem as if the unpleasant event is lasting longer than it actually is.

Poor Observation Conditions. Many identification errors are due to the circumstances of the observation. A major factor influencing perception is the duration of the observation period. Crimes in which the primary evidence is an eyewitness identification characteristically are brief, fast-moving events; the victim and witnesses consequently will have difficulty getting a sufficiently good "look" to allow them to process enough visual features of the event and the offender to make a reliable subsequent recognition.

Furthermore, visual efficiency drops dramatically when the observation occurs under poor or rapidly changing lighting conditions or over great distances, or in connection with distracting noises or other activity, forcing the already limited attentional capacities to be spread even thinner.

Stressful Situation. Another important environmental factor limiting the accuracy of perception is the stressful situation facing the victim. Although judges and juries often may be convinced by the victim's assertion that "I was so frightened that his face is etched in my memory forever," psychological research demonstrates that perception actually *decreases* when the observer is in a fearful or anxiety-provoking situation.

Studies have shown that an increase in anxiety generally produces a number of certain physiological responses. The frightened victim or eyewitness may report increases in heart rate, rapid breathing and excessive perspiration, but usually does not notice that the anxiety also has caused fixation of the eyes. This fixation reduces visual acuity.

Excessive anxiety also produces an attempt to cope with a frightening situation simply by rejecting it. This phenomenon of "perceptual defense" may cause a frightened victim to "close" his or her mind—and eyes—in order to block out and avoid recognition of stimuli that might produce anxiety. Even when still able to pay attention to the environment, the witness will concentrate on those aspects of a situation that are more important to his safety. Perception is so narrowed to this aspect of the experience that all others are missed.

Expectancy. Because the human mind can process only a small portion of what is visible at any given time, it develops the ability to form conclusions about what has been perceived based on limited amounts of sensory information. In essence, witnesses unconsciously reconstruct what *has* occurred from what they assume *must have* occurred. Consequently, they exhibit a pronounced tendency to perceive the expected.

Cross-Racial Identifications. Finally, considerable evidence indicates that people are poorer at identifying members of another race than of their own. Some studies have found that, in the United States at least, whites have greater difficulty recognizing black faces than vice versa. Moreover, the ability to perceive the physical characteristics of a person from another racial group apparently does not improve significantly upon increased contact with other members of that race. Because many crimes are cross-racial, these factors may play an important part in reducing the accuracy of eyewitness perception.

2. Encoding and Storage in Memory

Memory Decay over Time. People forget both quickly and easily. The more time that has elapsed since the perception of some event, the poorer a person's memory is of that event. Particularly with visual images, memory begins to decay within minutes of the event, so that considerable memory loss probably occurs during the many days—and often months—that typically elapse between the offense and an eyewitness identification of the suspect in a criminal case.

Filling Gaps in Memory. The mind combines all the information acquired about a particular event into a single storage "bin," making it difficult to distinguish what the witness saw originally from what he or she learned later.

In analyses of eyewitness reports in criminal cases we have seen the reports get more accurate, more complete, and less ambiguous as the witness moves from the initial police report through grand-jury questioning to testimony at the trial. The process of filling in is an efficient way to remember but it can lead to unreliable recognition testing; the witness may adjust his or her memory to fit the available suspects or pictures. The witness need not be lying; he may be unaware he is distorting or reconstructing his memory. In his very effort to be conscientious he may fabricate parts of his recall to make a chaotic memory seem more plausible to the people asking questions.

3. Retrieval of Information from Memory.

Inadequacy of Verbal Descriptions. When a witness is asked by the police to describe in his own words the event that occurred, the results are often vague and incomplete. On the other hand, as the questions become more structured in order to achieve completeness, the resulting responses become more inaccurate, because witnesses may feel compelled to answer questions completely in spite of incomplete knowledge.

Suggestion in the Composition of an Identification Test. In order to obtain identifications, police must rely on structured "recognition" tests such as lineups and photo display even though these procedures are notoriously unreliable. The witness often may treat the task as one of identifying the individual who best matches the witness' recollection of the culprit, even if that match is not perfect, rather than as one of identifying the true criminal.

The reliability of an identification made at a lineup, therefore, depends upon the similarity between the suspect and the other members of the lineup. If, for example, the witness described the assailant as "tall," and only one of the participants in the lineup could be considered tall, then the choice of that one individual has little meaning for the purpose of identifying the true criminal. In addition to the tendency of the defendant in a lineup to be dangerously dissimilar in overall physical characteristics to the other participants, he may also have one distinctive feature, which generally suffices to bias the witness toward identifying him. Some of the more common factors potentially exerting suggestive influences include any unusual physical characteristics such as scars or tattoos, differences in the clothing worn by the participants and their demeanor and facial expressions.

Suggestion in the Administration of an Identification Test. In addition to the possibility that the police will make and reinforce suggestions as to the "proper" choice by the manner in which they construct the lineup or photo display, police officers while conducting the identification procedure often themselves provide subtle clues. An officer who is aware of the identity of the prime suspect may influence the witness' choice simply by changes in voice intonation, increased attention to the response, the hint of a smile, or by more obvious gestures such as nodding agreement or asking the witness to take another,

[Loftus and Loftus, *Human Memory: The Process of Information*]

more careful, look if the "correct" identification has not been made. It is very difficult, if not impossible, to avoid giving such clues.

Social Psychological Influence. Various social psychological factors also increase the danger of suggestibility in a lineup confrontation. Witnesses, like other people, are motivated by a desire to be correct and to avoid looking foolish. By arranging a lineup, the police have demonstrated their belief that they have caught the criminal. Witnesses, realizing this, probably will feel foolish if they cannot identify anyone and therefore may choose someone despite some uncertainty.

Finally, witnesses are highly motivated to behave like those around them. This desire to conform produces an increased need to identify someone in order to show the police that they, too, feel that the criminal is in the lineup.

[Stephen A. Saltzburg, *Introduction to American Criminal Procedure*]

If the group reports have been clear and accurate, you should be able to answer the following true and false questions.

1. Stress causes a witness to give a very accurate description of an event.

   _____

2. People think that sudden, action-packed events happen very quickly.

   _____

3. A perceptual strategy often used is not noticing many details of our everyday lives. _____

4. We see best when under stress. _____

5. Often, we see what we expect to see. _____

6. As we have closer contact with members of another race, we are better able to see differences among members of that race. _____

7. Important events remain fixed and clear in one's memory. _____

8. A witness who "fills in" when describing a crime is intentionally lying. _____

9. When police questions become more structured, the witness's responses become more inaccurate. _____

10. A fair lineup would consist of similar suspects. _____

MNEMONICS

Any techniques (or tricks) a person uses to remember things are called *mnemonics* (from the Greek word *mneme* which means "to remember"). Have you ever known someone who tied a string around his finger to remind himself of some errand? Do you remember how you learned the number of days in each month? You may be familiar with the rhyme:

Thirty days hath September, April, June, and November,
All the rest have thirty-one
Save February alone, which hath twenty-eight, in fine,
'Till leap year give it twenty-nine.

There are several techniques which are commonly used to aid one's memory.

Loci

An early technique developed by the ancient Romans and Greeks is called the system of loci. Loci is the plural of the word *locus*, which means "place," and refers to a system of imagining the placement or location of a group of items to be memorized. Let's try it, and see if it helps you to remember.

On a separate sheet of paper, make a list of 25 common items. Exchange your list with that of a classmate. Study your classmate's list for exactly 60 seconds. Then, without referring to the list, try to produce as many items from it as you can remember.

How many items were you able to recall correctly? _____

Now, still using your classmate's list, write several paragraphs which describe the placement of each item somewhere in your room at home. For example, if the word *flashlight* is on the list, you might choose to place it next to your bed (in case of a power failure). When you have completed these paragraphs using every item on the list, reread what you have written.

Now put the paper away, relax for several minutes, and once again try to remember as many items on the list as you can by taking a mental walk through your room and recalling where each of the items was placed.

How many items were you able to recall this time? _____

Explain the difference in your scores.

You might try this experiment again in a week. Do not refer to the paragraphs during that time. How successful were you at remembering a week later? Why?

Outrageous Associations

Another mnemonic device often used to remember unrelated items is to form an outrageous picture in your mind linking two items. For example, if two of the words on the list were *pig* and *toothpick*, you might form an image of a large pig using the toothpick to dislodge some food particles from his teeth.

Try it! Make up ten word pairs. Form an outrageous image for each pair. Check on the number of items you can recall by remembering the images you formed.

Discerning Patterns

Some things which you wish to remember form a pattern. If you understand the pattern, remembering is easier.

Look at the following two groups of numbers. Which is easier to recall? Why? Can you explain the pattern?

1	17
4	3
7	6
10	12
13	14
16	5
19	11
22	16

Categorizing

Suppose you were asked to memorize the following list of food items:

a. bananas
b. lamb chops
c. chocolate
d. pork
e. french fries
f. string beans
g. tomatoes
h. apples
i. soda
j. eggs

k. hot dogs
l. wine
m. bacon
n. grapes
o. oranges
p. chicken
q. lettuce
r. pizza
s. peaches
t. spaghetti

u. watermelon
v. cereal
w. cucumbers

x. lasagna
y. milk
z. cheese

You can organize these items into smaller groups, according to certain similarities. Each group will then form a different category.

How many useful categories can you think of to help you organize the foods listed above? Write the names of the categories on the lines provided and place each item from the list into the appropriate category.

_____ _____ _____ _____ _____

_____

Acronyms

Acronyms are mnemonic devices commonly used to remember names of organizations. MADD is an acronym for Mothers Against Drunk Drivers; AIDS is an acronym for AutoImmune Deficiency Syndrome. As you can see, an acronym is a word formed from the initial letters of words in a phrase.

Abbreviations of words can also help one remember things. The FBI is an abbreviation of Federal Bureau of Investigation; UNICEF stands for United Nations International Children's Emergency Fund.

If you had to memorize the three stages of memory as described earlier, you might try remembering the first letter of each stage—ARR—and use these letters as cues to the words they represent: acquisition, retention, retrieval.

Sometimes each letter is used as the first word in a sentence. Using the three stages of memory as an example, you might create a sentence such and "*A*nn *r*emembers *r*ight." The first letter of each word stands for one of the three stages.

Imagine That

You were an eyewitness to a robbery. You have been asked by the police to describe what occurred. Write a description of the robbery, using the signal words that indicate addition in order to describe each step of the robbery.

In this chapter you have learned several ways to approach the reading of a textbook. They include:

1. Previewing, in order to identify headings, subheadings, italics, indentation, and numbering.
2. Prequestioning, in order to give yourself a purpose for reading and to help you concentrate as you read.
3. Identifying signal words, to help follow an author's writing.
4. Using mnemonics, as an aid in remembering things.

Try using the first three techniques as you read your textbooks in school. The next time you are required to memorize something for a test, try using one of the mnemonic devices discussed in this chapter. It may help you get that A!

A Further Reading

The following is a description of a true incident in which eyewitness testimony determined the fate of the defendant. As you read, you will recognize many of the subtle influences which affected the outcome of the trial.

The Sawyer brothers, eighteen-year-old Lonnie and his twenty-year-old brother Sandy, came from the small town of Mint Hill, North Carolina. To their horror, they were arrested for a kidnapping that took place on May 15, 1975. Robert Hinson, assistant manager of Collins' Department Store in Monroe, North Carolina, was forced into a car by two men, one of whom pointed a gun at him and demanded that he lie down in the back of the car. He got only a glimpse of his abductors before they pulled stocking masks over their faces, preventing any further view. The men planned to drive Hinson to the store where he would open the safe for them. However, Hinson convinced them that he did not know the combination, and they then took thirty-five dollars from his wallet and let him go.

Hinson had little to say about his abductors. He reported that one of them looked Hispanic, that they drove an off-white 1965 Dodge Dart, that the car was similar to one owned by a woman who worked at the store. He claimed that one kidnapper looked similar to a man who had recently applied for a job at the store, and from the bits of information he could provide, a composite sketch of one of the suspects was created.

Three days after the incident, the police stopped a 1965 white Plymouth Valiant and arrested the driver and passenger, Sandy and Lonnie Sawyer. The

Valiant looked similar to a 1965 Dodge. However, neither man looked like the composite sketch, neither had applied for a job at the store, and both vehemently denied knowing anything about the kidnapping.

At their trial, the prosecution introduced the testimony of the victim, Robert Hinson, who positively identified the Sawyers as the men who kidnapped him at gunpoint. Like Sacco and Vanzetti, the Sawyers had alibis. Four witnesses testified that Sandy was at home at the time of the kidnapping, and four witnesses testified that Lonnie was at a printing plant, where he was visiting his girlfriend. After two hours the jury was deadlocked, nine for conviction. The judge instructed the jurors to try hard to reach a unanimous decision, and within a few minutes all twelve jurors voted to convict. The younger brother was sentenced to twenty-eight to thirty-two years, and the older one received thirty-two to forty years (in part because of a prior conviction). As the boys were led out of the courtroom, Lonnie yelled to his father and mother, "Momma, Daddy, appeal this. We didn't do it."

Ordinarily there would not be much hope. But because of the perseverance of their family, friends, a tenacious private detective, and a television producer who had become interested in the case, the Sawyers did have a chance. These people all believed in the results of a lie detection examination indicating that the brothers had nothing to do with the crime. And then in 1976 a prisoner at the youth center where the Sawyers were taken swore that Robert Thomas, an inmate, had admitted to being one of Hinson's kidnappers. With this rumor in hand, the private detective talked further with Hinson and discovered important information that he had initially given to the police but that the police had kept from the defense. This included Hinson's first description of the abductors, the composite sketch produced by the police, and Hinson's thought that one of the men resembled somone who had recently applied for a job at the store.

The detective searched the job applications on file at the store and found one, dated a week before the crime, that had been filled out by Robert Thomas, the inmate who had supposedly admitted to being one of the kidnappers. The detective would later find out that Thomas had a friend whose mother owned a 1965 Dodge Dart. The pieces were coming together, but the job was not over.

Those trying to free the brothers were still puzzled by one fact. During the trial a large number of witnesses said that the Sawyers could not have been the kidnappers, and only one—the victim—disagreed; yet the jury believed the one rather than the many others. Why? Several jurors were interviewed and subsequently confessed that they had eventually caved in to the majority, voting guilty simply because they were tired.

From that point it should have been easy: there was a new suspect, new evidence, and the jurors' admission that they had not voted their consciences. But it was not easy. The Sawyers were almost granted a new trial, but a judge ruled, despite the existence of new evidence, that too much time had passed. The defense attorneys petitioned the governor for a pardon. Robert Thomas confessed in writing and on camera, then recanted, then recanted his recantation. It was not until January 7, 1977, that the case was finally over. On that day the governor of North Carolina pardoned the Sawyers, but only after the brothers had lost nearly two years of their lives, their impovershed family had collected and spent thousands of dollars, and many people had suffered through a nightmare.

[Elizabeth Loftus, *Eyewitness Testimony*]

Suggested Readings

Coxe, George Harmon. *Eyewitness*. New York: Alfred A. Knopf, 1950.

A detective story in which news-photographer Kent Murdock has to move fast to stay alive.

Cozzens, James G. *The Just and the Unjust*. New York: Harcourt, Brace, and Javonovitch, 1960.

The progress of a murder trial in a small eastern city is the background and substance of this novel.

Levin, Meyer. *Compulsion*. New York: Simon and Schuster, 1956.

Using fictionalized names and probing deeply into the psychological aspects of the crime, this is a retelling of the story of a notorious murder case in Chicago in the 1920s.

Rose, Reginald. *"Twelve Angry Men"* in *Six Television Plays*. New York: Simon and Schuster, 1956.

A jury decides the fate of a teenage boy accused of murder. Were the eyewitnesses believable? Is there reasonable doubt?

Stein, Sol. *The Magician*. New York: Delacorte Press, 1971.

Japhet, a bright Ossining, N.Y. high school student, is beaten up by a gang of rough-necks from this same school following the midwinter prom, during which the boy had performed some tricks of magic. The gang leader, Urek, then sneaks into the hospital and tries to kill Japhet. In the ensuing trial, Urek's sharp lawyer succeeds in getting him off scot-free. Urek once again attacks Japhet and, in the scuffle, Japhet kills him. In desperation, the boy turns to the same lawyer to defend him.

Tillet, Dorothy Stockbridge. *Eyewitness*. New York: Doubleday and Company, Inc., 1961.

A murder mystery. The eyewitness was Lily Logan, an actress, who told the police what she had seen—and played her most important role during a week filled with terror.

Traver, Robert. *Anatomy of a Murder*. New York: St. Martins, 1958.

Not the usual murder mystery, but a review by the lawyer for the defense from the time he takes the case of an army lieutenant, who admits to having killed the man who raped his wife, until the end of the trial.

Uhnak, Dorothy. *The Witness*. New York: Simon and Schuster, 1980.

This novel is about the murder of a young black law student who is active in civil-liberties demonstrations. A New York cop finds the gun in his hand. The city, especially the black population, cries for revenge. But one person saw the gun shoved into his hand—Christie Opara, a detective. The Mayor and the Chief of Detectives work to avert the consequences of a long, hot summer.

CHAPTER 2

Photo Researchers, Inc.

"Doctor, doctor, will I die?"
"Yes, my child, and so will I."

DEATH AND DYING

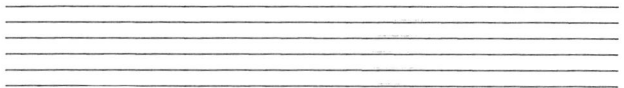

Most people feel uncomfortable when thinking about the subjects of death and dying. You might even wish you could skip this chapter. On the other hand, you might be curious as to what you will find in the following pages. We think you will find it interesting and thought-provoking.

In this chapter you will read about the emotional stages a dying person goes through. You will also read a discussion of the dying person's right to stop life-sustaining measures—in other words, the right to choose death. There is also a copy of a "living will" which you may decide to sign.

In addition, this chapter will show you how to find the main ideas of reading material. You will also have a chance to continue practice in the use of headings and prereading questions as aids to understanding what you read.

Have you ever thought about your own death? Suppose a doctor told you that you were suffering from an incurable disease, and you had only six months to live.

1. What feelings do you imagine you would have on hearing that news?

_____

_____

_____

_____

2. Would you change the way you are living now? In what ways?

_____

_____

_____

_____

3. Have you ever discussed death and dying with a member of your family? Why or why not?

_____

_____

_____

_____

4. In your opinion, why are many people afraid of death?

_____

_____

_____

_____

5. Working with a few other students, list as many euphemisms for death and dying as you can think of.

_____

_____

_____

_____

_____

_____

In Your Opinion

Why are euphemisms so commonly used with regard to the topic of death?

_____

_____

_____

_____

_____

_____

_____

Write a sentence which deals with the topic of death.

Death is a peaceful end to life.

Your instructor will list each student's sentence on the blackboard. As a class, decide on a method for organizing these sentences into groups, or categories. Describe the differences among the groups of sentences the class has created.

Choose a sentence from one of the categories. Use this sentence as the beginning of a paragraph which develops the idea expressed in the sentence you have chosen.

_____

_____

_____

_____

_____

_____

_____

_____

_____

_____

_____

_____

Your instructor will now ask several students to read their paragraphs aloud, omitting the first sentence. If each paragraph has developed the idea expressed in the first sentence, you should be able to determine to which category it belongs.

The opening sentences you worked with are examples of main

idea sentences. The main idea sentence is made up of two parts: first, the topic (in this case, death), and then a statement, or assertion, about the topic.

Writers, however, do not always use the first sentence of a paragraph as the main idea sentence. The main idea may be found embedded in the paragraph, or as the last sentence, often following a group of examples to illustrate the main idea. It is even possible to find paragraphs that contain no main idea sentence. In that case, that author expects you to understand the unstated main idea from the reading.

In order to find the main idea sentence of a paragraph, first decide what the topic of the paragraph is (what the paragraph is about); then find the sentence that makes a statement about that topic. The rest of the paragraph should be about the main idea.

In each of the following paragraphs underline the main idea sentence.

Since every turning point in life represents an encounter with the unknown, everyone develops ways of coping with the fear that accompanies it. As Stanley Keleman notes in his book *Living Your Dying*, "There are no turning points that are not accompanied by feelings of dying; no self-forming occurs without endings and loss." Keleman calls these events "little dyings"—the crucial occasions, such as one's first day at school, when old connections are broken and new connections are formed; bringing about new feelings and patterns of behavior. Through many "little dyings," he says, a person learns to deal with crisis and change and prepares for the "big dying" that is to come.

[Robert Emmett Kavanaugh (consultant), *Essentials of Life and Health*]

There nevertheless exists a great deal of curiosity about death. Although it is considered morbid and distasteful to dwell on the subject, most people want to know "what it's like" to die. Such curiosity usually consists of equal parts excitement and dread: people want to know, yet fear knowing for certain. Death, after all, remains throughout one's lifetime an unknown factor, and fear of the unknown is a familiar human trait.

[Robert Emmett Kavanaugh (consultant), *Essentials of Life and Health*]

Increasingly, Americans have come to expect and even to seek out scenes of death in the media. They enjoy watching earthquakes, burning skyscrapers, sinking ships, and gangland executions—all from a safe distance. The average American child is thought to witness 25,000 to 30,000 "media deaths" before reaching adulthood.

[Robert Emmett Kavanaugh (consultant), *Essentials of Life and Health*]

Whether you die at a young age or when you are older is less important than whether you have fully lived the years you have had. One person may live more in eighteen years than another does in eighty. By living, we do not mean frantically accumulating a range and quantity of experience valued in fantasy by others. Rather, we mean living each day as if it is the only one you have. We mean finding a sense of peace and strength to deal with life's disappointments and pain while always striving to discover vehicles to make more accessible, increase, and sustain the joys and delights of life. One such vehicle is learning to focus on some of the things you have learned to tune out—to notice and take joy in the budding of new leaves in the spring, to wonder at the beauty of the sun rising each morning and setting each night, to take comfort in the smile or touch of another person, to watch with amazement the growth of a child, and to share in children's wonderfully "uncomplexed," enthusiastic, and trusting approach to living. To live.

[Elisabeth Kübler-Ross, *Death: The Final Stage of Growth*]

Grief is the other side of the coin of love. If you are capable of love you are capable of grief. Only the person who is incapable of loving another is entirely free of the possibility of grief. We would not want to think of life without love. But when you love you become vulnerable, because the one you love may suffer and die and part of you suffers and dies along with him. When anyone dies we all die a little, for we are all diminished and reminded of our own mortal status. But this is not a hopeless state; the death we experience in our grief can be overcome at least in part by healthful mourning whereby our inner being is restored to normal. So grief is normal for normal people.

[David L. Bender and Richard C. Hagen, *Death and Dying: Opposing Viewpoints*]

Death is not final extinction for a Hindu, and has therefore no terrors for him. Life to him is the coming together of the body and the soul, and death to him is the dissolution of the body with the hope that his soul would migrate into another physical organism. He knows that he does not live only once but goes through a cycle of births, deaths and rebirths till at last his individual soul merges into the Universal Soul. This is the truth enunciated and affirmed in all the religious books of the Hindus . . . and this is what is clearly imprinted on his mind.

[David L. Bender and Richard C. Hagen, *Death and Dying: Opposing Viewpoints*]

Death is the ultimate problem because it erases us as experiencing beings. We do not think. We do not feel. We are insensible to the further course of time and event. For people who hold this view of death and for whom the inner life is of great significance, it is difficult to imagine a fate worse than death. All other considerations become secondary or even nonexistent. Death is far and away the greatest of calamities, for it closes down the theater of inner experience.

[Robert J. Kastenbaum, *Death, Society, and Human Experience*]

STAGES OF DYING

Elisabeth Kübler-Ross is a physician who has become well known as an authority on death and dying. She has worked with patients, family members, doctors, and nurses in order to help them deal honestly with death. Dr. Kübler-Ross has developed five stages common to dying patients.

Glance through the reading selection which follows and list the five stages of dying on the lines below.

Stages

1. Denial
2. Anger
3. Bargining
4. Depression
5. Acceptance

As you read Dr. Kübler-Ross's discussion, follow the procedure below.

1. Before reading each section of the article, think of two questions which might be answered in the text. Write these in the spaces provided.
2. Read the portion of the selection.
3. Answer the questions which you have asked.
4. If you are unable to answer any of your questions, explain the reason why you could not.

Prereading Questions

1. Why do people deny death?

2. How do people act in the denial stage?

Responses

1. _People deny death because of disbelief_

2. _The go on but slip back_

First Stage: Denial . . .

Among the over two hundred dying patients we have interviewed, most reacted to the awareness of a terminal illness at first with the statement, "No, not me, it cannot be true." This *initial* denial was as true for those patients who were told outright at the beginning of their illness as it was true for those who were not told explicitly and who came to this conclusion on their own a bit later on. . . . Denial, at least partial denial, is used by almost all patients, not only during the first stages of illness or following confrontation, but also later on from time to time. Who was it who said, "We cannot look at the sun all the time, we cannot face death all the time"? These patients can consider the possibility of their own death for a while but then have to put this consideration away in order to pursue life.

[Elisabeth Kübler-Ross, *On Death and Dying*]

1. The author compares looking at the sun all the time with facing death all the time. What do these two situations have in common?

   You cannot concentrate on one thing
   all the time, other things are going
   _on._

Prereading Questions

1. _Who are people angry at?_

2. _how is this anger expressed?_

Responses

1. _People are angry at there situation_

2. _The anger is expressed by complianing_

Second Stage: Anger

If our first reaction to catastrophic news is, "No, it's not true, no, it cannot involve me," this has to give way to a new reaction, when it finally dawns on us: "Oh, yes, it is me, it was not a mistake." Fortunately or unfortunately very few patients are able to maintain a make-believe world in which they are healthy and well until they die.

When the first stage of denial cannot be maintained any longer, it is replaced by feelings of anger, rage, envy, and resentment. The logical next question becomes: "Why me?" . . .

In contrast to the stage of denial, this stage of anger is very difficult to cope with from the point of view of family and staff. The reason for this is the fact that this anger is displaced in all directions and projected onto the environment at times almost at random. The doctors are just no good, they don't know what tests to require and what diet to prescribe. They keep the patients too long in the hospital or don't respect their wishes in regards to special privileges. They allow a miserably sick roommate to be brought into their room when they pay so much money for some privacy and rest, etc. The nurses are even more often a target of their anger. Whatever they touch is not right . . . .

The problem here is that few people place themselves in the patient's position and wonder where this anger might come from. Maybe we too would be angry if all our life activities were interrupted so prematurely; if all the buildings we started were to go unfinished, to be completed by someone else; if we had put some hard-earned money aside to enjoy a few years of rest and enjoyment, for travel and pursuing hobbies, only to be confronted with the fact that "this is not for me." What else would we do with our anger, but let it out on the people who are most likely to enjoy all these things? People who rush busily around only to remind us that we cannot even stand on our two feet anymore. People who order unpleasant tests and prolonged hospitalization with all its limitations, restrictions, and costs, while at the end of the day they can go home and enjoy life. People who tell us to lie still so that the infusion or transfusion does not have to be restarted, when we feel like jumping out of our skin to be doing something in order to know that we are still functioning on some level!

[Elisabeth Kübler-Ross, *On Death and Dying*]

2. The author claims that this second stage is difficult to cope with because the anger is displaced and projected onto the environment. Who is mentioned as becoming the target of the patient's anger?

   The Nurse

3. What is the reason given for the patient's anger?

The anger is at being cut-off
before there time

4. Can you think of a time in your own life when you were angry and let it out on someone else (displaced anger)? Describe what happened.

I had a bad day at school
and I was angry that things
didn't go my way. I was harsh
with everyone even though they
didn't do anything.

Prereading Questions

1. _Who do the people bargin with?_

2. _What do they bargin for?_

Responses

1. _The people bargin with God_

2. _An extension of life or to stop the pain_

Third Stage: Bargaining

The third stage, the stage of bargaining, is less well known but equally helpful to the patient, though only for brief periods of time. If we have been unable to face the sad facts in the first period and have been angry at people and God in the second phase, maybe we can succeed in entering into some sort of an agreement which may postpone the inevitable happening: "If God has decided to take us from this earth and he did not respond to my angry pleas, he may be more favorable if I ask nicely." The patient's wish is most always an extension of life, followed by the wish for a few days without pain or physical discomfort.

The bargaining is really an attempt to postpone; it has to include a prize offered "for good behavior," it also sets a self-imposed "deadline" (e.g., one more performance, the son's wedding), and it includes an implicit promise that the patient will not ask for more if this one postponement is granted. None of our patients have "kept their promise"; in other words, they are like children who say, "I will never fight my sister again if you let me go." Needless to add, the little boy will fight his sister again.

[Elisabeth Kübler-Ross, *On Death and Dying*]

5. With whom does the patient bargain?

God

6. What is the purpose of bargaining?

extentend time

Prereading Questions

1. _How long does the depression last?_

2. _What breaks the depression?_

Responses

1. _Doesn't say about length of_

2. _Acceptance breaks the depression_

Fourth Stage: Depression

When the terminally ill patient can no longer deny his illness, when he is forced to undergo more surgery or hospitalization, when he begins to have more symptoms or becomes weaker and thinner, he cannot smile it off anymore. His numbness or stoicism, his anger and rage will soon be replaced with a sense of great loss. What we often tend to forget, however, is the preparatory grief that the terminally ill patient has to undergo in order to prepare himself for his final separation from this world.

The patient should not be encouraged to look at the sunny side of things, as this would mean he should not contemplate his impending death. It would be contraindicated to tell him not to be sad, since all of us are tremendously sad when we lose one beloved person. The patient is in the process of losing everything and everybody he loves. If he is allowed to express his sorrow he will find a final acceptance much easier, and he will be grateful to those who can sit with him during this state of depression without constantly telling him not to be sad.

[Elisabeth Kübler-Ross, *On Death and Dying*]

7. Why is it important to allow a patient to be sad?

   he will learn to accept his
   death

8. In what ways can a person help the patient through this stage?

   let him be sad and don't tell
   them to look on the sunny side.

1. _Is acceptance giving up?_

2. _Are the people happy_

Responses

1. _____

2. _____

Fifth Stage: Acceptance

If a patient has had enough time (i.e., not a sudden, unexpected death) and has been given some help in working through the previously described stages, he will reach a stage during which he is neither depressed nor angry about his "fate." He will have been able to express his previous feelings, his envy for the living and the healthy, his anger at those who do not have to face their end so soon. He will have mourned the impending loss of so many meaningful people and places and he will contemplate his coming end with a certain degree of quiet expectation. He will be tired and, in most cases, quite weak.

Acceptance should not be mistaken for a happy stage. It is almost void of feelings. It is as if the pain had gone, the struggle is over, and there comes a time for "the final rest before the long journey" as one patient phrased it.

There are a few patients who fight to the end, who struggle and keep a hope that makes it almost impossible to reach this stage of acceptance. They are the ones who will say one day, "I just cannot make it anymore," the day they stop fighting, the fight is over. In other words, the harder they struggle to avoid the inevitable death, the more they try to deny it, the more difficult it will be for them to reach this final stage of acceptance with peace and dignity.

[Elisabeth Kübler-Ross, *On Death and Dying*]

9. Underline the words in this section that describe the feelings of someone who has reached the fifth stage of dying.

Check the statements in column A below with which you agree. Then read the next article, which describes the death of the author's mother-in-law. After reading the article, check those statements in column B with which the author would agree. Be prepared to discuss your choices in class.

Column A   *Column B*

_____   _____   1. There can be dignity in dying without putting up a fight.

_____   _____   2. Fight til the last gasp.

_____   _____   3. Easier said than done.

_____   _____   4. Illusion is an important part of our lives.

_____   _____   5. Young time is short; old time is fast.

_____   _____   6. What people actually experience is the opposite of what you might think they should.

LAST RIGHTS

Death with dignity. Who could possibly be against it?

My problem with the DWD movement does not lie with its specific goals but with an underlying philosophy that attempts to impose a comforting rationality on death. This philosophy borders on a religion and is derived in large measure from an enormously influential book, *On Death and Dying*, by Dr. Elisabeth Kübler-Ross. Dr. Kübler-Ross, considered the founding mother of the DWD movement, described her therapeutic work with terminally ill patients who pass through stages that include denial, anger, bargaining, depression and, finally, acceptance of death.

"Those who have the strength and love to sit with a dying patient in the silence that goes beyond words," she wrote, "will know that this moment is neither frightening nor painful, but a peaceful cessation of the functioning of the body. Watching a peaceful death reminds us of a falling star; one of a million lights in a vast sky that flares up for a brief moment only to disappear into the endless night forever."

Pretty thoughts, pretty words. But they have nothing to do with death as I have seen it.

Five years ago, when I was a smugly healthy 30-year-old, death and I weren't even on speaking terms. Then my mother-in-law got cancer. My husband and I, wanting to help and knowing nothing about serious illness and death, found the idea of death with dignity very appealing. My mother-in-law was uncharacteristically silent on the subject until she remarked tartly that most of the DWD promoters seemed to be vitamin-packed 25-year-olds in jogging suits.

Nor, it seemed, did she care very much about working her way through all of the stages leading to acceptance of death. She was angry at the start and angry when she died two years later. She was still showing up for work in her mid-70s in spite of the debilitating effects of cancer chemotherapy. On the night before her death, she struggled wildly against the cloth bonds that were preventing her from falling out of her hospital bed. It was a frightful sight, but there was something noble about the last spark of energy she invested in the struggle.

No, there is nothing peaceful or dignified about a life disappearing into the "endless night forever."

What is the harm, one might ask, in the illusion that death can be stripped of its pain, whether emotional or physical? The same harm, I think, that is inherent in another popular notion of the "Me Decade"—the idea that good sex is simply a pleasant form of recreation. In both instances there is an attempt to divest basic human experiences of their power and, inevitably, of their moral significance.

Too often, the DWD promoters have presented the choice between death and artificially sustained life in the simplest possible terms—the question of whether to "pull the plug" on a patient whose brain is already dead. The more common and much more complex dilemma is that of the sick human being who must weigh the physical and psychological stress of medical treatment against the possibilities—and uncertainties—of the future.

When my mother-in-law discovered she had cancer, I had serious doubts about the wisdom of radiation and chemotherapy "at her age." I know now that my concern was in part a mask for my own fear of death and disease. Some of her time was good and some was bad, but it was *her* time, and she died with the dignity of struggle rather than resignation.

In the end, I was glad she had listened to the voices of poets rather than psychotherapists. For those of us facing the inevitable struggle, no one has ever said it better than Dylan Thomas:

> Do not go gentle into that good night,
> Old age should burn and rave at close of day;
> Rage, rage against the dying of the light.

Susan Jacoby

Write a paragraph describing what the author admired about her mother-in-law's way of dealing with death.

The daughter in law admired the Fight her mother inlaw put up for her life even though she died. Her mother in-law didn't accept death but fought it all the way.

_____

_____

_____

_____

_____

_____

As you read the first-hand account that follows, decide which stage of dying the writer is in, according to Dr. Kübler-Ross's theory.

DEATH IN THE FIRST PERSON

I am a student nurse. I am dying. I write this to you who are, and will become, nurses in the hope that by my sharing my feelings with you, you may someday be better able to help those who share my experience.

I'm out of the hospital now—perhaps for a month, for six months, perhaps for a year—but no one likes to talk about such things. In fact, no one likes to talk about much at all. Nursing must be advancing, but I wish it would hurry. We're taught not to be overly cheery now, to omit the "Everything's fine" routine, and we have done pretty well. But now one is left in a lonely silent void. With the protective "fine, fine" gone, the staff is left with only their own vulnerability and fear. The dying patient is not yet seen as a person and thus cannot be communicated with as such. He is a symbol of what every human fears and what we each know, at least academically, that we too must someday face. What did they say in psychiatric nursing about meeting pathology with pathology to the detriment of both patient and nurse? And there was a lot about knowing one's own feelings before you could help another with his. How true.

But for me, fear is today and dying is now. You slip in and out of my room, give me medications and check my blood pressure. Is it because I am a student nurse, myself, or just a human being, that I sense your fright? And your fears enhance mine. Why are you afraid? I am the one who is dying!

I know you feel insecure, don't know what to say, don't know what to do. But please believe me, if you care, you can't go wrong. Just admit that you care. That is really for what we search. We may ask for why's and wherefore's, but we don't really expect answers. Don't run away—wait—all I want to know is that there will be someone to hold my hand when I need it. I am afraid. Death may get to be a routine to you, but it is new to me. You may not see me as unique, but I've never died before. To me, once is pretty unique!

You whisper about my youth, but when one is dying, is he really so young anymore? I have lots I wish we could talk about. It really would not take much more of your time because you are in here quite a bit anyway.

If only we could be honest, both admit of our fears, touch one another. If you really care, would you lose so much of your valuable professionalism if you even cried with me? Just person to person? Then, it might not be so hard to die—in a hospital—with friends close by.

Anonymous

1. In what stage of dying is this person?

   _____

2. To whom is this written?

   _____

3. What is meant by the "Everything's fine" routine?

   _____

   _____

   _____

4. According to the author, how is the dying patient seen by the medical staff?

   _____

   _____

   _____

THE RIGHT TO DIE

A decision about dying is the last important choice a person has in life. If you are going to die, modern medicine can often prevent you from doing so for a very long time. It has the devices to prolong existence, but the question is: Are we really prolonging life?

"Suppose you were told that you would live until the age of 90, but that after 70 you would be unconscious and have no physical movement except for such vital functions as breathing" (Michael Bayles, "The Value of Life— By What Standard?").

1. Would you choose to survive to 90 or to die shortly after lapsing into the coma? Why?

   _____

2. What effects would your decision have on your family? Explain.

_____

_____

_____

_____

_____

_____

Is there a difference between refusing treatment when you are near death—and refusing treatment when you are reasonably healthy? All of us are constantly refusing treatment in one way or another, or at least we have that choice. None of us is forced to consult physicians or take medicine. Some of us work long hours, smoke, overeat, undersleep, or go without exercise (Arthur J. Dyck, "The Value of Life: Two Contending Policies"). Do you have any habits which are detrimental to your health? Have you ever ignored a doctor's advice or refused to take a prescribed medication? If you were dying, would you want to have fewer rights than you have now? Often nobody listens to the dying when they try to assert their right to refuse treatment.

Many people are concerned with this lack, and organized movements to protect the rights of the dying person believe that euthanasia should be accepted in our society. Euthanasia, also called mercy killing, is the act of putting to death painlessly a person suffering from an incurable and painful disease or condition.

> In today's medical, legal, and theological circles it is generally accepted that there are two basic forms of euthanasia: direct (or positive) and indirect (or negative). Direct euthanasia is defined as a deliberate action to shorten a life. Injecting air into a dying person's bloodstream and causing an air embolism, for example, would be a direct euthanasia, a positive action shortening life, a "mercy killing." As current laws stand, this type of action is considered murder. Still, many feel that it should be permissible.

Indirect euthanasia is a much more common, and complicated, action which, while difficult to prove as murder, might be vulnerable to malpractice suits. In indirect euthanasia death is not induced, rather it is permitted. In other words, death is accomplished through the omission of an act or acts rather than by commission. Indirect euthanasia can take one of several forms: halting treatments that prolong the life of the patient or altogether withholding treatment.

[David Hendon, *Death as a Fact of Life*]

The paragraphs above compare two types of euthanasia. Below is a chart which indicates both types. We have provided the information which describes direct euthanasia. You fill in the empty blanks with the appropriate words to complete the comparison.

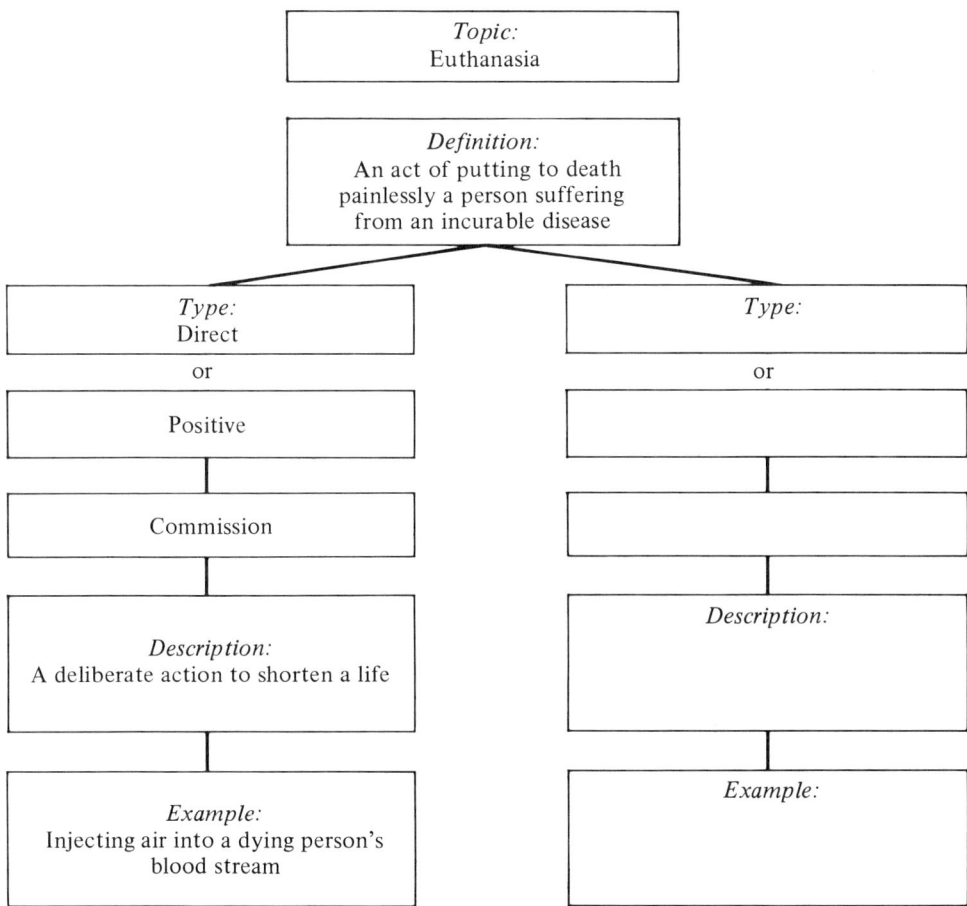

```
                    ┌──────────────────────────┐
                    │         Topic:           │
                    │       Euthanasia         │
                    └──────────────────────────┘

              ┌──────────────────────────────────┐
              │           Definition:            │
              │     An act of putting to death   │
              │   painlessly a person suffering  │
              │     from an incurable disease    │
              └──────────────────────────────────┘

┌──────────────────────────┐          ┌──────────────────────────┐
│          Type:           │          │          Type:           │
│          Direct          │          │                          │
└──────────────────────────┘          └──────────────────────────┘
            or                                    or
┌──────────────────────────┐          ┌──────────────────────────┐
│         Positive         │          │                          │
└──────────────────────────┘          └──────────────────────────┘

┌──────────────────────────┐          ┌──────────────────────────┐
│        Commission        │          │                          │
└──────────────────────────┘          └──────────────────────────┘

┌──────────────────────────┐          ┌──────────────────────────┐
│       Description:        │          │       Description:        │
│ A deliberate action to    │          │                          │
│   shorten a life          │          │                          │
└──────────────────────────┘          └──────────────────────────┘

┌──────────────────────────┐          ┌──────────────────────────┐
│        Example:          │          │        Example:          │
│ Injecting air into a      │          │                          │
│ dying person's            │          │                          │
│ blood stream              │          │                          │
└──────────────────────────┘          └──────────────────────────┘
```

Terms:

omission	negative
indirect	death is permitted
withholding treatment	stopping treatment

Opponents of euthanasia stress the sanctity of life and ask whether it is ever morally right to take the life of another human being, even if he begs to die. Might not the sufferer be only temporarily depressed and have a different outlook the following day or week or month? Might not the physician be wrong about the hopelessness of the case? If euthanasia were approved, would hard-pressed families facing economic ruin or the necessity of sacrificing the education of their children because of the patient's costly illness be encouraged to decide that the sufferer's life should be ended? What of the temptation to unscrupulous persons who stand to inherit under a patient's will? And finally, might a society in which life comes to be held cheap someday find reasons other than compassion for eliminating the old and unproductive or others whom the state considers a burden or a threat?

[American Friends Service Committee, *Who Shall Live?*]

In Your Opinion

Are either, or both, forms of euthanasia acceptable to you? Give reasons for your opinion.

_____

_____

_____

_____

_____

_____

_____

_____

_____

_____

It is possible for people to decide while they are healthy, to put in writing—as with a will—the circumstances under which they would want medical intervention and under what circumstances they would wish to have no further intervention.

For example, Concern for Dying is an organization which favors the individual patient's freedom of choice and provides the following statement of intent:

To My Family, My Physician, My Lawyer and All Others Whom It May Concern

Death is as much a reality as birth, growth, maturity and old age—it is the one certainty of life. If the time comes when I can no longer take part in decisions for my own future, let this statement stand as an expression of my wishes and directions, while I am still of sound mind.

If at such a time the situation should arise in which there is no reasonable expectation of my recovery from extreme physical or mental disability, I direct that I be allowed to die and not be kept alive by medications, artificial means or "heroic measures". I do, however, ask that medication be mercifully administered to me to alleviate suffering even though this may shorten my remaining life.

This statement is made after careful consideration and is in accordance with my strong convictions and beliefs. I want the wishes and directions here expressed carried out to the extent permitted by law. Insofar as they are not legally enforceable, I hope that those to whom this Will is addressed will regard themselves as morally bound by these provisions.

Signed _____

Date _____

Witness _____

Witness _____

Copies of this request have been given to _____

_____

_____

_____

Would you sign such a document? Explain your answer. _____

_____

_____

_____

_____

_____

_____

_____

_____

_____

The "living will" has its own drawbacks. There is no way to tell whether the person who signs such a document when he's healthy may change his mind about being kept alive when he is very sick. "You can pass living wills around a roomful of young people and 95 percent will sign them," says Seattle internist Dr. Normal K. Brown. "But pass them around a nursing home and you'll get a different response."*

1. According to Dr. Brown, would the majority of people in a nursing home sign a living will? _____

2. Assuming that Dr. Brown's statement is correct, can you give an explanation for it?

_____

_____

_____

_____

_____

_____

_____

*Copyright 1981, by Newsweek, Inc. All Rights Reserved. Reprinted by Permission.

Here are some real cases in which decisions had to be made by patients, doctors, and family members. What would *you* have done?

Case 1

Doctors at a university hospital examined a 10-year-old boy whose bone cancer of the upper arm had recurred in spite of radiation treatments. The physician advised amputation of the limb and warned that without the operation, the child would almost certainly die. But the boy, an enthusiastic Little Leaguer, begged his parents and the doctors to let him keep his arm so that he could continue to play baseball.

[*Newsweek*]

If you were the parents, what instructions would you have given the doctors?

_____

_____

_____

_____

_____

_____

This is what actually happened: The family decided against surgery. Now, nearly a year later, the boy is receiving radiation and chemotherapy—and playing baseball. Physicians say it is too soon to estimate his chances of recovery.

[*Newsweek*]

Case 2

Since the age of 19, when she suffered kidney failure, Diane Moore had had to go to a hospital three times a week for dialysis treatments. [This is a painful procedure in which the patient is hooked up to a machine for several hours, while the machine purifies the patient's blood, eliminating wastes. This purification is the normal function of a healthy kidney.]

At age 31, she decided she could no longer endure life under those conditions. She told her doctor that she was discontinuing the dialysis but, knowing that without medical help she would die in agony, she asked him to care for her in her final days. He could not treat her, he said, unless she was in a hospital. Once in the hospital, however, she was ordered put on the dialysis machine again. Because she refused, the hospital discharged her. Home nursing care was then obtained for her, since she lived alone. With a nurse on hand, the doctor could ease her pain and be on call in case of need. Diane died nine days after her last dialysis treatment.

[Elizabeth Ogg, *"The Right to Die with Dignity"*]

If you were Diane would you have made the same choice? Why or why not?

_____

_____

_____

_____

_____

_____

_____

Case 3

A 42-year-old man, the surviving parent of three children, was hospitalized terminally ill with brain cancer. Suddenly he suffered cardiac arrest, but an alert intern got the man's heart beating again and the patient lived another month.

[Patrick Young, *"What's Right?"*]

Did the doctor do the right thing in resuscitating the man? Why or why not?

_____

_____

_____

_____

Choose three of the following statements. For each, write a sentence or two about an imaginary person and the circumstances under which he/she might have said it. What motive might have caused him/her to express this point of view?

1. "I've been a fighter all my life and I intend to keep right on fighting to the end."
2. "Come on now, things are not so bad."
3. "Why did she have to get sick now, when the kids are still so young?"
4. "If I had only sent him to the doctor earlier. . . ."
5. "I am not a judge and I am not God."
6. "A lot of time is wasted on these patients—we're wasting precious time on people who cannot be helped any longer."
7. "Is there anything specific I can do to make you more comfortable?"
8. "We shall have to learn to refrain from doing things merely because we know how to do them."

1. _____

_____

_____

_____

2. _____

_____

_____

_____

3. _____

_____

_____

_____

Now that you have completed this chapter you have some understanding of the stages a dying person goes through. You have also considered various viewpoints on euthanasia.

You learned that the main idea of a paragraph is made up of two parts: the topic and a statement about the topic. You also discovered that the main idea may be found anywhere in a paragraph. The ability to find main ideas in paragraphs (or longer selections) will enable you to understand the most important ideas an author wants to convey.

In addition, you continued to use two approaches to reading which assist in your understanding of the material: using headings and prereading questions.

A Further Reading

I *HAD* TO PLAY GOD

Treating a child who was more dead than alive, this physician faced an agonizing choice—and made the only decision he could honestly make.

The surgical service was frantic that weekend. As an attending physician on emergency-room duty, I'd admitted five major cases in 24 hours. I was sitting at the E.R. desk and catching up on paperwork when I heard the wail of another approaching ambulance. The adrenaline started pumping again.

The slamming of doors and the rush of the attendants as they wheeled in a stretcher confirmed my forebodings. I moved quickly to the bedside, where an unconscious 5-year-old girl lay in blood and grime. A rapid examination revealed occipital hematoma, flail chest, deformities of the right clavicle and thigh. Efficient residents and nurses immediately started intubation, oxygen, intravenous fluids, and other support measures.

Minutes earlier, the blond girl's fragile little body had been a vehicle of play. But it had carried her into the street, into the path of a much larger and sturdier vehicle. Now she was deep in coma. The slow, writhing movement of her limbs was broken by intermittent spasms that thrust her head and heels back, her body forward. An X-ray confirmed a serious head injury. And there was other serious trouble. Five ribs were broken on the right side. . . . The right clavicle and femur *were* fractured. [In addition there were many other complications.]

I called in surgical and neurological specialists. An orthopedist placed the femur in traction. I performed a tracheostomy, inserted a Rusch tube, and had the child connected to a respirator. A chest surgeon inserted a bilateral thoracotomy tube and the girl's breathing improved markedly.

In the middle of the night, however, her neurological condition sharply deteriorated. During an emergency operation, a neurosurgeon drilled bur holes and found generalized swelling and hemorrhaging. He placed drains for skull decompression. The girl's condition stabilized.

The next morning, the ECG monitor showed a strong and regular heartbeat. In unhappy contrast was the flat line drawn by the EEG.

There was no family physician on the case, so it was my job to talk with the young parents of this only child. I now had some time to do it. The situation was serious, I told them. The brain injuries had caused unconsciousness. I spelled out the other injuries and assured them that, with six specialists and a top-notch I.C.U. team on the job, their daughter was getting the best of care. We'd done everything we could, and now we'd just have to wait and see. Sometimes people in a coma wake up and come around again.

But as Day 3 dawned, I approached rounds with trepidation, aware this was almost certainly a losing battle. That morning the little girl looked to be sleeping peacefully. It was an illusion disturbed by the rhythmic wheeze of the respirator and the surgical dressing that had replaced her golden hair. The sight of that lovely child tore at my heart. She would never function again. She could only lie there like a delicate doll.

The girl was connected to many of the technological marvels of the 1970s, and they worked efficiently. From all appearances it seemed as if we'd snatched a life back from the grave. But there was no ignoring that straight-line EEG.

The days passed in agony, and the parents haunted the I.C.U. round the clock. On the fifth day, the EEG repeated its grim verdict: brain death. After separate examinations of the patient and reviews of her chart, two neurosurgeons wrote identical opinions: "The patient is terminal and beyond neurological retrieve."

The primary neurosurgical consultant accompanied me as I tried to explain the hopelessness of the situation to the parents. "We think your child is terminal and that there's no hope she will ever function again," I said. "We also believe it's time to start thinking about turning off the artificial life-support systems."

"We don't care what you think," said the young father adamantly. "Don't give up, Doctor. Please, keep doing everything you can." The parents insisted and I agreed. They simply loved their child and wanted her alive again.

Day 8. Neurosurgical note: "Patient remains at medullary level with coma and dilated, fixed pupils. Again conveyed hopeless status to father, mother, and relatives."

All medical and therapeutic efforts continued, and so did the couple's suffering. The child's normal electrolytes, blood pressure, and temperature seemed to guarantee that we could maintain her lifelike appearance indefinitely.

I talked to the parents as often as I could, and they asked me many questions. While in the I.C.U., the father kept examining the strip of ECG graph paper, which recorded a healthy cardiac output. I was afraid he would realize this and ask me, "If she's terminal, why is her heartbeat so good?" But he never did.

The straight line of the EEG ran on to the 11th day. Due to the unusual circumstances, I asked the hospital administrator for an opinion on whether the life-support equipment could be turned off. There was no policy on how to handle such a situation, either at the hospital or the local medical society.

The administrator and the chief of surgery met with me and reviewed the case. Later, after phoning the hospital attorney, they gave me this instruction: "All efforts to keep the child alive should and will continue at this facility."

Legally, I suppose that they couldn't have said anything else, no matter how they really felt. I'm sure they didn't want the child to occupy that bed forever—she absorbed a tremendous amount of nursing and support care—but there was nowhere else to put her. The administration was just trying to dodge a potential lawsuit, and that left me more perplexed than ever. "Who's holding the bag now?" I wondered.

The Karen Ann Quinlan case kept coming to mind. When the lawyers and courts tried to answer the question of how long to maintain life artificially, their wrangling lasted a year. Then they pulled the plug—and Karen Ann got along without the respirator. I decided to confront the parents with another explanation and sound them out once more.

At this point, they were walking around like zombies, mentally and physically exhausted. I felt sorry for them. "Have you thought about when we should stop this effort?" I asked. "The child is not getting anywhere, and she's not going to. You people are numb with fatigue. How long do you think this can go on?"

I again detailed the child's injuries and restated the fact that she was terminal. I discussed the crippling financial blow that further hospitalization would deal to them. And I made a plea for giving a salvageable patient the benefit of the I.C.U. bed and nursing care. I wished for the right words to convince them the struggle was futile. Medical school and surgical residency had not prepared me for this meeting.

The father was even more insistent than before. "We want you to do everything you can," he said. "And if you can't keep our daughter in your intensive-care unit, we'll take her to another hospital."

The hazards of a transfer aside, I could visualize six more specialists being called in, more useless medical and surgical efforts, and the manipulation of publicity in which the parents would be pawns in a media game. I advised them against the transfer.

Day 12. Neurosurgical note: "Status unchanged. Patient remains at medullary level with no respirations initiated. Straight-line EEG with no brain activity."

"How long can this go on?" The question echoed inside my head while making rounds that night. "It could be three more weeks, or three more months, or longer. And it still won't matter. The girl won't get any better. Both parents will probably fall ill from the physical and emotional drain. The father may lose his job. It simply can't go on like this."

And so, in the shadows of the night, in the confusion of the nursing shift change, with the curtains drawn, a trial removal of the respirator was carried out. I turned off the machine. "There's no hope," I told myself. "Let's get it over with."

The zigzag on the ECG monitor gradually flattened out until it ran parallel with that day's straight-line EEG tracing. The couple had borne enough anguish. Now the torment was finished. I started the respirator again and completed my rounds in a mild state of shock. Perhaps, in lifting the decision from the parents' shoulders, I also took on some of the guilt they may have had to endure. No, I'm not God—I'm human!

Later that night, I talked to the couple again. "Fortunately, the ordeal is over," I told them. "The nurses' notes say your little girl passed away quietly a short time ago. You can both go home now and get some sleep for a change. If there's anything I can do, well—I just want to say I'm very sorry." The mother cried a bit, and the father supported her. But the duration of the deathwatch left them stunned. They expressed more relief than grief. None of us had much to say. Like the parents, I too felt inadequate.

The couple never suspected that I had pulled the plug, and I kept the truth from them for what I considered the kindest of reasons. Being in charge of that case was like being the captain of a sinking ship. It's largely a technical job that forces one to do the logical thing, despite the hysteria around him. I don't believe in waiting for miracles. I had to make decisions.

The autopsy provided some justification for the final choice I made. "The brain is semiliquid with massive necrosis," the report said. I let the couple know there'd been absolutely no hope for recovery. Had the post-mortem shown a healthy brain, I don't know how I might have reacted.

If you'd been in my shoes for those 12 days, what would you have done?

Anonymous

Suggested Readings

Alsop, Stewart. *Stay of Execution.* New York: Reader's Digest Condensed Books, 1974.

A writer for *Newsweek*, suffering from leukemia, describes his last months.

Bayley, Joseph. *The View from a Hearse.* Elgin, Ill.: D. C. Cook, 1973.

Many views of death are discussed as well as death-related subjects such as terminal illnesses, funeral parlors, and grief. The viewpoint presented is religious.

Becker, Ernest. *The Denial of Death.* New York: The Free Press, a division of Macmillan Publishing Co., Inc., 1973.

This study explores the concept that man's innate fear of death is a principal source of his activity.

Gunther, John. *Death Be Not Proud.* New York: Harper Row and Co., 1949.

A father's memoir of the last year in the life of seventeen-year-old Johnny Gunther, a brilliant student, afflicted by a brain tumor.

Kübler-Ross, Elisabeth. *On Death and Dying.* New York: Macmillan Publishing Company, 1969.

Dr. Kübler-Ross discusses the five stages of dying and records interviews with patients who are terminally ill.

Leach, Christopher. *Letter to a Younger Son.* New York: Harcourt, Brace, Jovanovich, 1981.

The elder son, Jonathan, of the author of this book died at the age of eleven from an attack of asthma. The author has tried to give meaning to his son's death in writing this book.

Lear, Martha. *Heartsounds.* New York: Simon and Schuster, 1980.

M. Lear describes her physician husband's heart disease, how a doctor becomes powerless as a patient viewing medicine from the other side.

Lund, Doris Herold. *Eric.* Philadelphia: Lippincott and Company, 1974.

A mother's account of her son's battle with leukemia.

Moody, Raymond. *Life After Life.*

The author interviews people who have experienced clinical death and have been revived. In this book, they recount their near-death experiences.

Morris, Jeannie. *Brian Piccolo: A Short Season.* Chicago: Rand McNally, 1971.

The story of Brian Piccolo, a member of the Chicago Bears, who lost the battle against cancer.

Phipps, J. *Death's Single Privacy: Grieving and Personal Growth.* New York: Seabury Press, 1974.

Phipps tells her personal story of dealing with her husband's death, telling her children their father is gone, handling difficult finanacial problems, and coming out of the experience with a different sense of self and viewpoint on life.

Plante, David. *The Country.* New York: Atheneum, 1981.

This story has a son, David, returning home from abroad first to visit his ill and aging parents; later he comes home again to attend his father's funeral.

Wertenbacker, Lael Tucker. *Death of a Man.* New York: Beacon Press, 1974.

When L. T. Wertenbacker's husband was diagnosed as having cancer, they made a pact. When the pain of living with disease and death became too much, she agreed, at his request, to help him end his life. This book is the story of a loving, last journey together.

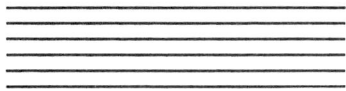

CHAPTER 3

"Games is just for a little while.
Your face and teeth is all your life."
—Muhammed Ali

VIOLENCE IN SPORTS

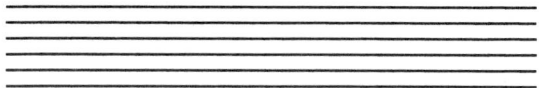

In this chapter you will read about the types of injuries encountered by football players and boxers. Does society create the need for this violence? Are the athletes at fault? Is aggression an instinct or is it learned behavior? You may find the answers to these questions in the following pages.

The reading skills you will use are those of making inferences and identifying examples an author uses to clarify main ideas. You will also learn a method of underlining to help you in reading textbooks.

1. Have you ever participated in a team sport? Which one? What things did you enjoy about being a member of the team?

_____

_____

_____

_____

_____

_____

_____

2. Were there things associated with team sports which you disliked? Explain.

_____

_____

_____

_____

_____

3. Was there a coach or physical education teacher who supervised the team? What was his/her attitude toward winning and losing?

_____

_____

_____

_____

_____

_____

4. Do you enjoy watching sports? Which ones?

_____

_____

_____

_____

_____

_____

_____

5. Why do you think so many people enjoy athletic events?

_____

_____

_____

_____

_____

_____

_____

6. Have you ever watched a football game? What was the most exciting moment? Why?

_____

_____

_____

_____

_____

_____

In Your Opinion

Do males and females tend to prefer different sports? If you think they do, which sports do males prefer? Females prefer? Can you think of a reasonable explanation for this difference in preferences? Explain.

_____

_____

_____

_____

_____

_____

_____

_____

_____

_____

_____

FOOTBALL

Football is one popular sport that most people would agree is violent. Author Don Atyeo, in his book *Blood and Guts: Violence in Sports*, includes these facts:

A physicist has determined that when a 240-pound lineman capable of running 100 yards in 11 seconds collides with a 240-pound back capable of covering the same distance in 10 seconds, the resultant kinetic energy is "enough to move 66,000 pounds, or 33 tons, one inch." When players stagger about the field mumbling to themselves after a play—"having your bell rung" in football parlance—the likelihood is that they have been hit on the helmet by a blow approaching 1,000 Gs (1,000 times the force of gravity). Astronauts on takeoff experience around 10 Gs and pilots tend to black out at about 20. Tests run on Detroit linebacker Joe Schmidt reportedly showed that he had to cope with blows which registered at 5,780 Gs.

According to the *Encyclopedia of Sport Sciences and Medicine* of 1971, from 1931 to 1965 there were 642 football fatalities (348 high school players, 54 college players and 72 professionals and semiprofessionals). A similar accounting by the National Collegiate Athletic Association determined that from 1931 to 1975 (excluding 1942) there were 821 fatalities directly related to football, with a further 400 or more indirectly related (the player collapses but does not die until at least four days later). Each season at least 50 and, according to one survey, as many as 86 out of every 100 high school players receive injuries serious enough to keep them off the field for more than a week. Another survey has estimated that each year 32 college and high school students become paraplegics as a result of playing football. Any boy who plays the game throughout both high school and college stands a 95 percent chance of a serious injury. Not so long ago, doctors at the University of Iowa examined 108 college freshmen recruits over a four-year period and discovered that more than a third of them had suffered neck and spinal injuries while playing high school football. Players at Ohio State University alone consume three thousand *miles* of surgical tape each season, mostly to pad and repair their injuries. According to the Occupational Safety and Health Administration, football players from all ranks—high school, college or pro—are two hundred times more likely to be injured than coalminers. As neurosurgeon R. C. Schneider wrote in 1973, "there is probably no better experimental or research laboratory for human trauma in the world than the football fields of our nation."

Statistics detailing the frequency of injury, of course, convey only the bare bones of football's violence. What must also be taken into account is the nature of these injuries. "I never saw such injuries, even in my intern years in the emergency rooms of inner-city hospitals," exclaimed Arnold Mandell. "Huge bruises spread over big slabs of the body." According to Dr. Alan Strizak, whose work at New York's Institute of Sports Medicine and Athletic Trauma brings him into close contact with several professional teams including the Jets, the toll pro football exacts on hands and head is "enormous." "If you ever see a lineman, the first thing you'll probably notice is that his hands are totally deformed . . . broken fingers, dislocated fingers." Players such as Lloyd Voss, who retired in 1973: near the end of his career Voss took to taping up each individual fingertip because his fingernails kept getting torn out. "Concussions, too," said Strizak, "they happen a lot." As do shoulder separations, broken limbs and dislocated hips. Knee ligaments are especially vulnerable, collapsing under the strain of body blocks which, as one surgeon reported, "are comparable to the thrust of a railroad tie against the unsupported knee."

One week before the final game of the 1976-7 season, the Jets' training ground provided a stark illustration as to the rigors of pro football. After a grueling losing season, the number of crippled Jets far exceeded the healthy. Of the twenty-three defensive players on the roster, only ten were fit enough for action. In the medical room the rows of stainless steel beds were in constant use, with players lining up to take their turn under the heat lamps and massage equipment.

INFERENCES—READING BETWEEN THE LINES

According to what you just read, more high school students died in football games between 1931 and 1965 than did professional and college players.

What conclusion(s) about high school football can you draw from this?

_____

_____

_____

_____

_____

How did you arrive at your answer? Although the author did not give the answer in the reading, you were able to figure it out. You were making an inference.

An inference is an educated guess. As you read the facts and ideas stated by an author you are "reading the lines"; when you put the facts and ideas together to draw conclusions, you are reading "between the lines." You are making an *inference.* Inferences are based on given information and leads you to a reasonable conclusion that has not been explicitly stated by the author.

People are making inferences all the time—that is, they are drawing conclusions from what they see. For instance:

- If you saw a father playing ball with his son on a Sunday morning, what kinds of inferences would you make?

_____

_____

_____

- If you were listening to a football game on the radio and heard a loud cheer from the stadium, what inference would you make about what had just happened?

_____

_____

_____

1. List the types of injuries Atyeo includes in the statistics he gives.

_____

_____

_____

_____

_____

2. Which of the injuries on your list would you consider most serious? Least serious?

Most serious: _____

_____

Least serious: _____

_____

In among this assembly was quarterback Joe Namath, shortly to be traded to the warmer climes of California.

Even in the exacting world of NFL football, Namath's medical history has set him slightly apart from his colleagues. His particular cross has been his knees, which remain today as a pinnacle of surgical ingenuity. His knees severely battered during college, Namath was told by doctors that if they survived four years of professional football he could count himself fortunate. Up to that point, with the help of an unnerving number of operations, he had held them together for twelve, although, as he confessed, they were giving him a little trouble. By this Namath meant that he had difficulty stepping sideways or walking up a flight of stairs (a complaint he shared with another pro footballer, Leon Donahue, who was eventually forced to move out of his split-level home). The knee joint wasn't designed to be able to take a lateral blow or a medial blow, Namath explained. Whenever a big man hits you and has some power behind the hit, something's got to give. And with the object of the whole exercise being, in Namath's own words, to kill the quarterback, the blows have come painfully hard and fast.

But knees are only one episode in Namath's painful career. Worse still was the nerve injury in his leg which happened around the time of his first knee operation:

> I used to get a jolt from my foot up my body every five seconds or so. It went on for about three weeks and almost drove me crazy. Medication wouldn't help it, morphine wouldn't help it. I lost thirty pounds. It was remarkable. One day I went into the doctor's office and I put the pills down and said, "Doc, I can't take any more medicine. This stuff's killing me." Thirty pounds light! That was the roughest. Then I lost the feeling in my foot. The neurosurgeons all assured me that the feeling would come back, and it has. But it took more than three years.

Namath's other injuries included separations of both shoulders, a broken wrist, a broken cheek bone, a dislocated finger and a broken ankle. His current problem was a torn hamstring muscle.

"This one here," he said, pointing to what looked to be a heavily strapped thigh underneath his trousers. "It's balled up right there. I can't extend my leg like that more than two or three strides. Then it pulls up and you can't run on it."

I asked him if he had to wear the bandage all the time.

"There's no bandage," he grinned, grabbing my hand and running it over the bulge on the back of his leg.

What at first sight had appeared to be a bulky arrangement of pads and straps was in fact a solid knot of muscle the size of a half baseball.

"*Jesus Christ!*" I muttered.

"Yeah. The whole muscle just tore and rolled down. Looks like a damn grapefruit, don't it?"

"What will happen to it? You're just going to leave it like that?"

"They could fix it, but it's not necessary. It would take a major operation, and for what we do in everyday life it's fine. I just can't run at all."

"How long has it been like that?"

"Three years."

I looked at Namath in amazement and he grinned again. "This is a rough game," he said, "people *have* to get hurt. You can't keep track of the hits. When you come off the field it can be bad, but it's not as bad as it is that night or the next day. When you try to get out of the bed the next morning it's a bitch."

Although the name of the game may be quarterback killing—and indeed, one of the most enduring spectacles in American football is that of a quarterback disappearing under a welter of clawing bodies just as he releases the ball—everybody, said Namath, suffers. "Running backs . . . they want to jack'em up and give'em a good hard hit and if it puts them out of the game, well . . . that's a shame. When I see defensive linebackers and cornerbacks taking the kind of blows they take, I can't understand how they can get up and come back the next play. Every play they're getting hit from one side or another. As long as it's a good hard hit, that's the incentive. Make the guy not want to get up, not want to come back the next play."

Namath was phlegmatic about football's physical toll, a toll which, according to Dr. Ronnie Sue Stangler of the University of Washington, cuts twenty years off the life expectancy of NFL players. Like many other NFL stars he was resigned to living with his injuries long after the cheering had stopped. He frankly admitted that by the age of 50 he fully expected to have difficulty merely putting one foot in front of the other, let alone negotiating a flight of stairs.

[Don Atyeo, *Blood and Guts*]

3. Joe Namath describes his professional football experience as "a painful career." What long-lasting physical disabilities has he suffered?

_____

_____

_____

_____

_____

_____

In Your Opinion

Why would someone choose to earn his living in such a profession?

_____

_____

_____

_____

_____

Imagine That

You are a parent. Would you want your son or daughter to play football? Why?

_____

_____

_____

_____

_____

_____

_____

_____

_____

In Your Opinion

What are some of the advantages of being a member of a football team? What are some of the disadvantages?

_____

_____

_____

_____

_____

_____

_____

_____

The following are quotes from professional athletes who have been actively involved in the game of football. As you read, note the similarities in the various points of view.

Said Alex Karras, retired star of the Miami Dolphins:

I hated everyone on the football field, and my personality would change drastically when I got out there. And that attitude was the only thing that kept me in the league. I'm not the biggest guy—I played at about 240, which is terribly light for a tackle—but I would hurt people. I had a license to kill for sixty minutes a week. My opponents were all fair game, and when I got off the field I had no regrets. It was like going totally insane. . . . Most linemen play it like that and most of them are very tough and very sadistic. In fact, the best linemen were all sadistic. They were like big docile dogs that were let loose on a football field and suddenly went crazy. Just like me.

Jerry Kramer wrote in his 1968 bestseller *Instant Replay:*

I don't really realize how brutal the game is until the off-season, when I go out to banquets and watch movies of our games. Then I see guys turned upside-down and backwards and hit from all angles, and I flinch. I'm amazed by how violent the game is, and I wonder about playing it myself.

NFL player Jean Fugett:

The game is *legalized* violence. Out in the real world you just can't go around beating on somebody's head the way we do. I can go into a game and just literally try to break somebody's neck.

Conrad Dobler, voted in 1978 the NFL's meanest player:

If you ever forget that football is a violent game, they'll catch you gazing at the stars and put your lights out.

Merlin Olsen, retired fourteen-year veteran of the Los Angeles Rams:

People ask, "You don't really hit that hard do you?" The answer is simply yes. The collisions are that violent, and the game itself is a very physical game. People who play for any length of time carry the scars for the rest of their lives. They may not be showing on the outside, but they'll have knees that are worn out, shoulders that don't work right, fingers that point in a different direction.

Robert Grant, associate professor of physical therapy at Ithaca College and a former college football trainer:

I would have to rate football as the most violent sport yet known. It's really almost undeclared war, and the way we play it in the professional game as well as in the high-pressure college games, it's just that—an organized, thoroughly campaigned and rigidly controlled game of outright violence.

Sports columnist and author Roger Kahn:

Football is terrifically violent. It's a game of impact, twisted knees and concussions. And whatever the mystique they try to put around it—that you have to be intelligent, that the scholar-athlete makes a good footballer—that's not really so. If you teach a gorilla to carry a football, he'd be the best running back in the history of the game.

A Game of Passion, an NFL publication:

Pro football is excessive. It's out of all proportion, beyond all bounds. It's an orgy of violence; an obsession with superiority; an excess of commitment, effort and discipline; a wallowing in flesh and will.

[Don Atyeo, *Blood and Guts*]

From the quotes you just read, list the words you would use to describe the personalities of most football players. Explain your choices.

_____

_____

_____

_____

_____

_____

_____

_____

_____

_____

A group of psychologists were interested in testing college football players to see if, in fact, they were more violent than other college students. The following article details their experiment and the results. Four tests were included in their experiment. As you read, place a check in the margin each time another test is described.

SEMI-TOUGH AND SUPERNORMAL

"I like my players mobile, agile, and hostile." This quote, by Jake Gaither, former football coach at Florida A & M University, lists three of the characteristics popularly ascribed to good football players. TV commentators, the sports pages, and books such as *Out of Their League* and *North Dallas Forty* have fleshed out the picture: football players have been described as basically conservative, willing to follow orders unthinkingly on the field, but a bit undisciplined in other areas, prone to beer busts and boasts of sexual prowess.

1. In the paragraph above, underline the stereotypes often used to describe football players.

During the 1980 football season, we decided to find out how college football players may differ in personality from other students.

Through the good graces of the athletic director and head football coach at a major university in the Southwest Conference, we conducted psychological evaluations of all 108 players on the football squad there. At first we were a bit concerned, afraid that testing by psychologists might make the players and staff ill at ease. Our fears were unfounded. We found no evidence of anxiety among them; this amalgam of muscle, crutches, pads, and bandages struck us as a harmonious group—just bigger than our customary subjects.

For comparison, we tested two other groups of students of the same age: 60 men who had earned at least one football letter in high school but had not lettered in college; and 60 men who had never received a varsity letter in any sport in high school.

We gave all of them four psychological tests. The first, the Profile of Mood States (POMS), is a list of 65 words or phrases—"carefree," "tense," "unable to concentrate," "grouchy"—that describe feelings. People taking the test indicate how well the term describes how they have been feeling during the past week by choosing one of five options ranging from "not at all" to "extremely." The result is a mood profile that covers six personality components: tension, depression, anger/hostility, vigor, fatigue, and confusion.

The football players came out very well. In sharp contrast with the stereotype, they showed considerably less anger and hostility than the other students, as well as less depression, confusion, and fatigue. Tension was about the same. They also showed a great deal more vigor and much less total mood disturbance.

Overall, the players' personality pattern was decidedly healthy. They seemed to be men intensely committed to life's challenges, who go about their business with a relaxed style and a clear sense of purpose.

The second test we gave the students indicates how much personal influence people believe they have over their lives, compared with chance or the actions of powerful others. The football players believed much more strongly than the rest of the students that other people had considerable control over their lives. Casual conversations with team members made it clear who some of these others were. The players obviously placed great stock in the advice given by the coaches assigned to their positions. In times of personal crisis, a strong safety looked to the defensive backfield coach for reassurance and emotional support, a halfback to the offensive back coach, and so on.

The California F-Scale, our third test, measured authoritarianism, broken down into nine characteristics that include conventionalism, superstition, submission, and aggressiveness. The football players scored significantly higher on nearly all of them. In brief, they were inclined to have rigid moral values and to be submissive to authority, willing to punish those who violate conventional values, and suspicious that a lot of illicit sex goes on unnoticed.

As a final test, we asked students how much they agreed or disagreed with nine statements about how important mental attitude was in winning games. Most of the nonplayers agreed strongly with the thought that "regardless of one's mental attitude, the person with the superior physical skill wins most athletic contests," and similar statements lauding matter over mind. The football players disagreed. Perhaps remembering that most of the opponents they had to deal with also were big, mobile, and agile (if not hostile), the football players felt that mental preparation—being strongly motivated, feeling happy, having mentally rehearsed what they had learned in practice—was vitally important in determining who won.

Some of our findings confirmed the stereotypes about college football players; more disputed them. We found most of the players we studied to be good psychological as well as physical specimens, if a bit dependent and conventional in their attitudes. Overall, they were free of debilitating stress and psychological distortion, and, least stereotypic of all, less aggressive than the average student. Coaches favoring "mobile, agile, and hostile" players may have to be content with more docile athletes. Or recruit only linebackers.

Jack R. Nation and Arnold D. Leunes

2. Fill in the chart below.

Test	*Purpose*	*Results*
1		
2		
3		
4		

3. Are the test results of the psychologists in agreement with the words you listed after reading the quotations of players? _____

BOXING

Another popular sport marked by much violence is boxing. Imagine what it would be like to be a professional boxer. Does the idea appeal to you?

Money—or social advancement—has long been the primary motivation behind boxing. It has traditionally been the sport of the poor man or the deprived. Indeed, the history of boxing can be read in terms of the continual upward shift of ethnic minorities: initially it was Jewish boys who were forced to turn to the ring in order to make money and gain respect; next it was the turn of the Irish; next it was the blacks. But today's comparative affluence has sapped boxing in the West of much of its motivation. Not only are there more "good trades" about, but for the deprived youngsters there is a whole new range of sporting outlets—pro football, basketball, soccer, baseball—offering better opportunities for fame and fortune than the ring, without the ring's incessant pain and violence. And so Western boxing is on the wane. . . .

Today it is the "hungry" countries of Latin America and South East Asia that are boxing's most enthusiastic supporters. In Bangkok there are three cavernous boxing stadiums which offer among them a bout every night of the week. In Mexico alone there are currently some seven thousand professional fighters, including five world champions. "They all have the same look," remarked the proprietor of one of Mexico City's nine flourishing boxing gymnasiums, "flat bellies and hungry eyes."

[Don Atyeo, *Blood and Guts*]

1. According to this author, boxing is not as popular in the United States as it once was. What reasons are given for this decline in the sport's popularity?

2. In Mexico, boxing is a very popular sport. What does the author mean by, "They all have the same look . . . flat bellies and hungry eyes?"

A boxer says:

> Back in Roman times, the gladiators—it wasn't so much a sport perhaps, but an exhibition of violence—they filled the arena and made the people go wild. I *think* it's the same urge with boxing. It's something innate in us. We can't change it. Now, I don't think anyone will tell you, "Sure I go to a fight because I just *love* to see somebody get knocked out!" And yet, in a fight, in a big fight, somebody goes down and whole arena goes wild. Same thing with car racing—car turns over and we all stand up. Perhaps it's bad for people to be that way, but unfortunately we are just that way. There's an accident on the street—somebody gets splattered on the corner somehow or other. Everybody from this block and around is going to come over here. They hate it. But they're looking at it, they're looking at the blood and the guts and everything. You can't explain that. You ask them, "You like that?" "Oh my God, I *hate* that! Jeez!" "Why are you looking at it?" "Oh, curiosity . . . " I think there's just a deep down thing in us that we have to see this stuff. It's fantastic for me because I make my living out of boxing.
>
> [Don Atyeo, *Blood and Guts*]

3. Have you ever witnessed a gory accident, a brutal fistfight, or a horror movie? Describe your reaction to one of these.

_____

_____

_____

_____

_____

4. Do you believe the boxer is correct when he says, "We are just that way"? Explain.

_____

_____

_____

_____

Some of the statements below refer to information given in the following poem while others are inferences. Decide in which category each statement belongs and place its number under the correct heading.

1. The boxer grew up in a poor home.
2. There are some boys practicing boxing in a gym.
3. A successful boxer achieves power and status.
4. The person to whom this poem is written had been a successful boxer.
5. The boys believe they will have a lot of money some day.
6. The fighter of the title probably belonged to a minority group.
7. This boxer was killed during a boxing match.

Stated	Inferences
_____	_____
_____	_____
_____	_____
_____	_____

Do you recognize in the following poem any concepts which you read about?

To a Fighter Killed in the Ring

In a gym in Spanish Harlem
boys with the eyes of starved leopards
flick jabs at your ghost
chained to a sandbag.

They smell in the air the brief truth of poverty
just as you once did:
　　　　"The weak don't get rich."

You made good.
Probably you were a bastard,
dreaming of running men down in a Cadillac
and tearing blouses off women.

And maybe in your dreams great black teeth
ran after you down dead-end alleyways
and the walls of your room
seemed about to collapse,
bringing with them a sky of garbage
and your father's leather strap.
And you sat up afraid you were dying
just as you had so many nights as a child.

Small bruises to the brain.
An accumulation
of years of being hit.

I will not forget that picture of you
hanging over the ropes, eyes closed,
completely wiped out.
Like a voice
lost in the racket of a subway train
roaring on under the tenements of Harlem.

Lou Lipsitz

EXAMPLES

There have probably been many times when you have used examples in your conversations. When writing or speaking, people frequently use examples to make ideas clear. Teachers certainly make frequent use of examples to help students understand important concepts. A common opening in many sentences in our everyday speech is, "For example. . . . "

When reading textbooks, it can be very helpful to identify examples. They usually are there to clarify a major concept (or main idea). Therefore, as you read you will be able to identify the *main ideas*, and use the examples as the author intended—to aid in your understanding. Usually an instructor will expect you to remember the main ideas. If you have a good grasp of these main ideas, you will probably be able to provide your own examples.

Let's practice using and identifying examples which clarify a main idea.

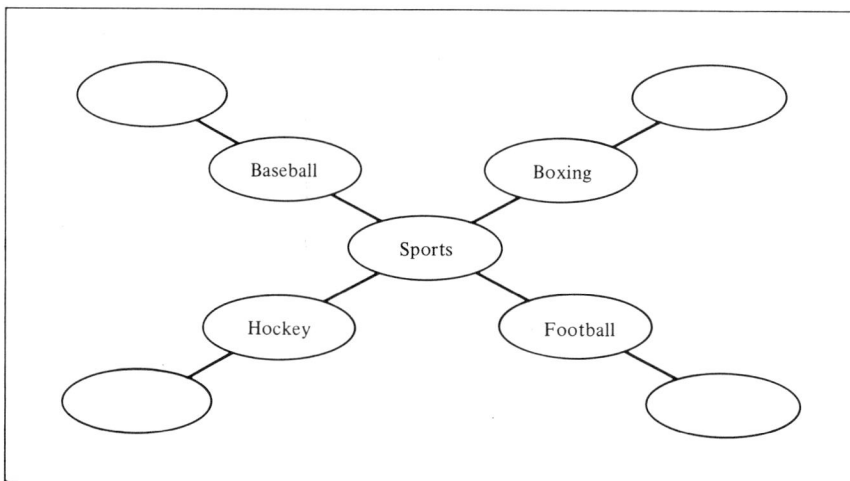

1. In this diagram, the central idea is _____ .

Hockey, boxing, football, and baseball are all *examples* of different kinds of sports.

2. In the blank circles, give *examples* of the types of equipment associated with each of the sports.

Look at these two statements about violence in our society.

> Violence has been a recurring feature of American society. As H. Rap Brown said, "Violence is as American as cherry pie."

> Since the Boston Tea Party and the inception of the American Revolution, violence has been a recurring feature of American society. Slavery was maintained through overt and covert use of violence. The Ku Klux Klan conducted terrorism throughout many areas of our society well into the twentieth century. Immigrant and ethnic groups in the large cities found that the "melting pot" was not free of conflict. The labor movement has often been involved in violence to achieve the proclaimed rights of laboring men and women. In the frontier and rural regions of America, a "dead Indian was a good Indian," and the use of vigilantes, the "law of the gun," and lynchings were mechanisms of social control. More recently, in the 1960s we have witnessed, often on color television, the violence of the Vietnam War, assassinations, brutality directed at civil rights demonstrators, and urban riots. As H. Rap Brown said, "Violence is as American as cherry pie."

> [Snyder and Spreitzer, *Social Aspects of Sport*]

You probably found the second statement more interesting because many examples are included to help make the main idea more vivid.

In the blank spaces, list six examples used by the author to support the main idea.

Violence has been a recurring feature of American society.

1. _____

2. _____

3. _____

4. _____

5. _____

6. _____

FIGHTING BEHAVIOR

Fighting behavior, or aggression, among human beings has been a source of worry for such a long time that some people have studied fighting behavior in animals to find out what happens, what causes it and whether it can teach us anything about fighting among men. In this exercise you will get an opportunity to read some of the findings of such research and to come to your own conclusions.

Here are five statements about fighting behavior. Read each statement carefully and decide whether you agree with it or not. Note down your answers in the column titled Your Opinion.

	Your opinion		Writers' opinion		
Statements	*Yes*	*No*	*Yes*	*No*	*Paragraph*
1. The only reason why animals fight is to win living space.					
2. Fighting in animals often leads to death or serious injury.					
3. Most animals run away to avoid injury in a fight.					
4. Fighting behavior is very similar between one species and another.					
5. Fighting behavior in animals is learned; it is not innate (inborn).					

[*Skills for Learning*]

Following are several writers' opinions on each of the statements. As you discover these opinions note them in the "Writers' Opinion" column. Include the letter of the paragraph which supports your choice.

Text A

Among vertebrates—from fish to man—fighting between members of the same species is practically universal. The reason seems to be that animals of the same kind, holding a similar position in the natural setting, must compete with each other for food, nesting places, and building supplies. When animals fight, therefore, it serves the function of separating, of spacing out, the animals in the area they occupy. This not only prevents overcrowding but allows animals sufficient space to live. Also, because fighting arises from competition for partners, the best animals—the strongest and the fittest ones—are left to multiply the species.

Text B

Another factor must be considered in fighting behavior among animals: fights occuring between animals of the same species rarely end in death and almost never result in serious injury to either animal. In fact, such fights closely resemble a competition with rules rather than a serious fight. There would be serious consequences, in fact, if the loser were killed or seriously injured because the loser need not necessarily be a less healthy or weaker animal; he may simply have the disadvantage of being a young, rather than a mature, animal.

Text C

If aggressiveness is learned behavior, it can be prevented by teaching or con-ducting. Research findings, both from fieldwork observation and from laboratory experiments, suggest, however, that aggressiveness is not learned by animals but is inborn (or innate). Furthermore, the pattern of fighting differs from one group of animals to another. A particular species or group of animals will thus follow its own fighting pattern.

Text D

Although serious fights do occur between animals of the same type, or species, they usually occur in species which have no weapons that can cause death. Animals which can kill or inflict serious injury on one another are usually the ones which can easily and quickly get away from a fight. Others may admit defeat by lying down in such a way as to show the other animal that he has won. For example, if a young dog lies on its back exposing its stomach, its stronger fighting partner will realize that he has won.

Text E

Most animals do not run away nor do they surrender (give up) to avoid fights in which they may be killed. Instead, they fight in such a way as to measure their strength without seriously hurting each other. This type of fighting is often referred to as ceremonial fighting.

[Skills for Learning]

In the next reading the author presents his view on the reasons for violence in our society, and the function of sports in controlling that violence.

Breakdown of Social Control

Social disorganization is based on social relationships. It is clear that a crowd of strangers who have not had time or opportunity to develop social relationships with each other, form a disorganized group compared with individuals who have either grown up with each other from birth or who have had long previous associations.

When we examine the incidence of destructive violence and fighting in our society, we find that it is associated with social disorganization of various sorts. The slum areas of our large cities—no matter which nationality or race they include—often include many immigrants who are complete strangers to each other, and there are many instances of broken and disorganized families. The skidrows of our big cities are inhabited by homeless wanderers without families. Even in the affluent areas of middle class suburbia, the extreme mobility associated with industrialized life, with families moving from house to house and even from city to city every two or three years, may result in a weakened form of social organization and a loss of control which may be expressed in forms ranging from drug-taking to outright violence and vandalism.

Finally, there is a built-in period of social disorganization which normally occurs in our society. The young person, and particularly the young male, breaks away from his parental family at about the age of 18 or so, and normally does not form a new family for several years later. It is this age period between 18 and 25 in which the highest numbers of crimes and violence occur, and it is also the time when there is the highest incidence of automobile accidents. Social control frequently breaks down in men of this age, which is also the age when sport is of greatest importance in our society and when it might play a great deal more important role than it does with respect to the control of aggression.

The Function of Sports in the Control of Aggression

Organized sports and games, whatever their nature, are a form of social organization; hence, they exert some degree of social control, both over the participants and over the spectators. It follows that sports by their very nature must counteract the factor of social disorganization as a cause of destruction and violence.

The function of sports and games is to prepare individuals for participation in adult life and particularly to provide ways for the control of undesirable aggression and violence. If you watch a group of very young children trying to play a game, you observe that most of their time is spent arguing about what the rules are and whether the players have conformed to them. This provides training in the practice of organized cooperative living according to rules and eventually of living according to laws. In many cases, the rules and concepts of childhood games are closely related to general concepts in our society. For example, the idea of "fairness" is very close to that of equal treatment under the law. Again, in adult-dominated contact sports, such as football and ice hockey, there are rules which define the limits of physical violence, and there are persons assigned to see that these rules are obeyed and to proscribe penalties for their violation. In short, games and sports are training grounds for the control of aggression.

[G. Kenyon (ed.), *Contemporary Psychology of Sport*]

Following are ideas which are stated or implied in the previous reading selection. They are followed by examples of these ideas. In Column A place a check if you agree with the statement. In Column B write the number of the statement which it illustrates.

1. A crowd of strangers who have not had time or opportunity to develop social relationships with each other form a disorganized group.
2. Frequent moves to new neighborhoods result in social disorganization.
3. A young adult of 19 or 20 years of age is experiencing a period of social disorganization.
4. Organized sports are a form of social organization.

A   *B*

_____   _____   1. There is a high incidence of vandalism in wealthy suburbs.

_____   _____   2. People who feel as if they don't belong to a social community are likely to show an interest in sporting events.

_____   _____   3. A typical bar on any Saturday night is a place of social disorganization.

_____   _____   4. The majority of men interested in sports are young adults.

As you read underline the five methods of controlling violence the author describes.

While the current situation in our society is far from encouraging, the fact remains that games and sports provide effective methods for the control of undesirable aggression.

First, games and sports are one way of organizing life along peaceful and non-harmful lines. This in itself combats one major cause of aggression—social disorganization.

Second, games and sports in childhood provide training in living according to rules; an essential technique for successful adult social life.

Third, rules learned this way, plus habits of participation in sports, are particularly valuable for the control of violent behavior in the young adult age group, which represents a built-in developmental period of social disorganization in our society. (Persons working with this age group have long known that sports participation is an effective technique, but we are now beginning to appreciate the theoretical reasons *why* it works, and hence to know its limitations as well as its advantages.)

Fourth, apart from their effect in combating social disorganization, games and sports work psychologically in two different ways. One of these is through passive inhibition: the mere fact of not fighting forms a habit of not fighting in a particular situation. The other is through exposing individuals to situations that normally elicit fighting, such as intense competition or pain, and teaching them to restrain themselves.

Finally, games and sports have the physiological effect of restoring normal physiological balance through violent exercise, when this balance has been upset by strong emotions such as fear and anger. Many sports actually provoke such emotions and then relieve them, which gives the player practice in dealing with such emotions.

[G. Kenyon (ed.), *Contemporary Psychology of Sport*]

Choose one of the five methods for controlling aggression, and give an example to illustrate it.

_____

_____

_____

_____

_____

_____

_____

Match each of the following situations with each of the methods for controlling aggression listed above.

1. The children attending summer camp were required to participate in sports activities every day. There was usually a peaceful atmosphere in the camp.

_____

_____

2. Bob had an argument with his boss. After work he stopped off at the gym to play a game of raquet ball before going home.

_____

_____

3. As children, Bill and Mary often played games with neighborhood friends. As adults they are always very careful not to break any law, no matter how small.

_____

_____

4. In the spring and summer, most of the families in our suburban town participate in a community softball league. In the winter they compete on bowling teams.

_____

_____

5. Sixteen-year-old Jack hopes to win a basketball scholarship to college; he plays basketball several hours each day. He thinks his peers are foolish for wasting their time getting into trouble with the law.

_____

_____

Aggression—(ə gresh′ en) n., 1. the practice of making assaults; forceful, often striking, behavior

---

1. List some words which describe an aggressive person.

_____

_____

_____

_____

_____

2. Now circle all the words you just listed which you consider to have a negative meaning attached to them.

3. Describe a situation in which aggression would be an appropriate behavior.

_____

_____

_____

_____

_____

_____

_____

Catharsis—(kə thar′ sis), n., 1. an action that encourages or permits the discharge of pent-up socially unacceptable behavior.

On Aggression

Sports enthusiasts believe that violent sports are one of the last safety valves for aggression left in our world. People need an avenue, so the argument goes, by which they can vent their hostilities and aggressions in a harmless and socially acceptable fashion. Without such an avenue, aggressions build up like a head of steam in a boiler until they burst out in antisocial directions—muggings, wife beating, warfare and other undesirable forms of behavior. By shooting a deer, boxing a few rounds or by watching a group of paid professionals locked in combat on a football field, people can relieve their pent-up hostilities, work out their aggressions and return home at the end of the day better for it. In other words, health through ventilation.

[Don Atyeo, *Blood and Guts*]

1. What are the examples given of undesirable forms of aggressive behavior?

_____

_____

_____

2. What are the examples given of acceptable forms of aggressive behavior?

_____

_____

_____

3. What does the author mean by "health through ventilation"?

_____

_____

_____

The theory of vented emotion—the catharsis theory—is by no means a modern discovery. It was first postulated by Aristotle (*catharsis* is derived from a Greek word meaning to purge emotion) who saw the dramatic stage as offering a means of dissipating "pity and fear." Later the theory was applied to sport. It is probable that the Roman rulers viewed the arena as a way of diverting the day-to-day hostilities of the public. . . . In rural England many sporting events were considered annual safety valves. There is also evidence that successive governments allowed the existence of the bare-knuckle prize ring in the hope of defusing the violence of the lower classes which on several occasions . . . brought England perilously close to revolution.

The catharsis theory enjoyed a rebirth earlier in this century following the discoveries of Sigmund Freud. In an attempt to explain the horrors of World War I, Freud decided that mankind was cursed with an inherent aggressive drive, a "death instinct," which when turned inward led him to destroy himself and when turned outward drove him to destroy others. Other authors took up Freud's idea and developed it further. . . . While acknowledging the existence of inherent aggression, they saw it as a potent drive, "not to be minimized, but to be dealt with; not to be denied, but to be converted; not to be hated, but to be harnessed" (Karl Menninger in *The Vital Balance*, 1963). One way of dealing with the build-up of aggression was by finding it an outlet. As early as 1948 Menninger's brother William was advocating that "competitive games provide an unusually satisfactory outlet for the instinctive aggressive drive." Bertrand Russell, an English philosopher, argued that there was a "savage" within each of us which must find expression through some means compatible with civilized life. He suggested sport. . . .

It was the Nobel Prize-winner Konrad Lorenz who brought the catharsis theory to full popular bloom. After a lifetime spent studying the habits of birds and animals, Lorenz came to the conclusion in his celebrated book *On Aggression* (1963) that man was "a dangerously aggressive species" whose innate aggression, while winning him supremacy over his primeval competitors, now threatened him with violent destruction of the species. Man's aggression was an instinctive appetite for fighting, or at least deterring, rivals, he wrote. This appetite built up in the same way as hunger or the sex urge, but whereas an animal could discharge its hostility through fighting or ritual displays of aggression, man's sophisticated weaponry meant that his fights or ritual hostilities inevitably led to bloody conflict. In the age of the H-bomb, the consequences were annihilation. The only hope for mankind lay in redirecting this damned-up aggression into acceptable outlets. As before, it was sport which suggested the perfect solution.

After *On Aggression* . . . Lorenz became famous, and catharsis—or "Drive

Discharge" as it was now being called—became very fashionable. It was made even more appealing by Lorenz's disciples. "It is obvious that the encouragement of competition in all possible fields is likely to diminish the kind of hostility which leads to war rather than to increase it," wrote British psychiatrist Anthony Storr in *Human Aggression* (1968); " . . . rivalry between nations in sport can do nothing but good." Philip Goodhart . . . in *War without Weapons* wrote:

> The contests will sometimes be far from peaceful. But sport is an outlet for the aggression that lurks beneath the surface in every society. . . . As the twentieth century devises yet more total means of mass destruction, it is not too fanciful to discern an instinct for self-preservation in the popular passion for representative sport. A kind of warfare perhaps. But war *without* the weapons.

"I think that if we could suit up the whole world in football uniforms," Pittsburgh Steeler Jack Lambert once said, "maybe we wouldn't have any more wars." It would seem that most athletes today would agree, perhaps not with Lambert's choice of sport, but certainly with the idea that athletic contest offers some form of therapy. Of all the sportsmen I spoke to, not one wholly rejected the idea of catharsis through sport, and many of them . . . considered it one of sport's major assets. "I think it's better for people to work out all their violence watching me smash into someone else rather than not to have this outlet and go home from the office and take it out on their families, beat their wives or something," said LA Ram Tom Mack.

In recent years the sporting press has heard many such utterances. When San Diego football coach Harland Svare was asked what he thought football was accomplishing for spectators after being howled off the field by a murderous crowd, he replied, "it's moving it from the front page to the sports page." "Football is the safety valve for these people. . . . There would be far more violence without football. I'm sure of that."

[Don Atyeo, *Blood and Guts*]

4. Explain the "catharsis theory."

_____

_____

_____

5. According to the selection you just read, what useful function is served by sports?

_____

_____

6. Many psychologists and researchers mentioned in the selection have written about catharsis and its function in sport. In the following exercise, match each person with his theory by writing the letter of the theory in Column B next to the name of the person in Column A.

Column A

1. Sigmund Freud _____

2. Karl Menninger _____

3. William Menninger _____

4. Bertrand Russell _____

5. Konrad Lorenz _____

Column B

a. Man has an inherent aggressive drive which must be dealt with.

b. There is a savage in each of us which must be expressed in a civilized way.

c. Our aggressive instincts are similar to the hunger or sex instincts. We are a dangerously aggressive species, threatened by violent destruction. We can only survive by redirecting this aggression into acceptable outlets.

d. Man has a death instinct which will either destroy himself or others.

e. Competitive games are an excellent outlet for aggression.

Think About This

Many games are organized like a war. Think of three ways in which a sport and a war are similar.

1. _____

_____

2. _____

_____

3. _____

_____

Other Research on Aggression

In some research directly addressing the relationship between sport and aggression, Sipes, an anthropologist from Southampton College, has found that heavy contact sport is positively associated with patterns of aggression in society and that there is no basis for the possibility that sport could ever serve as a substitute for destructive aggression such as war. After randomly selecting 10 warlike and 10 peaceful societies throughout the world, Sipes was interested in discovering whether "combative sport" was present to the same extent in all of them or whether it was more likely to be found in one or the other. Contrary to what might be expected using a model based on the ideas of Freud, he discovered that in the 10 warlike societies, 9 had combative sport and in the 10 peaceful societies, only 2 had it. To verify his cross-cultural findings, he then looked at the relationship between the extent of military activity and the popularity of various types of aggressive sport in the United States from 1920 to 1970. Again, he found a positive relationship.

[Jay J. Cookley, *Sports in Society*]

1. True or False: The catharsis theory would suggest that a society with many aggressive sports would be a peaceful society.

2. Do the studies of Sipes support the concept of the catharsis theory?

UNDERLINING

Some people think that as long as they look at words on a page, they are reading. They think of reading as a passive activity which requires no more effort than passing their eyes over words. If you have ever "read" a page and then felt that you did not understand what you had read, it was probably for this reason.

Reading is really a very active process. Think of it as similar to playing ball. When someone throws a ball to you, you must actively catch it. If you do not, the ball will go past you. An author has thrown ideas out to you by writing words. Your role, as the reader, is to actively catch the ideas. Otherwise, they will not register in your mind—they will go past you.

One effective method of reading actively is to underline parts of the material. Because so many students do not understand the purpose of underlining, they end up underlining too much.

There are several purposes for underlining:

1. Underlining keeps you reading actively. You are constantly identifying concepts and making decisions as to what should

be underlined. You cannot fall asleep while you are doing this.
2. <u>Underlining saves time when reviewing for exams.</u> Instead of rereading long sections of a text, you need only reread underlined portions.

Now that you have some understanding of the purposes for underlining, here are some suggestions for <u>how to</u> underline.

1. Underline all <u>key terms</u> (often printed in italics or boldface) and <u>definitions.</u>
2. Underline <u>main ideas</u> and <u>important concepts.</u>
3. <u>Do not underline examples</u> (However, you may want to indicate examples, using "ex." in the margins.)
4. <u>Keep underlining to a minimum.</u> Remember, when reviewing you want to be able to read only what you have underlined. What you underline <u>should be important</u> and <u>make sense.</u>

If you look back over the preceding explanation of underlining, and read only the underlined words, you will see that all the key concepts stand out. The underlined words give you very clear, direct information.

The next selection, taken from a psychology textbook, describes various psychological theories on the subject of aggression. Glance through the excerpt and create an outline using the headings.

_____

_____

_____

_____

As you read, underline all the important terms and definitions and indicate examples in the margins.

Biological Instinct Theory

Based upon their research studies of animal behavior, ... Konrad Lorenz, Robert Ardrey, and Anthony Storr conclude that aggression is instinctive or genetically determined.

Another important concept (developed from the study of animals) is that man is a territorial animal who will fight to defend his own territory. This idea appeals quite naturally to those persons interested in sport behavior because the concept of territory is utilized in several sports, the purpose of which is to encroach on another's territory while protecting one's own. Perhaps a football team gives ground more grudgingly near its goal line because its members become more aggressive as a result of the greater threat to their territory.

Social Learning Theory

Social learning theory hypothesizes that aggressive behavior is learned. . . . Aggression research indicates that aggression is a contagious aspect of behavior . . . and that aggression and violence, once seen or perpetrated, tend to be reinforced in a *circular effect.*

In sport, if we place great value on toughness and (fighting), if the norm for successful sport behavior is violence and intimidation, and if the successful sport role models are visibly aggressive, then an environment for learning aggression is created. The behavior models just described will reinforce aggression in observers, who see the aggressive acts; and because of the circular effect, reinforcement of themselves and of others will take place with increased frequency and intensity. Several of the recent attacks made by athletes and ex-athletes on the game of football testify to the circularity of violent and aggressive behavior.

Further reinforcement of learned aggression is provided by the incentives that sports place on aggressive behavior (consider the "bit hit" award for the player making the most forceful block or tackle).

It is reasonable to expect that in sports where aggressive behavior is called for, the strength of the aggression habit will be increased. . . .

[Leonard Berkowitz, *"Experimental Investigations of Hostility Catharsis"*]

Physiological Theory

[This theory holds that] a person's aggressiveness depends upon the state of his nervous system, which in turn determines his mood. When a person is happy, only a small number of different things can make him angry. When he is irritable, a great many things can throw him into a rage. But even on an irritable day, it takes a specific stimulus to make a person act aggressively. Fighting does not take place in a vacuum.

However, the appropriate stimuli are not the only factors that determine whether a person will behave aggressively. The appearance of aggressive behavior is also dependent upon the state of the neural systems (in the brain) that govern this behavior. When these systems are active *and* the appropriate stimuli are present, the person will act aggressively.

This interaction between a person's environment and his nervous system is the key to [this] model of human aggression.

[K. E. Moyer, *"The Physiology of Violence"*]

On the line before each of the following statements place a "B" if it supports the biological instinct theory, an "S" if it supports the social learning theory, and a "P" if it supports the physiological theory.

     1. When Mr. Brown and his neighbors heard that the city was planning to build a major highway through their neighborhood,

they wrote petitions, called a neighborhood meeting, and threatened to sue the city.

_____ 2. If a person doesn't get enough sleep and doesn't eat regularly, s/he will probably be easily provoked to act aggressively.

_____ 3. Children who watch a lot of violence on television tend to be more aggressive with their peers.

Construct a test consisting of at least eight questions on this selection. The test might include the following kinds of questions:

1. Identification and/or definitions of different theories of aggression.
2. Examples to support ideas.
3. True and false questions.
4. Multiple choice questions.

Now that you have made up test questions, your instructor will ask you to form groups. As a group, organize the questions into categories according to the theories discussed. List the questions in the appropriate spaces below.

Biological Instinct Theory

_____

_____

_____

_____

_____

_____

Social Learning Theory

_____

_____

_____

_____

Physiological Theory

_____

_____

_____

_____

_____

In Your Opinion

Do you think that violence is a desirable part of sports? Why?

_____

_____

_____

_____

_____

_____

_____

_____

If you think that violence is *not* necessary in sports, what can be done to help eliminate this excess?

_____

_____

_____

_____

_____

_____

_____

_____

_____

_____

For each of the poems which follow, provide a title which expresses it's meaning. Explain the reasons for your choices.

> *Soon fades the spell, soon comes the night,*
> *Say will it not be then the same,*
> *Whether we played the black or white,*
> *Whether we lost or won the game?*
>
> **—Lord Macaulay**

My Title: _____

> *When the One Great Scorer*
> *comes to write*
> *Against your name—*
> *He marks—not that you*
> *won or lost—*
> *But how you played the game.*
>
> **—Grantland Rice**

My Title: _____

In this chapter you learned the following important ideas about reading:

1. When you "read between the lines" you are making inferences.
2. Authors frequently include examples in their writing to make main ideas more understandable.

3. Underlining serves two important purposes: it keeps you involved in the reading and helps you in reviewing for exams. In this chapter you learned how to underline effectively.

This chapter also looked at the personalities of athletes, at different theories on aggression and society's influence on aggression.

A Further Reading

The first time that I was made aware of the realities of boxing was in 1974 when Muhammad Ali fought George Foreman for the world heavyweight crown in the ramshackle city of Kinshasa, Zaire. Until then I had always thought boxing a game, in which the contestants—even the heavyweights—were more or less normal human beings whose punches were tactical weapons and therefore somehow less painful than punches thrown in anger during, say, a bar-room brawl. Then again the closest I had ever been to a major heavyweight bout was six feet from a television set, which, as I soon discovered, was about as useful for understanding boxing as trying to study the surface of the moon through the wrong end of a telescope.

The first blow to my preconceptions came when George Foreman entered the gymnasium for his first training session. The thing about Foreman was that he was unlike any other person in the room, sparring partners included. He was a monster, the heavyweight champion of the world, a man-machine who exuded doom and destruction like the sweat which trickled down his enormous shoulders. The punches that he landed as he attacked the big punching bag were equally inhuman. I had tested the bag earlier, punching it as hard as I could. I had not been able to leave more than the slightest dent in its leather surface; in fact, the thing had barely moved on its heavy chain. Before Foreman began his assault he had his manager, Dick Saddler, grasp the bottom of the bag and lean into it with his shoulder. The first punch he threw jacknifed the bag like a snapped breadstick and sent Saddler reeling back a dozen paces. It was an awesome display of power. I saw the champion cripple the punching bag and shook my head in sorrow for Ali's probable fate, but the thought that Foreman might actually snap Ali like a breadstick never really entered my mind. Boxing was, after all, only a game.

The first punch which caught Ali's rib cage disabused me of that simple-minded belief. It landed with a sickening crunch which cut through the shouts of the crowd like a laser beam through butter. Seated at ringside a yard away from the two fighters, I could see Ali's face contort with agony and hear the rush of air as he tried to suck in his next breath. He lay back on the ropes directly above my head and Foreman went to work using the same staggering blows which he had used to destroy the big bag. For the first time I realized why people pay so dearly for ringside seats at heavyweight title fights. When you are close enough to be showered by sweat after each blow it becomes stunningly obvious that boxing is not sport but mortal combat, a primitive blood battle in which two giants smash at each other with their fists with all their might. It is savage, bloody and cruel, and also entirely mesmerizing.

Foreman kept up his lethal barrage for seven rounds. In the end he was beaten by the uncontrollable rush of his own brute power which slowly drained away as he hammered Ali, a fighter whose own iron physique had been carefully disguised by the graceful proportions of his body. Foreman was a man trained to bludgeon to pulp anything that stood in his path; Ali was a fighter who had trained solely to absorb punishment. On that night in Zaire Ali's training proved the more effective. It was as simple as that. Early in the eighth round, with Foreman's misguided bombs still whistling around his head, Ali stepped forward and landed two lightening punches flush in Foreman's puffed and bloody face. They connected with the pistol crack of leather against bone and they sent the champion spinning helplessly to the canvas. He tried to get up but he couldn't. I could see his body quivering with the effort.

I returned to London a few days later and caught a cab at the airport. I began chatting with the cabbie and inevitably the conversation turned to Zaire and the fight. I gave him a few impressions of the fight and at the end he half-turned in his seat and said with a knowing grin, "But it was a fix though, wasn't it." "Come on," he continued as I looked at him in astonishment, "you can't tell me they were *hurtin'* each other in there. Big George Foreman bangin' away? Jeez, I coulda done better myself! And that last bit where Ali put'im down, those punches wouldn't've hurt my bleeding grandmother." He had seen it all with his own eyes, he said. He had paid ten pounds and taken his seat in a cinema showing a live relay of the fight on one of those larger-than-life closed-circuit screens. "You see everything on them," he declared. "See right up their bleeding noses if you want."

How can you argue against ten-foot video? I turned away and stared out the window, remembering poor George mumbling inanities in his dressing room after the fight, and how the morning after Ali had kept getting up from his seat in the sun on the banks of the Zaire to check whether he was still pissing blood.

[Don Atyeo, *Blood and Guts*]

Suggested Readings

Corbin, Richard. *Requiem for a Heavyweight.* In *Twelve American Plays* New York: Scribner and Sons, 1973.

An original T.V. script about the destruction of a once successful heavyweight champion fighter.

Cousy, Bob. *The Killer Instinct.* New York: Random House, 1975.

Bob Cousy, basketball superstar and professional coach, takes readers into the dark corners of his own life to show how destructive the killer instinct can be.

Gardner, Leonard. *Fat City.* New York: Farrar, Strauss, 1969.

The story of two third-rate fighters, one just thirty, trying desperately to make a comeback, the other a raw kid just starting out. The two men whose lives touch on each other briefly, the seedy world of boxing hangers-on and managers, the women in their lives, and the frantic ways they try to turn a buck all come to life with blistering accuracy.

Gardner, Paul. *Nice Guys Finish Last—Sport and American Life*. New York: Universe Books, 1975.

A book of stories about sports teams and those who control them.

Heinz, W. C. *The Fireside Book of Boxing*. New York: Simon and Schuster, 1961.

An anthology of stories about boxing.

Lipsyte, Robert. *Assignment: Sports*. New York: Harper & Row, 1968.

John Pappas, about seventeen years of age, pale and thin, appeared on the second day of spring training. He had come to Florida to be a pitcher for the N.Y. Mets. Nobody knew what to do with him.

Lipsyte, Robert. *Sportsworld*. New York: Quadrangle, The New York Times Book Co., 1975.

Lipsyte describes the world of sport as a rich, dark corner of our national psyche, joyous and oppressing, idealistic and hypocritical, giving and greedy.

Lorenz, Conrad. *On Aggression*. New York: Harcourt, Brace, Jovanovich, 1974.

A study of aggressive behavior in animals.

Mailer, Norman. *The Fight*. Boston: Little, Brown and Co., 1975.

Mailer tells the story of a major boxing event when Mohammed Ali and George Forman met in Zaire, Africa for a fifteen-round, heavyweight title fight.

Morris, Jeannie. *Brian Piccolo: A Short Season*. Chicago: Rand McNally, 1972.

A biography of a young football player for the Chicago Bears who lost a seven month battle against cancer.

Odets, Clifford. *Golden Boy.* In *20 Best Plays of the Modern American Theatre* edited by John Gassner. New York: Crown Publishers, 1965.

The development of a young prizefighter.

Schaap, Dick. *Sport*. New York: Arbor House, 1975.

Dick Shaap has been a professional sports writer for years. In this book he presents a collection of columns which have appeared in the newspapers featuring well-known sports personalities such as Mohammed Ali, Fran Tarkenton, Joe Namath, Tom Seaver, and others.

Schulberg, Budd. *The Harder They Fall*. New York: Random House, 1947.

A relentless disclosure of the fight racket and of the men and women involved in it. It is the story of Eddie Lewis—a story of violence, of evil, and yet of understanding, of pity, and even of the beauty of tragic fury.

Tatum, Jack, with Bill Kushner. *They Call Me Assassin*. New York: Everest House, 1979.

Jack Tatum, of the Oakland Raiders, played the game according to the rules. "I am supposed to hit people and destroy the play, and the harder I hit them, the better I can do the job." Tatum, involved in a terrible accident which paralyzed another player, reflects on the nature of the game.

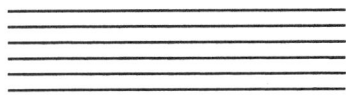 # CHAPTER 4

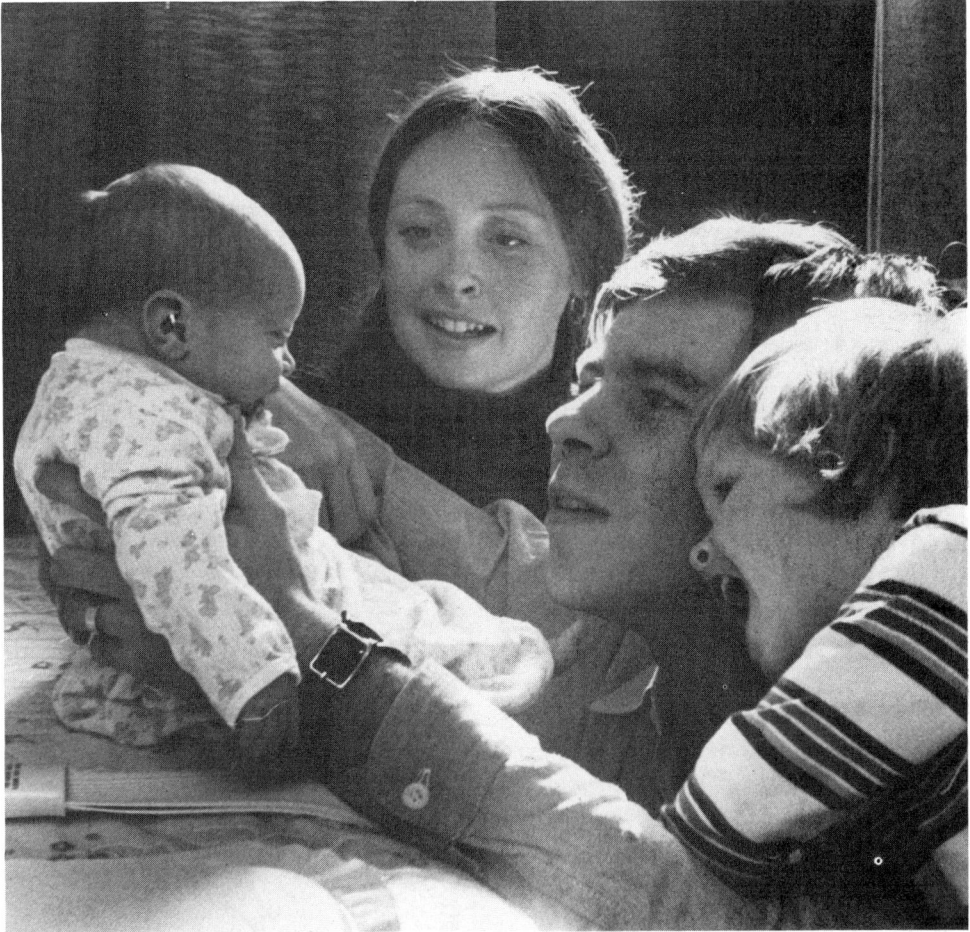

Every man can be a father,
but not every man is a daddy.

ADOPTION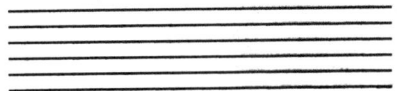

As a reader, one of the important areas in which you need to develop an awareness is that of points of view. This means that you need to be able to

a. Recognize when an author is presenting a point of view.
b. Recognize what the particular point of view is.
c. Recognize your own point of view on the issue (if you have one).
d. Keep your point of view separate from that of the author.

A simple experiment will illustrate this. Take three items from your food shelf at home (for example, a soup can, a cereal box, and a soda bottle), and place them on a table. Have four people sit at the table, one on each side. Ask each person to write a detailed description of what he or she sees—shapes, words, colors, and so on. When all four people have completed their descriptions, read them aloud. You will find that they are all different. Which one is right? Could they all be correct? Why?

The following excerpt from a book on child care will illustrate this idea of points of view in written material. (As soon as you read the words "child care" your own point of view about this topic was called up in your mind.)

> There is a sensible way of treating children. Treat them as though they were young adults. Dress them, bathe them with care and circumspection. Let your behavior always be objective and kindly firm. Never hug and kiss them, never let them sit in your lap. If you must, kiss them once on the forehead when they say good night. Shake hands with them in the morning. Give them a pat on the head if they have made an extraordinarily good job of a difficult task. Try it out. In a week's time you will find how easy it is to be perfectly objective with your child and at the same time kindly. You will be utterly ashamed of the mawkish, sentimental way you have been handling it.

> [John B. Watson, *Psychological Care of Infant and Child*]

As you read the preceding paragraph, you realized that the author has a particular point of view concerning the handling of children. How would you describe his point of view? Do you agree with it?

_____ A tough unloving view of child car

_____ No

(By the way, the advice to parents in the paragraph above comes from a book written in 1928 by a psychologist named John Watson. He was a "behavioral psychologist" who had a tremendous influence on child-raising practices in the United States at that time.)

Here is another author's point of view about the same topic.

> Don't be afraid to love him and enjoy him. Every baby needs to be smiled at, talked to, played with, fondled—gently and lovingly—just as much as he needs vitamins and calories. That's what will make him a person who loves people and enjoys life. The baby who doesn't get any loving will grow up cold and unresponsive.
>
> [Benjamin Spock, *Baby and Child Care*]

What is the difference in the point of view of these two writers?

One writer believes in a loving

approach the other believes

in a unemotional approach

What is *your* point of view on this topic?

I agree with the second point

of view.

In this chapter dealing with adoption, you will find differing points of view. Be alert to possible motives which help explain each. Explore your own ideas, imagine yourself in someone else's shoes, reflect upon the ideas offered and draw your own conclusions.

"Every man can be a father, but not every man is a daddy."

1. What do the words "father" and "daddy" (or "mother" and "mommy") mean to you?

> Father - A ascribed role.
> daddy - a loveable person
>
> Mother - Same + Housework
> Mommy - Loving

2. Do you believe that the responsibilities of a father and a daddy are different? Explain.

> yes
> father is Finacial and material
> responsibility
> Daddy - loving caring , unworried

Sometimes parents give birth to a child and find it necessary to give it up for adoption. Adoptees grow up with two sets of parents.

In Your Opinion

If you adopted a child, would you tell him/her that he/she was adopted? Why?

Yes, because I wouldn't want the child to think I was ashamed because it was adopted

If you were an adopted child, would you want to know that you were adopted? Why?

Yes, because I would probably have differnt characteristics than the rest of the family and I would woonder why.

The following article by Dr. Brazelton, a professor at Harvard Medical School, deals with the interaction between parent and infant.

What It Means to Adopt a Baby

[1] It seems to me harder work to raise an adopted child than it is to raise your own. The rewards can be just as great, but the inevitable periods of failure, imagined or real, seem to hit harder.

[2] Parenting a child is never easy. There are wonderfully rewarding good times, but they are liberally mixed with those in which feelings of failure predominate. Every time the child has a temper tantrum, lies about a broken vase or steals and hides money from your pocketbook, you are bound to question your worth as a parent. In the end, though, because the child is your own offspring, you tend to be accepting of certain kinds of defects as part of his inheritance and you can justify them to yourself. With an adopted child it is difficult to see the defects as anything but a failure in your parenting or a result of his shady past.

[3] In other words, an adoption carries with it an *adjustment*—that of seeing that the child is indeed an individual, with all the faults and idiosyncrasies of any human being.

[4] Since preparation for parenting in our culture is so meager—with little opportunity for being actively involved with small children as we grow up, with few societal backups for new parents, with the generation gap working against the kind of support from the extended family that other cultures offer new mothers and fathers—it seem important to outline some of the adjustments that will be necessary to an adoption. I shall describe some of these in the hope that by doing so it will enhance the pleasure and decrease the pain of making such adjustments.

[T. Berry Brazelton, *"What It Means to Adopt a Baby"*]

1. In the paragraph above, underline the three examples of how preparation for parenting in our culture is meager.

2. True or False: There is a difference between raising a child who is your own offspring and raising an adopted child. Explain.

   False — raising adopted or real kids you run into the same problems

3. Can you think of any "backups for new parents" offered by our society? List them.

   Child Care
   Religion

[5] During a pregnancy expectant mothers and fathers go through a predictable turmoil. They tend to question themselves, to wonder whether they'll ever be adequate parents, to be afraid that they will repeat what they conceive of as their own parents' mistakes, to regret, perhaps, that they let themselves in for such an upheaval and for such a change in their lives. During the nine months, however, these questions tend to be resolved, and the turmoil the husband and wife have experienced actually energizes them for coping with the new baby.

[6] Parents who are about to adopt a baby go through the same kind of self-questioning, of wondering whether they are making the right decision and of feeling inadequate to the role of mother and father. But there is not the length of the pregnancy to work out these doubts. The baby is usually presented to them suddenly, the turmoil has to be resolved and the energy refocused on the baby right away. No wonder the first few days are often a nightmare of readjustment.

[T. Berry Brazelton, "*What It Means to Adopt a Baby*"]

4. What reason is given by the author for referring to the first few days as a "nightmare of readjustment"?

During pregnancy most of these differences are resolved but not in adoption

[7] Prospective parents should be forewarned that the first weeks are bound to be tumultuous, but that this will also be a period of learning for all the participants. Rather than feeling the failure that most new parents feel in such a period, they can see this as an important time of readjustment to one another, of learning how to get upset and how to calm down together. Living *through* a disorganized period can be the most rapidly effective way of achieving togetherness. In addition, if the adopted baby is not newborn, the period of adjustment can be expected to take longer.

[T. Berry Brazelton, "*What It Means to Adopt a Baby*"]

5. How can the first few weeks, which are bound to be tumultuous, be a period of learning for parents?

yes, learning how to cope with the baby and each other can wear on a person

.

[8] None of nature's built-in processes that lend themselves to bonding to a new baby—such as labor, delivery and breast feeding—are available to help adoptive mothers over this initial hump. And I believe that most parents think they ought not to feel anything but positive about the new baby lest they end up not liking him. Of course, that's not true. One is bound to feel angry at and tired of any child at times.

[T. Berry Brazelton, *"What It Means to Adopt a Baby"*]

6. What examples of bonding are mentioned in the paragraph above?

labor, delivery, breast feeding

[9] We have been studying the rhythms of reciprocity basic in the interaction of parents and babies as they learn about one another. We have identified the rhythms of a small baby, his looking at an observer and looking away, smiling and then waiting, cooing and then quieting, that are necessary to maintain himself in the face of the excitement he feels as he interacts with his mother and father or other important person. These very subtle rhythms get locked with his parents' rhythms of movement, of looking, of vocalizing, to form a feedback system that each participant depends on for knowing about the other. We think that these rhythms may be partly inherited and partly entrained in the uterus, so that at birth they are ready to be put into effect in a natural mother-infant interaction.

[T. Berry Brazelton, *"What It Means to Adopt a Baby"*]

7. What does "feedback system" mean?

Talking back to one another in words and actions

[10] In an adoptive situation, a longer period of adjustment may be necessary before the baby's and the mother's rhythms can be interlocked. So I usually warn adoptive mothers that initially they are apt to feel lost and unable to feel out their baby, but that if they can see the synchrony as a goal rather than as something that should be there from the beginning, the period of adjustment may not be so disturbing.

[11] As far as difficulties in adjustment are concerned, however, I would venture that *all* adoptions will be fraught with some kind of imbalance—between the eager parents who want so desperately to reach the baby and that baby, who has developed rhythms, expectations and thresholds of his own. With the disruption of losing an environment to which he has become accustomed, one can expect the baby to regress, to become unreachable or upset. He may show such symptoms as colic or crying, feeding problems or sleep problems, and in toddlers, even toilet-training problems. All these can be expected and even respected. For they mean that the child is conserving his resources and reorganizing his response patterns and expectations.

[T. Berry Brazelton, "*What It Means to Adopt a Baby*"]

8. In the paragraph above, underline the examples of a baby's regression.

9. According to the author, are all signs of regression bad? Explain.

They aren't all Bad the
child is just reorginizing
his energy

[12] An example of another adjustment at a later period might be subsumed under the question: When should a child be told he is adopted? I think the fact of adoption should be treated as a normal part of a child's background from the first and should not be saved to "expose" to him at a special time when he is "ready." He will feel that if it has been hidden, it must imply something wrong—ergo, wrong with him. If the adoptive parents can present the idea that they wanted him enough to care for him—someone else's child—as *theirs*, that through their growth together as a new family they have forged links to one another in all sorts of now-indissoluble ways, his concerns about his "bad blood," about his rejection by his natural parents, can be eased.

[T. Berry Brazelton, "*What It Means to Adopt a Baby*"]

10. When does the author think a child should be told that he or she is adopted?

A time when he is ready

[13] Sooner or later adoptive parents must also be able to discuss the child's questions about who he really is, who his real parents are and why these parents gave him up. Certainly these questions and the feelings that underlie them can never be completely eradicated, but opportunities should be provided for discussing them all along the way—even when there can be no real answers.

[14] In times of stress or of bursts of autonomy, the child will be likeliest to test these questions against his parents. He needs to do this to reaffirm their commitment to him and to be reassured that they find him a valued, solid person. For "Will you give me up too?" may be implied by his testing.

[15] In order to do this, to reassure their child that his fears of being deserted, of being worthless, of turning out to be unfortunate like his fantasied real parents, all are groundless, adoptive parents should be ready in their own minds. They must discuss and deal with their own questions about his background—about why his parents were willing to give him up, about whether his "inheritance" may indeed predispose him to acting out later on. If they have settled their own concerns, they will be ready to help the child with his.

[16] Coming to terms with such issues will be necessary before the parents can be firm and consistent about disciplining the child and establishing limits. For the child may demonstrate that he needs his parents to stop him in order for them to show how much they care about him. Too many adoptive children are "spoiled" by their mothers' and fathers' inability to set such limits, and this certainly is an injustice to them. Limits and discipline are an important way for parents to demonstrate their caring, and are a necessary part of all children's learning to set limits for themselves.

[T. Berry Brazelton, "*What It Means to Adopt a Baby*"]

11. In what ways are limits and discipline important for children?

they show caring and are a part of learning

[17] Giving their child the continuity of a caring family, of a sure background in which to grow and test himself, is the goal for all parents. Adoptive

parents may find that the achievement of this goal is more difficult, especially at the beginning, but they can be sure it is just as satisfying.

[T. Berry Brazelton, *"What It Means to Adopt a Baby"*]

Below are six sentences which express the main ideas of six different paragraphs in the selection you just read. Match each statement with the appropriate number.

Main Idea Sentence	*Paragraph Number*
a. It is more difficult to accept the defects of an adopted child then one's own child.	16 *e*
b. The turmoil felt during pregnancy prepares parents for the birth of their child.	9 *C*
c. There is a natural system of rhythmic communication between the mother, father and the infant.	7 *f*
d. Parents who adopt do not have an extended period of time to work through their turmoil.	5 *b*
e. Setting limits and behaving consistently is a way for parents to show their love.	1 *A*
f. The turmoil experienced during the first few weeks after adopting a child can be a time of achieving togetherness.	6 *D*

Explain the steps you used to do the exercise you just completed.

_____ Scanning to Find the answer _____

_____

_____

_____

Compare your method with that of another student. Did you both do it the same way? _____ If not, was one way more efficient than the other? Why?

_____

_____

_____

_____

Another view of the problems that accompany adoption in our society is presented in the next selection.

ADOPTION: ADOPTING PARENTS, ADOPTED CHILDREN—A REAL FAMILY?

[1] How many families do you know, among your own relatives and close friends, in which there is an adopted child—a child who has completely become a member of her new family but who has no kinship ties at all to her adoptive parents? Probably you can think of several families, some of them with more than one adopted daughter or son. Most Americans think adoption is a good thing.

[2] Recently it has also become quite common for a husband to adopt his wife's children born of an earlier marriage, especially if they are still small. They know who their birth father is, but usually they carry their adoptive father's name. Far more rarely, as yet, a wife may adopt her husband's children born of another marriage. In one such case the judge hearing the woman's petition to adopt was frankly puzzled. "Why are you doing this?" he inquired. "It isn't necessary. It doesn't change anything."

[3] "Oh, but it does," the adopting mother insisted. "It makes us all one family—a *real* family!"

[4] For us, as Americans, this—making a real family—is at the heart of adoptions, particularly those about which we hear most often in which the birth parents are neither relatives nor friends of the adopting family, but strangers unknown to the adopting parents and the adopted children alike. Taking these children, often as young infants, to become our own children, we pray that they in turn will accept us as their true parents. We want to create a real family, and one, we hope, that will be less troubled than are so many real—that is, birth—families.

[5] Nowadays adoptive parents are counseled to explain to the child as early as possible that she was adopted and for this very reason is especially precious. However, not so long ago the fact of adoption was one of the best-kept social secrets—until the day the tale was told. Naturally, every adult close to the family and almost every neighbor knew the truth. But they honored the illusion and tacitly conspired with the new parents to keep the secret. Then all too often it was another child—a taunting child who had heard whispered gossip—who broke the news: "You don't really belong. You're adopted!" And all too often this news shattered the fragile identity of the family and traumatized everyone—parents and children—who had believed that their family was "real." Only a fortunate few ever recovered completely.

[6] Partly in rebellion against painful experiences of this kind, many young couples over the last generation have deliberately adopted children who are so startlingly unlike each other and the adoptive parents that there can be no possible doubt that theirs is a family formed by choice, not by birth. It is a practice that has distressed social workers in adoption agencies, who had been trained to believe that a good match between parents and children was necessary for the adoptive relationship to work out successfully. Disregarding this, many prospective parents sought out not only American-born Black or Hispanic babies for

adoption, but also Japanese, Korean, Chinese or Vietnamese infants or the mixed-race children fathered and abandoned by our soldiers during foreign wars.

[7] The obvious physical difference certainly did away with one kind of secrecy. But the aim remained the same. The child's birth parents were even more remote, strange and untraceable. And the new parents hoped that with so much out in the open, the adults who chose and the infants who were chosen—because they were *not* required to match physically—would be joined together through shared love as a real family.

[8] This is a daydream it would be very easy for almost any of us to share. What very few of us realize is that it is a very American daydream. The dilemma of wanting and not having a child—or of lacking many healthy children—is virtually universal. But in different societies people have found the most various solutions. Ours is only one, and it is a rare and unusual solution at that.

[9] In general, it provided a humane and workable answer to the problems of a great many married couples who have longed for children, and to the problems of children in desperate need of a family. However, good social institutions are open to criticism, and adoption as we have institutionalized it is no exception.

[10] From the beginning, many prospective parents who have been rejected by placement agencies, for whatever reason, have looked for black-market babies, a practice that has often fostered corruption and sometimes has led to blackmail. Other prospective parents have objected strenuously because they have been refused a child of another race or ethnic background or even of a religion other than their own. In still other cases the rigid separation of foster care and adoption, as we all know, has led to tragedies for caring adults and the children they love. And finally, today there are many adults adopted as babies who want to know something about their origins: who their birth parents were, why they were given up for adoption, whether they have sisters and brothers. Yet our present laws forbid the breaking of silence on this whole subject.

[11] Today our most basic beliefs about adoption—that children should "match" their adoptive parents, that an adopted child should not know who her birth parents were, that foster parents may not adopt their foster children—are under attack from all sides. And now we must face the question, Where do we go from here?

[Mead and Metraux, *Aspects of the Present*]

1. Why are adoptive parents encouraged to tell their children that they are

adopted? _____

_____

_____

_____

_____

2. Why do people adopt children who look different from them?

_____

_____

_____

_____

3. According to the authors, who is disturbed by interracial adoptions? Why?

_____

4. What do social workers consider a "good match"?

_____

_____

_____

_____

5. In paragraph 10, four specific problems related to adoption are described. Signal words are used to introduce each problem. Circle the signal words and underline each problem.

Here are two different points of view of women who gave their children up for adoption:

Mrs. Bryant's Story

A 48-year-old married mother of five put it this way: "My social worker told me I was doing the best thing for the baby by placing her for adoption. She assured me I would forget the pain, and that after I married and had a family, I would never think of this baby anymore. She was dead wrong. You never put such an experience behind you. No matter how happy I am, or how good I feel about my family, I will always wonder about that first baby, and wish that somehow I could see her and know how she is. I would give anything if she wanted to meet me. I could tell my family. My husband knows, and my children would understand. I don't feel that I have the right to interfere with her life. I wish that it could have been different but I had no choice but to give her away. That doesn't mean that I don't continue to love her and to want to know her. If she's out there looking for me, I hope she find me."

[Baran et al., *The Dilemma of Our Adoptees*]

Think About This

1. Why did this woman put her child up for adoption?

   _____

   _____

2. How did she feel at the time she put the child up for adoption?

   _____

   _____

3. How does she feel now about it?

   _____

4. Is this woman happy with her family?

   _____

   _____

5. Does her family know about this child? How do you know?

   _____

   _____

6. What sex is the child she put up for adoption?   _____

Mrs. Marco's Story

I was wondering if you have any concern or respect for the natural parents. I will explain my situation. I am twenty-two years old and will be twenty-three in December. I gave up my daughter when I was seventeen. My parents left the decision up to me. They wanted me to keep her. I fed her all the time I was in the hospital. I must admit it was a tough decision. I felt that at that age it wouldn't be fair to a baby to be brought up without a father or be brought up in the company of a baby-sitter while I worked. I knew that I could spare my feelings by keeping her, but she would suffer with one parent. I knew that if I gave her up I would suffer, but if she needed a new pair of shoes she would have them. There are many wonderful people who are willing to accept another person's children and love them as their own. I knew she would have a chance for a college education if she wanted one. I knew I could not give her this. I suffered a severe depression for a year and a half after giving my child up. I do not feel that it is fair for a woman to knock on my door fifteen years from now telling me she is my daughter. I do not feel it would be fair to my husband or children either. Mentally I do not think I could handle this. I forfeited everything to give this child a loving home and a fair chance and now people like you start movements like this. Why? No child has its full birthright unless it is born gleefully wanted by both parents. Would you do me a favor and show this letter at your next meeting to those who are seeking their natural parents? I am now in tears. I will never live a comfortable life without being full of fear that the adoption records will be obtainable.

[Henry Ehrlich, *A Time to Search*]

Think About This

1. Why did this mother give her child up for adoption?

2. How did she feel about it at the time?

3. Does she want to meet her daughter? Why?

Imagine That

You have given up a child for adoption. Do you think you would share the feelings of Mrs. Bryant or Mrs. Marco? Explain.

_____

_____

_____

_____

_____

_____

_____

_____

_____

_____

_____

_____

_____

In an adoption situation other people are involved besides the birth mother. Here are the views of parents who have adopted children.

Mrs. Johnson's Viewpoint

The wish to search for biological parents is one of those thoroughly understandable, absolutely human impulses. But it seems to me that in most circumstances it's an impulse that needs to be controlled. Adoptees who begin this search often do not recognize the anger they feel unconsciously for their biological parents—especially for their mothers, who in our culture still have prime responsibility for child nurturing. The wish to find one's mother may very well be an unconscious way to punish her. "Don't think I'm going to let you get away with what you did," the subconscious mind says in its pain. "You'll pay, all right. The happier you are right now, the guiltier I'll make you feel."

[Eda LeShan, "*Should Adoptees Search for Their Real Parents*"]

1. Does this mother feel that her adopted child should be encouraged to search for her birth mother?

_____

2. What reasons does she give for her opinion?

_____

_____

Mrs. Perez's Viewpoint

If we had known that there was a possibility of the records being opened, we never would have adopted. We did not adopt our children to be caretakers or baby sitters for the natural mothers who gave them up for adoption. We adopted because we were guaranteed total anonymity, and we feel that promise must be honored. I am sure that most adoptive parents feel as we do, and view your work as meddlesome and dangerous. I'm sure that none of you are adoptive parents, for you have no understanding of how adoptive parents feel.

[Sorosky et al., _The Adoption Triangle_]

1. What does this parent mean by "we adopted because we were guaranteed total anonymity"?

_____

_____

Mrs. Wright's Viewpoint

Unsealing the records threatens the safety and happiness of all the women who relinquished their children for adoption. We feel such love and compassion for that woman who could not keep our little boy. We feel she deserves protection forever from having to fear that her life will be disrupted at some future date. How could she live in peace? How could she make a new life for herself, if she was waiting for a stranger to ring her doorbell and break her heart?

[Sorosky et al., _The Adoption Triangle_]

1. In this parent's opinion, who will be most hurt by encouraging the child to find the birth mother?

_____

Some adoptive parents feel differently about their children's search for roots. Mr. Fisher says:

My relationship with the kids has been established by the fact that I have been with my adopted daughter for thirteen years. I don't know that her relationship to her friends or anybody else particularly affects her relationship with me. That is well established. I am not afraid. Eventually she is going to get out and live her own life. But she does have another set of parents. That is a fact, and it concerns her. Since it does, I want her to find out as much as she can about it and I'll help her do it.

[Sorosky et al., *The Adoption Triangle*]

1. List several words which you think would describe Mr. Fisher. Why did you choose each one?

_____

_____

_____

_____

_____

_____

_____

Sometimes an adoptive parent assumes an even more active role in a child's search for a birth parent. To whom is the following letter written?

Dear Friend,

After all these years she is coming to see you. Her name, as you probably know by now, is Barbara. Your daughter—and mine.

"The biological mother," the Children's Home calls you. I am "the adopted mother." Cold, impersonal titles, I feel. But not a cold, impersonal agency. I'm particularly grateful for the way they're handling this meeting—having Barbara and you get acquainted on neutral ground. "They can take it from there," Miss Haynes said, indicating that either you would decide to see each other again in more intimate surroundings, or you would settle for the single encounter. I honestly don't know which way I hope it goes.

"You'll always be my mother," Barbara told me, sliding into my room in that awkward, diffident way she has, "but there are things I've got to find out. Like . . . " She did not finish that sentence.

Although she'll be 19 next month, I still cannot quite let her go. "Honey, you can't hold her by the hand forever," my husband tells me. Nor will she let me. Still, I do not want her to be hurt. Not by her boyfriend. Not by her boss at the shop where she works part time. Not by you.

She has made you a gift. Please, answer her questions, even if they hurt you. There are things, as she says, that she needs to know.

I must confess to some curiosity about her background myself. To pick just one harmless thing. What collection of ancestors came together to give her that charming Slavic face, those almond eyes, and that wonderful Sophia Loren mouth?

Miss Haynes revealed that you were at first reluctant to see Barbara. I can understand: You have your life, your family. Children you were able to keep and love. None of them knew. Now you've had to tell them. This disturbed you. But surely there is some relief there, too. Expecially since, as Miss Haynes told us, they are all supportive of you.

To be frank with you, I did not approve of Barbara's joining Birthrights Unlimited. Such a militant group, I thought. Asking questions. Taking legal action. Opening records. Spading up the past. Disturbing things. Disturbing people. People like me. People like you. But I've come around. I've thought hard about it, and I recognize that it would drive me crazy to know that I had another family living out their lives without my knowing where or even who they were. I'd need to find out. So does Barbara.

Whatever you do, please don't make her feel unwanted. I would like to ask you to welcome her, to give her some sign of love. There is, after all, a bond between you that neither can deny. Nor, for that matter, can I.

With best wishes,
Caroline

[Shirley Cochrane, "Letters to the Other Mother"]

1. Why is this mother afraid to have her daughter meet her birth mother?

_____

_____

_____

2. What is meant by "she has made you a gift"?

_____

_____

_____

Imagine That

You have adopted a child. Would you want your child to search for the birth parent?

1. What concerns would you have for your child?

_____

_____

_____

_____

_____

2. What concerns would you have for yourself?

_____

_____

_____

_____

_____

_____

You have just read several selections which express a variety of parental emotions dealing with the child who has been adopted. Like the parents, these children have many strong feelings about who they are and where they come from.

Imagine That

You are an adopted child.

1. Would you want to find you birth parents? Why?

_____

_____

_____

_____

_____

2. If your answer to the preceding question is "yes":
   a. Would you search if your adoptive parents were opposed?

   _____

   b. What kinds of disappointments might you find?

   _____

   _____

   _____

   _____

   _____

   _____

3. If your answer to question 1 is "no": Do you think other adoptees should have the right to find their natural parents? Why?

   _____

   _____

   _____

   _____

   _____

4. Within your family, how do you think you might feel different from other children who are not adopted?

   _____

   _____

   _____

   _____

   _____

_____
_____
_____
_____

The next few selections reflect the feelings and concerns of some adoptees.

John's Viewpoint

Even though you have wonderful folks and live in a loving home, no one can convince me that an adopted child will not always have a yearning to know just who he really is. He will always, deep within himself, have a fear, a haunting of who he really is. For he is like a twig broken from the trunk of life that bore him, and if he is not put in rich soil, he can wither into nothing. They say, "as the twig is bent, so shall it grow." I don't give a damn how you twist a twig that you have taken from a tree other than the family tree it came from, it will grow in the direction of its natural birth. You cannot take inherited instincts and destroy them; they will surface.

Then there is the old question of diseases. I worried about my health. I had no idea what diseases I might have inherited from my biological parents. Any time I did anything that was improper I worried. Were my real kinfolks really bad-natured people? Maybe I would inherit bad ways. I felt unwanted and alone. I had no identity other than the one I made up for myself. I even worried about maybe marrying a relative—how would I know? Because of this I did not marry until I was thirty-five years old. I was a "mongrel."

[Sorosky et al., *The Adoption Triangle*]

1. What are some of the fears John expresses?

_____
_____
_____
_____

2. John compares an adopted child to a tree twig. What similarities does he see?

_____
_____

3. What does John mean by "I was a 'mongrel'"?

_____

_____

_____

_____

Kathy's Viewpoint

I, for one, would highly resent the intrusion by my biological parents into my present life, for they mean absolutely nothing to me. I feel about them the same way I do about the stranger on the street—general indifference. Quite frankly, I really do not understand why there is such a problem. What difference does it make whose seed started what entity? What is of prime importance, however, is who cared for and nurtured the child with their love. My real parents are the two people who gave me that love.

Sometimes I think that adoption is used by individuals as an excuse to keep from coping with problems encountered by all individuals throughout the course of life—if it were not the adoption complex, it would be something else. Society, however, just happens to be very sympathetic to homeless waifs—many people who do not know about adoption put adoptees in that classification, applicable or not.

I feel pity for adoptees who spend so much of their life dwelling on the identity of their biological parents rather than living. To have an individual believe that such knowledge is essential to their self-identity is tragic. Self-identity is supposedly a state of mind based on establishment and knowledge of one's goals and values rather than on details of the conception of that person.

[Sorosky et al., *The Adoption Triangle*]

1. List five words that you would use to describe yourself. Put them in order from the most important to the least important.

_____

_____

_____

_____

2. List three people who have played an important part in helping you to feel the way you do about yourself.

_____

_____

_____

3. What does Kathy mean by self-identity?

_____

_____

_____

4. Do you agree or disagree with Kathy's ideas about self-identity? Explain.

_____

_____

_____

_____

_____

_____

_____

_____

_____

_____

_____

_____

_____

Jake's Viewpoint

When I was little I couldn't really understand what being adopted meant. It was hard for me to comprehend that I had another mother somewhere. It finally stuck when I was 6 or 7. If I adopted a child, I'd tell him he was adopted from the beginning, but I'd wait a few years to explain the details.

I know some information about my birthmother, but not that much. I've heard what she looks like, her approximate age, and where she lived. She was very musical, quite beautiful, and just starting college when I was born. I guess she knew she was doing the right thing—that she couldn't have given me a very good life. I admire her because I think it takes a special vision to be able to see way ahead. I mean, if you had a tiny baby, it would be easy to say, "Well, I can handle this. After all, how much room can he take?" At the time, I wasn't much bigger than a football, and could have fit into the drawer of a night table. I don't know anything about my birthfather, and I don't wonder about him at all.

You know, I never really think about having another mother. I just consider the mother I have as my mom. When I was little I used to think about my first mother more often. Whenever I got mad I'd say, "Oh, you're not my real mother—you can't punish me like that!" And my mother would say, "Yes, I *am* your real mother. Even though you had a birthmother, I am you real mother now."

Around Christmastime, if I had been really bad, I used to worry, "Oh dear, Santa Claus is going to put coals in my stocking, and worst of all, Mom's going to take me back to the adoption agency," Of course my parents told me it wasn't true, but I still thought it.

My little brother goes around telling everybody he's adopted. I'll be walking home from school with him and someone will say, "Oh, you two don't look anything alike," and he'll always scream out, at the top of his lungs, that we're adopted. Everyone always turns around, and it makes me blush. It also makes me want to beat him up.

Some of my friends ask me questions like I was some freak or oddball, but I just say, "What's wrong with being adopted?" and they say, "Well, it's just that you're different," and I tell them, "No, it's not different, it's special," and after that they don't usually bring the subject up again.

Being adopted can be very embarrassing at times. For example, there's another kid I know who's adopted, and he's always getting into trouble. It really makes me upset when people say to me, "Oh, you're adopted just like him—you two should stick together!" He's a kid who talks back to teachers and writes on the wall—stuff like that. I don't even want to be near him.

I don't think I'll ever search out my birthmother. Maybe she would be awful and I'd just be disappointed. If she searched for me, I wouldn't particularly like it, but I don't think I'd mind. I'd be willing to go out for dinner with her, and I'd probably like to ask her a few questions. But I wouldn't want to stay with her or anything like that.

[Jill Krementz, *Blessed are the Children*]

1. Underline some of the examples which indicate how Jake feels about being adopted.

2. How old do you think Jake was when he was adopted? _____

Holly's Story

At about 1:30 in the afternoon, the telephone rang and the voice on the other end asked for my mother. It was a Saturday and I was home alone. I said she was out, so the caller asked me to write down her name, address and telephone number. Then the woman who was on the other end of the phone said, 'Fourteen years ago I had a baby that I gave up for adoption. I believe you are my daughter.''

I was in total shock, and as we talked, my mind was in a different world. She asked me a lot of questions about myself and filled me in on what had happened to her. She said she was 5'4", had blond hair and green eyes, and that she worked for a management consulting company. And she explained why she had put me up for adoption. She was 17 when she met and fell in love with my birthfather, but by the time she found out she was pregnant they had broken up. She wanted to keep me, but her mother talked her out of it. She told me she had gotten married since then, to someone else, but was presently divorced and she didn't have any other kids. We talked for about an hour, and after I hung up I started sobbing. One of my father's friends came in the door looking for my parents, and I put my arms around him and just kept on crying and crying. I wasn't crying because I was sad. I had planned on searching when I got a little older, and my parents were going to help me. In fact, it was something we had talked about very recently. So I was happy that my birthmother had found me, but I never expected it to be so all-of-a-sudden. I always figured I had a few years more before I really had to deal with it.

I was finally able to tell my father's friend about the phone call, and he drove me over to where my adoptive mother was working. On the way over we met my dad, but I was still crying so hard I couldn't explain what had happened. He thought someone had died until I was finally able to tell him. Later, my mom and dad and I talked and decided it would be best to begin a relationship slowly— that we would just exchange information and photographs by mail for a while. We did that for about two months. I was still wandering around in a daze during this time, and I was worried about how my life might change. My mother said I should just think of Alison, my birthmother, as a friend, and that I should try to put myself in her position, so that's what I tried to do.

Six months later we finally met. We invited Alison to stay with us for a few days. My parents and I met her at the airport, and that was really weird. After we got home she gave me a picture of my birthfather and also the little bracelet they had put on my wrist when I was born. She had kept it all these years.

We spent the weekend talking about what she had been doing since I was born and how she had found me. It took her eight months and a lot of work, calling around and checking records. I showed her my scrapbook and told her about my school—stuff like that. We had a good visit, and after she left, we wrote letters back and forth. The following month, I went to visit her for a week. That was really exciting because I had never been to New York before, but it upset me when her friends would say stuff like, "So you're Alison's daughter." I didn't know what to say. I sort of went along with it because I didn't know what else they could call me, but by not saying anything, I felt like I was taking away something from my mom. It's confusing because I don't know how to categorize my relationship with Alison. I don't want to think of it as purely biological, but I don't know how else to define it. I feel ridiculuous introducing her as "my friend," and yet I certainly don't think of her as my mother.

In my view I have only one mother and that's the mother who raised me and mothered me—who gave me food and shelter and love while I was growing up. That's my definition of a mother. Alison is the person who gave me my heredity and my life, and while I don't want to push her away, I don't want my mother to feel any loss of prestige.

The past two years have been real hard on my parents. I get the feeling that sometimes they're thinking that they're losing me, and that's the last thing in the world I want them to feel. It isn't true. And most of all, I don't want to lose them. Once, when my mother and I were having a fight—the way all mothers and daughters have arguments—my mom said something like "Well, you can just go and live with Alison." Even though I knew she didn't mean it, I felt really hurt. That's the sort of thing that can't ever be said—not even in the heat of an argument.

I think I'm probably mature for my age, so I've been able to handle this fairly well. My main concern for the future is that Alison may expect more out of me than I can give. I would be sad if she wanted to make me the center of her existence, because I can't do the same thing for her. Alison has told me I don't need to worry—that all she wants is for us to be honest and open with each other. I hope that's true because right now I'm feeling real protective about my mom, and I'd hate to feel I have two mothers.

[Jill Krementz, *Blessed are the Children*]

1. How do you feel about the birthmother in this story?

_____

_____

_____

_____

2. What do you think of the reactions of the adoptive mother?

_____

_____

_____

_____

Now that you have a variety of points of view, use the space below to express your own point of view about whether or not birth records should be available to adoptees.

_____

_____

_____

_____

_____

_____

_____

_____

_____

_____

_____

_____

_____

_____

_____

_____

_____

Decision making is an important part of our lives. Every day we make decisions—sometimes based on the flip of a coin, sometimes according to what our "intuition" tells us to do, sometimes after carefully examining various alternatives and then choosing among them.

In the exercise that follows, you are to work with three other students in your class. Each person in the group should choose one character listed and either position A or B. Write a list of arguments supporting your point of view and be prepared to act out the character you have choosen.

ROLE PLAYING

Characters	A. Open the records	B. Keep records sealed
Judge		
Birthparent		
Adoptee		
Adoptive parent		

In this chapter you learned the importance of recognizing an author's point of view, recognizing your own point of view, and keeping these separate. A variety of viewpoints concerning adoption were explored.

This chapter also gave you the opportunity to use the skills of underlining, finding main ideas and examples, using signal words, and making inferences.

A Further Reading

I TAKE AFTER SOMEBODY; I HAVE REAL RELATIVES; I POSSESS A REAL NAME.

In the fall of 1943, when I was a year and a half old, I was adopted by Elizabeth and Henry Baines. I went from a Roman Catholic orphanage to the home of a middle-class Virginia family.

The Baineses were very proud of their family history. The paternal side of the family traced their ancestry to one of the first families of America, and they were listed in the Southern social register. (The names of places and persons have been changed to conceal identities. Only the author's name remains unchanged.) My adoptive parents placed great emphasis on lineage. When I turned 12, they managed to get a listing for me, saying that it would improve my marriage prospects. To them, this listing was a sign of good breeding, but whose? Certainly not mine.

My adoptive parents frequently reminded me that I was special. Many children were not wanted, but I had been chosen. Despite my special standing, I occasionally asked about my natural parents. The Baineses regarded such questions as signs of immaturity, poor psychological adjustment, and worst of all, ingratitude. All I ever found out about my past was my birth date, the name of the orphanage in which I had stayed, that I had been born in Richmond, Virginia, and that I had always been named Mary.

The Baines's lack of response to my inquiries was not entirely defensive. They had little information. The social workers who had worked on the adoption had discouraged questions and told them that persistent inquiry indicated a need for counseling. There was also the threat that the adoption would be blocked. No wonder they now regarded my own questions with such dismay.

The laws of the State of Virginia (and many other states) require the sealing of nearly all official documents once an adoption becomes final. No one can legally view sealed records without a court order, and few adoptees are successful in persuading a judge to unseal their records.

Normal Curiosity. For years I feared that if I searched for my natural parents, I would be giving in to the morbid curiosity the social workers had warned against. I tried to convince myself that I was not interested. But by the time I reached 30, I decided that my intense curiosity was normal and that to stifle it was neurotic.

I began the search for my past by telephoning St. Christopher's Infant Home and asking if I could look at my records. I explained that I wanted to find out everything I could about the circumstances of my adoption and about my natural parents. The social worker at St. Christopher's, Mrs. Walker, said they would search for my records. After some days, she reported that they could not find my file. She thought perhaps my records were filed under my original name. Since I did not know what that was, she said, she could go no further. However, St. Christopher's sometimes took in babies from other crowded orphanages. It was possible, according to Mrs. Walker, that my records were kept by another adoption agency.

I began a systematic canvass of the Catholic adoption agencies in the immediate vicinity of St. Christopher's. Because some of the agencies no longer existed, this was a tedious job. I would contact an agency, wait impatiently for several days while they searched their files, and then be told that they had no record of my adoption.

I decided to try another, more speculative approach to finding out my original last name. Chances were that my birth would have been recorded under my parents' surname. After some checking, I found that Richmond City Hospital was the only Richmond hospital with a maternity ward at the time of my birth. I asked the hospital for a listing of all female births on March 16, 1942. This was public information and they had no objection to supplying it. However, the hospital had moved within the previous year and had stored their old records in a warehouse. They were uncertain whether they could retrieve this information and if so, when.

In the meantime, my persistence at the Catholic adoption agencies paid off. A social worker at one of the agencies told me that the Adoption Reports Section of the State Department of Welfare kept a registry of all adoptions. She consulted the Section and found out that my adoption had indeed been handled by St. Christopher's. But that was not all. The Department of Welfare had their own file on my case, and one of their documents was not sealed. It was open to my inspection.

Three days later, on Wednesday afternoon, I was in Richmond at the welfare department identifying myself to an official who would show me the only document in my file that was not sealed. She warned me that the document I was allowed to see contained little, if any, useful information.

Glimpse of the Past. But I was exhilarated; for the first time I would have a glimpse of the past. Seated in front of the microfilm reader, I scanned the "Report of the Commissioner's Investigation regarding the adoption of Mary Francoeur." There it was, my last name, the single most important piece of information the document could have contained.

I felt excitement and a sense of unreality. I repeated the name over and over to myself. Half a dozen times within the next few hours I pulled my copy of the Commissioner's Report out of my briefcase and reread it.

The welfare official had suggested that I visit the court through which the adoption had been handled. I might be able to see the final order of adoption, which might contain my parents' full names. I doubted that I could walk into the courthouse and look at sealed documents, but it was worth a try.

Early the following morning, on my way to the courthouse, I stopped by St. Christopher's. At the orphanage I met Mrs. Walker, the social worker. I gave her my original name and asked that she try again to locate my file. She asked me many questions about my adoptive parents, the home in which I had grown up, my present occupation and marriage. She seemed enthusiastic to discover that I was a professor of sociology with a special interest in family problems.

Indirectly, and then more pointedly, Mrs. Walker spoke of the benefits of sealed records. Gradually, her position became clear. She felt that adoptees should not search for their natural parents. Mrs. Walker spoke of the shame and guilt I would cause my mother if I should ever locate her.

If my presence became known, she said, it would ruin her life and bring down the moral outrage of the community.

I tried to explain that my determination to find out about my parents did not necessarily mean that I would contact them. I could not decide about that until I learned what sort of people they were and the nature of their present circumstances. Should I decide to call them, I promised, I would be discreet. Only my natural mother and father would know who I was.

After some pressing on my part, Mrs. Walker admitted that she had found my file in her first search. Her claims that she could not locate it were false. She had never expected that I would discover my original name and had assumed that the issue was closed. I was dismayed by her willingness to have me travel several hundred unnecessary miles in search of my name. Her hour of questions concerning my past had been pure deception; she had only wanted to discover how one of St. Christopher's adoptees had turned out.

Smug and Sadistic. Mrs. Walker finally volunteered that not only had she located my file, but she had read it. I was outraged. She had the information that I needed to fill in my life and was deliberately choosing to withhold it. Her smugness was detestable. There was no need for her to read the file, but having read it, it was sadistic of her to tell me that she had read it but intended to share none of the information.

One of the results of the secrecy about my adoption and the identity of my natural parents was that early in childhood I had developed the belief that I was illegitimate. The reaction of this social worker strengthened my suspicions; she always referred to my mother, not to my parents. Maybe, I thought, she was giving more information than she intended. Perhaps I did not have an acknowledged father. I explained to Mrs. Walker that I did not share society's moral outrage toward the out-of-wedlock mother. When my pleadings and reasoning met with stony obstinacy, I left Mrs. Walker to her smug convictions.

I drove immediately to the courthouse, but with little hope that I could persuade the court clerk to let me see the final order of adoption. At the courthouse, I found an amiable middle-aged woman who searched for an hour before she found a file containing the records relevant to my adoption. To my surprise, she handed me the file, cleared off a desk and invited me to sit down and study the contents. I could barely contain myself as I read through that file. The most important items to me were the name of my natural mother, Michelle Francoeur, and a brief summary of the circumstances surrounding the adoption. My suspicions were correct; I was illegitimate. In the words of the affidavit filed by the orphanage, ". . . the natural father of the said Mary Francoeur has neither acknowledged her nor contributed to her support." The worst was known. I was both relieved and amused to discover that I had been right, but I was also filled with pity and compassion for Michelle Francoeur. The scorn of the Mmes. Walker of 30 years ago must have been difficult to bear.

I knew my original name, my mother's name, and that I had no legal father. Now I needed the address of my mother at the time that she gave birth to me. I had earlier contacted the public library and discovered that they had issues of the local newspaper for 1942 on microfilm. They also had back issues of a city directory, which listed all city residents who are heads of households and their spouses.

I consulted the directory and found there was only one family named Francoeur in Richmond in 1942. The Francoeur family consisted of a husband, William, who was employed as a policeman, and his wife, Mary, unemployed. Perhaps William and Mary Francoeur were Michelle's parents, which would mean that I had been named for my grandmother. The directory listed no Michelle Francoeur. In a 1940 edition of the directory, I found the same Francoeur family residing at the same address.

Blind Alley. The newspaper listed the birth of four girls on the day that I was born. But none of the girls was born to a Francoeur. Disappointed, I looked closer and found that one of those girls was born to a Mr. and Mrs. Thomas Blackward who lived at the same address as the Francoeurs. Since I now knew that I was illegitimate, I felt that I might have discovered my father's name. But the directory listed no Blackward family in Richmond around the time of my birth; I had come to another dead end.

I stopped looking for my father and returned to the search for my mother, hunting through all issues of the directory for Michelle Francoeur. I needed to determine the relationship, if any, between Michelle Francoeur and the Richmond family with the same name. The Francoeurs appeared in the directories for every year that the library carried, but never did Michelle Francoeur's name crop up. The library had no directories published after 1964.

It was late Thursday when I returned to my hotel extremely tired, but keyed up. Friday morning I took the train home. I spent the three-hour ride going over the pieces of information I had acquired, trying to fit them together into a plausible story of my past and deciding what to do next.

Given the length of time I knew William and Mary Francoeur had lived in Richmond, I speculated that they might have lived there even longer. Men in police work are usually longterm community residents. If Michelle Francoeur were their child, she might have been born in Richmond. Records had to exist somewhere. But in order to locate her birth certificate, I would have to know the date of her birth.

Friday afternoon, I phoned the Richmond operator and asked for the names and numbers of the rectories of some Catholic churches in Richmond. When I contacted a rectory, I said that I was Michelle Francoeur and asked if they had a copy of my baptismal certificate. Since Catholics often want their own copies of documents commemorating religious events, I figured that my request would not raise suspicion and I was right.

When I located the correct church, the woman who searched the records volunteered that they also had Michelle Francoeur's marriage certificate as well. "You are Mrs. Joseph Celler?" she asked. I said that I was and she offered to send me copies of both documents. The baptismal certificate and marriage license arrived the next day. My hunches were correct. Michelle was the daughter of William and Mary Francoeur. The marriage certificate indicated that Michelle Francoeur had married a Lt. j.g. Joseph Celler in 1944.

I looked in a Richmond telephone directory but found no listing for either William Francoeur or Joseph Celler. On Monday, I contacted the Richmond Police Department. I explained that I was trying to locate my grandfather, who was a retired policeman. They had a list of retirees, with their current addresses. William Francoeur still lived at the address listed in the directory, and Information gave me his number.

All I had to do was phone the Francoeurs and ask for Michelle Celler's number. This step proved difficult, and just plain scary. I thought about it for two days. When I finally screwed up my courage, I used a pay telephone at the public library in a neighboring town. I decided to call person-to-person to Michelle Celler so that the operator would have to do the talking. I figured that if Michelle Celler answered the phone I would just hang up. If she were no longer married to Joseph Celler, I hoped that whoever answered would, supply her present name and number. The man who answered, quite probably my grandfather, said that Michelle no longer lived in Richmond and gave me her telephone number in a city some 1,500 miles distant. I then phoned the information operator in that city and found that the number listed for Joseph Celler matched the one I had.

I did not call the number. For days I hesitated, torn between my desire to contact Michelle Celler and my fear of jeopardizing her present way of life.

At last I dialed the number. When a man answered the phone, I pretended to be conducting a telephone survey. By asking my survey questions, I discovered that Michelle Celler worked part-time as a clerk and that she held moderate political views. I found that I had two half-brothers and a half-sister, all married, all white-collar workers, and all living in other cities.

I have never spoken to my mother, but I no longer have an urgent need to contact her. Instead, I find myself wanting to protect her. A sudden call from the past could have severe consequences. She may have a husband who could not forgive an illegitimate birth. Or she may just want to forget the past.

Although I would like to meet the woman who gave birth to me, my story has been told. I am apparently named for my grandmother. Maybe my sleuthing ability comes from my grandfather. I take after somebody; I have real relatives; I possess a real name. My sense of living in a void has given way to a sense of my past, and that is very comforting.

Mary Howard

Suggested Readings

Bawden, Nina. *Familiar Passions*. New York: Wm. Morrow & Co., 1979.

Bridle Starr is discarded by her husband of thirteen years who had married her as a widower with two children. Her relationship to those children, whom she had regarded as her own, is now uncertain. An adoptee herself, she is uncertain of her relationship to her parents, and determines to discover her origins.

Blank, Joseph P. *Nineteen Steps Up the Mountain: The Story of the DeBolt Family*. New York: J. B. Lippincott Co., 1976.

The story of a family who has adopted many children from various national backgrounds and with different kinds of handicaps.

Buck, Pearl S. *Children for Adoption*. New York: Random House, 1964.

In this book Miss Buck unfolds the unhappy picture of thousands of illegitimate and unwanted children born every year in this country. Possible solutions are examined.

Chinnoch, Frank W. *Kim: A Gift from Vietnam*. New York: World Publishing Co., 1971.

The adoption of a Vietnamese child by an American family. At times a painful and often amusing love story.

Ehrlich, Henry. *A Time to Search*. New York: Paddington Press Ltd., 1977.

The moving stories of eleven adoptees who searched for their roots.

Fisher, Florence. *The Search for Anna Fisher*. New York: Fawcett Publications, Inc. 1981.

The author is a pioneer in the fight for the rights of adoptees to see the records of their birth. Ms. Fisher, herself, searched for her natural parents—and found a happy ending.

James, P. D. *Innocent Blood*. New York: Charles Scribner's Sons., 1980.

A mystery tale of a young woman who searches for and finds her biological mother—in prison.

Krementz, Jill. *How It Feels to Be Adopted*. New York: Alfred A. Knopf, 1982.

Interviews with nineteen adopted children in which they discuss the advantages and disadvantages of growing up "just a little bit different."

Lifton, Betty Jean. *Lost and Found: The Adoption Experience*. New York: Dial Press, 1979.

This book is a plea for the right of the adopted to know their true origins. It includes a list of adoptee search groups and a Bill of Rights and Responsibilities for everyone involved in adoption.

Margolies, Marjorie, and Ruth Gruber. *They Came to Stay*. New York: Coward, McCann and Geoghegan, Inc., 1976.

The story of one woman's fight to adopt a Korean orphan.

Savage, Thomas. *I Heard My Sister Speak My Name*. Boston: Little Brown & Co., 1977.

This novel tells of the efforts of Amy McKinney Nofzinger to trace her parentage and win acceptance from a clan that had never been aware of her birth.

Sorosky, A., A. Baran, and R. Pannor. *The Adoption Triangle*. New York: Anchor Press/ Doubleday, 1978.

A discussion of the three parties vitally concerned with adoption—the birthparents, the adoptive parents and the adoptee.

Whitney, Phyllis A. *The Golder Unicorn*. New York: Doubleday & Co., Inc. 1976.

After losing her adoptive parents, Courtney Marsh becomes determined to find her natural mother and father. Courtney uncovers the secret of her birth and becomes involved in a family scandal that almost causes her death.

CHAPTER 5

Photo Researchers, Inc.

One shot or one joint is too much,
a thousand reefers, a thousand shots aren't enough.

DRUGS

In this chapter you will read what drug users have to say about their reasons for using drugs and their experiences as drug users. You will also find out the facts about marijuana, one of the most widely used illegal drugs in our country today. There is an explanation of society's role in causing people to turn to drugs, and arguments are presented in favor of and against the legalization of marijuana.

In addition to continued practice in using headings, signal words, and main ideas to help you comprehend what you read, you will learn about cause–effect relationships in this chapter.

To begin, here are 17 questions to test your knowledge about drugs and drug abuse. It is not important that you answer all of the questions right. You might be surprised when you check the answers. But they are the facts.

Mark your answers, then turn to the end of the quiz to find out if you're right.

Are You a Drug Quiz Whiz?

1. The most commonly abused drug in the United States is

    _____ marijuana

    _____ alcohol

    _____ cocaine

    _____ heroin

2. People who are dependent upon heroin keep taking it mostly to

    _____ experience pleasure

    _____ avoid withdrawal

    _____ escape reality

    _____ be accepted among friends

3. Which of these is *not* a narcotic?

    _____ heroin

    _____ marijuana

    _____ morphine

    _____ methadone

4. Which age group has the highest percentage of drug abusers?

_____ 10–17

_____ 18–25

_____ 26–35

_____ 36–60

_____ 61 and over

5. Which drug does not cause physical dependence?

_____ alcohol

_____ morphine

_____ peyote

_____ secobarbital

_____ codeine

6. Most drug users make their first contact with illicit drugs

_____ through "pushers"

_____ through their friends

_____ accidentally

_____ through the media

7. What is the most unpredictable drug on the street today?

_____ PCP

_____ heroin

_____ LSD

_____ alcohol

8. Which of the following is *not* a stimulant?

_____ amphetamine

_____ caffeine

_____ methaqualone

_____ methamphetamine

9. Which of the following poses the greatest health hazard to the most people in the United States?

_____ cigarettes

_____ heroin

_____ codeine

_____ LSD

_____ caffeine

10. Which of the following poses the highest _immediate_ risk to users?

_____ marijuana

_____ nicotine

_____ LSD

_____ inhalants

11. When does a person become hooked on heroin?

_____ first time

_____ after four or five times

_____ 20 times or more

_____ different for each person

12. What sobers up a drunk person?

_____ a cold shower

_____ black coffee

_____ a traffic ticket

_____ time

_____ walking

13. Which of the following should *never* be mixed with alcohol?

_____ amphetamines

_____ sedatives

_____ cocaine

_____ cigarettes

14. Medical help for drug problems is available without legal penalties

_____ if the patient is under 21

_____ under the protection of Federal law

_____ in certain states

15. How long does marijuana stay in the body after smoking?

_____ one day

_____ 12 hours

_____ up to a month

_____ one hour

16. The use of drugs during pregnancy

_____ should be limited to tobacco and alcohol

_____ may be harmful to the unborn child

_____ should cease at 26 weeks

17. What makes marijuana especially harmful today?

_____ younger kids are using it

_____ it is much stronger

_____ it could affect physical and mental development

_____ none of these

_____ all of these

Answers to Drug Quiz

1. *Alcohol.* It is estimated that about 10 million people in the United States are dependent on alcohol. About two-thirds of all adults are occasional drinkers of either wine, beer, or some other alcoholic beverage. About half of all junior high school students have tried some type of alcoholic drinks.

2. *Avoid withdrawal.* When heroin addicts are deprived suddenly of the drug, they develop physical withdrawal symptoms. These symptoms may include shaking, sweating, nausea, runny nose and eyes, muscle spasms, headaches, and stomachaches. Sudden withdrawal from certain drugs can be dangerous. For instance, a person who has been using barbiturate sedatives for a long time should not attempt withdrawal without a physician's assistance.

3. *Marijuana.* Marijuana was legally declared a narcotic in the past but it is not now. The way the drug works on a person's mental and physical system differs from the effects of narcotics.

4. *18-25.* The findings from the 1979 National Survey on Drug Abuse showed that of the three major age groups surveyed (12-17, 18-25, and 26 and over), illicit drug abuse was more prevalent among young adults, ages 18-25.

5. *Peyote.* The active ingredient of the peyote cactus is mescaline, a hallucinogen. Physical dependence on this class of drugs has not been verified.

6. *Through their friends.* The pressure from friends to experiment with drugs can influence many people to try drugs, especially young people. Being accepted by friends is strong pressure. But showing friends that you care when they feel bad about themselves and their lives, and helping them solve problems can prevent them from becoming involved with drugs.

7. *Phencyclidine (PCP).* This illicit drug can produce unpredictable, erratic, and violent behavior in users. These actions can be directed at themselves or at others, and, in some cases, have led to serious injuries and death. Drownings, burns, falls from high places, and automobile accidents have also been reported. Since the drug is usually manufactured illegally, users cannot be certain of its purity.

8. *Methaqualone.* This is a nonbarbiturate sleep-inducing drug called a "lude" or "soper" on the street. Abuse can lead to convulsions or coma.

9. *Cigarettes.* There are over 50 million cigarette smokers in the United States. It is estimated that 300,000 deaths each year are related to tobacco use.

10. *Inhalants.* These compounds are found among common household products. Sniffing these substances can result in immediate death, irregular heartbeat, and interference with breathing can cause suffocation. This can happen the first time or any time a person uses these substances.

11. *Different for each person.* The time it takes for a person to become dependent on heroin varies. But repeated use will eventually cause physical dependence. Some people become hooked on heroin after using it a few times. Developing an addiction to any drug varies with the form and potency of the drug, the dosage, the frequency, the pattern of use, and the personality of the user.

12. *Time.* There are no shortcuts to sober a drunk person. Once alcohol is in

the bloodstream, it takes time for the body to rid itself of the alcohol. This process, called metabolism, takes about 2 hours for each drink taken.

13. *Sedatives.* (Also known as tranquilizers and sleeping pills.) Most people do not realize that alcohol is a sedative drug. Combining sedatives with alcohol increases their effects. . . . This can result in comas and death.

14. *Under the protection of Federal law.* Under Federal law persons can seek help for drug problems. Federal law in most instances requires doctors, psychologists, and drug treatment centers to keep confidential any information received from drug patients, if the drug treatment program is federally assisted.

15. *Up to a month.* The major active ingredient in marijuana is tetrahydro-cannabinol (THC). Scientists have discovered that THC accumulates in the fatty tissues of the cells and is eliminated slowly. It takes approximately 4 weeks for the body to rid itself of THC.

16. *May be harmful to the unborn child.* Pregnant women should be extremely careful about taking drugs, even aspirin, without consulting a physician. Research has shown that heavy smoking and drinking can harm the fetus. Babies born of narcotic- and barbiturate-dependent mothers are often born drug-dependent and must receive special care.

17. *All of these.*

"Sure it's real stone-ground wheat. Harry here was stoned when he ground it."

[From *The Wall Street Journal*, Permission—Cartoon Features Syndicate]

1. Are drugs an every day part of your life? (Think carefully.) Why?

_____

_____

_____

_____

_____

_____

_____

_____

_____

_____

_____

_____

_____

2. Have you ever smoked cigarettes? _____ Do you smoke now? _____
Can you recall the circumstances under which you took your first cigarette?
_____ Describe this incident including your age, the place, the reasons,
and so on.

_____

_____

_____

_____

_____

_____

_____

3. Under what circumstances do you drink alcoholic beverages?

_____

_____

_____

4. What causes you to drink at those times?

_____

_____

_____

There are many reasons why people use various drugs. In the following selections drug users explain their reasons for taking drugs. After each reading, write the reasons which caused that individual to try drugs.

Hector Rodriguez

I started taking narcotics in the Bronx, when I was eleven. I was curious, but I wasn't using them that much—I was just taking marijuana once in a while and snorting; I wasn't shooting it up, I was just skinning it then. Skinning is just where you hit anywhere in your body and shoot the dope in. That's with heroin. And snorting is where you snort it up your nose, just like if you're sniffing something. And burning marijuana, that's like smoking a cigarette, the only thing you inhale it, you don't let it out, you just try to hold it in.

I was using it up there, and then when I moved down here, I was still using it, you know, but I didn't have no habit or nothing. Like when I started going to school, I would go to school high, and I learned how to read a little high. You know, like I wanted to learn something, the things I need in life, but the teachers wouldn't teach me. They used to ignore me, and pay attention to the other kids. Then when I didn't want to learn, they used to come and try to teach me how to learn. Like I couldn't see that; it used to burn me up. I used to go to school high and start nodding all over the classroom, get drowsy, and that's when I started staying out of school; I didn't go to school no more than three or four months in a year.

That's when I started mainlining, when I got to be fifteen.

[Jeremy Larner, *The Addict in the Street*]

_____

_____

_____

Dom Abruzzi

I guess it was sort of a lark. At that time anyway, we were all off on a kick. I was sixteen years old exactly, and I was walking with one friend on Henry Street, and he asked me, have you ever smoked pot before? I didn't know what pot was, and I had to ask him, so he told me it was marijuana and I almost fell with shock. But then he talked about it, and he explained to me it was nothing to worry about, and three days later I was smoking my first weed. Three months afterward, I started snorting heroin. I got in on that because it was so cheap—a dollar and a half apiece to split a three-dollar bag—and everybody was getting so high and seemed so happy. I just indulged, I put in my dollar and a half, and the first time I got high on horse I was sick as a pig. I couldn't see, I kept vomiting all over the place, and a few months after that I took my first shot. That was a skin-pop, and followed a week later by a mainline. But for the first few years I would say I was an oddity, because I kept myself in check; I didn't get a habit. I was going out with a very wonderful girl at the time, and I wanted to marry her. But in the next few years that followed, I got arrested once, then a second time, and the girl and I broke up. After we broke up, we had money in the bank, in a joint account. I took it all out and spent it on dope, and that's how I acquired my first habit.

[Jeremy Larner, *The Addict in the Street*]

_____

_____

_____

_____

Nancy Steward

When I was in the sixth grade, a detective, complete with a badge, came into our class armed with various samples of drugs: little red pills, white powder, and some greenish-brown pot. They were all enclosed in plastic boxes attached to a board, and he pointed to each one in turn, explaining how each substance constituted a threat to our lives. He even went so far as to burn some marijuana, so that each of us would be able to recognize the pungently sweet aroma and we would know enough to stay away from any place where that smell could be found. I believed everything he said; marijuana was surely an evil. How could anyone do something illegal like smoking pot, not to mention risking harm to their brain?

In junior high the same thing happened, this time with the health teacher. But what the teacher doesn't realize is that by telling kids how bad it is she will just raise their curiosity. You just sit there and think: what is it like to get high? What does she mean by euphoria? So all the curious kids went and got high because nobody could explain how it felt.

My first experience came shortly after that. Two close friends of mine, both a year older than me, asked if I wanted to try it. I knew that Marie, who was like a cousin to me, had smoked previously. At first, I was quite shocked and disappointed in her, but gradually the newness of the confession wore off, and I no longer viewed it in the same alarming light. Already the logic was setting in; if so many people smoked pot, and nobody seems to be harmed by it, how can smoking pot be so bad?

[William Novak, *High Culture*]

Tommy Bennett

I don't go for the argument that pot is safer than alcohol or cigarettes. I don't go for the argument that pot makes you a better person—that you become more creative, and nicer, and all of that. I don't smoke because I'm unhappy with myself. I've been allowed to drink since I was sixteen or so, I'd guess. I could try sherry when I was small, a kid. I started drinking a couple of years ago because I liked the feeling; my parents do all the time, and my brother does, and we all relax. I take pot for the same reason. My friends use it. My girl friend does. The guy who teaches us sociology does, the guy who teaches the writing course does, and the graduate student who works with us in the chemistry lab does. Now are *they* all mixed-up teenagers? God, we're sick of those doctors leaning over and trying to be so cool and reasonable and understanding, and talking about adolescents, adolescents, adolescents. They don't know how they sound to us—us adolescents: preachy, oh so worried, and, most of all, full of themselves and their moralisms that come out, one after the other.

[Brenner et al., *Drugs and Youth*]

Lisa Johnson

I smoke pot because I enjoy the idea that one minute my mind and body are tired, confused and depressed, and the next minute it doesn't matter. The high has built up unknowingly while I've been smoking, and the doors of my mind have been opened. My problems and frustrations don't go floating away, but rather, they are no longer important for a while. I can still conjure them up if I want; there are, after all, still bills to pay, doctors to visit, relatives to deal with. But where does such worrying get you?

[William Novak, *High Culture*]

Linda Field

I smoke with my friends, and my boy friend, and his friends. It's not really to be sociable. It's because we want to be more natural and honest, and it's hard to be that way—the way you are when you're alone and doing some thinking—when you're with other people. I honestly wish my parents would take grass with me. Then we'd settle some of these things, I believe we would. They would stop for a minute and *think*; and I wouldn't feel we were in two different worlds, them and me. I try to talk with them, but they want to talk about facts—about grades, and money, and what a boy's father *does*. I try to get them to sit back, and relax, and smile—I mean smile at themselves, and me, and this whole sad, funny world. But my mother begins to get nervous, and she wants to know why I'm so *philosophical*. When they heard I was using marijuana—I told them—they blamed everything on that. How silly can you get? They said I was in a "daze" a lot of the time, and I was becoming a "radical" in politics, and I wasn't taking good care of myself: I wasn't as neat as I used to be, especially my hair—it's stringy—and I wear sandals all the time, and blue jeans, and a dress practically never. I told them that everything they were saying—*everything*—had nothing to do with smoking grass. I reminded them that they'd been criticizing me all the time about all of those things, and more, and that I'd only tried grass a few months ago; and that, if anything, I was less up-tight than before, and so I could talk easier with them.

No, I don't believe that marijuana solves your problems. How could it? All I claim is that sometimes a few of us get together; we turn on and we enjoy it—we really do. We don't want to take heroin, or cocaine, or LSD, either. Why does everyone say we're going to do that—everyone who's never tried smoking grass? I can't believe what I read about marijuana—what people say, what my own parents say. How can anyone believe the most obvious lies and crazy exaggerations? Wouldn't you be insulted if someone came and told you that because you have a drink or two every *week*—not every day—that you'd soon be a drug addict, and uncurable, the way addicts are? That's what my dad said;

he said I'd soon be taking worse drugs, and I'd lose all my "values and goals." I jumped him on that. I told him that's what I wanted; I wanted to talk with him about my values and his, my goals and his. But he dropped it like a hot potato; he just kept on telling me how *dangerous* marijuana is. I think it's more dangerous that he and I can't talk honestly, and that he believes only what he wants to believe, what he reads—stuff written by people who cater to his prejudices, rather than give him sensible information and try to challenge him to go find out things for himself, and be his own judge of what's true and what's false.

[Brenner et al., *Drugs and Youth*]

Betty Green

The Greens' colonial-style house in Springfield, Massachusetts, had been built according to a plan Betty and her husband had drawn up themselves with the help of an architect. Ultramodern on the inside, it was equipped with everything imaginable from a stereo hi-fi, color TV, and pool and Ping-Pong tables in the game room, to a bar that would have been the pride of any restaurant. Electrical appliances simplified nearly every housekeeping chore, but still a maid came in five days a week; so Betty had almost nothing to do. Though it might seem impossible that anyone could be bored in a house that had everything but its own movie screen, everyone was.

Betty's husband was the least bored, but he spent the least amount of time at home. As vice-president of a large electronic instrument company, he had to travel fairly often, play golf with customers, and entertain a great deal both at home and outside. The children all had after-school activities of some kind. Betty's son was on the swimming and baseball teams; the girls were cheerleaders and were often on committees for school dances or acting in school plays. Betty was the only one who was not obliged to do anything at all. Of course, she played bridge and belonged to various clubs for women, but she didn't particularly enjoy those activities. She had neither school nor office to demand her time and attention, and between the appliances and the maid, she was not really needed even at home. Because her children spent the largest part of their time at school or watching television, her role seemed purely social and decorative, except for chauffeuring the children to and from various appointments.

The traditional role of mother in the Greens' home had been taken over by television, school, and the children's friends, since, to be popular, the children had to do exactly the same things their friends did, they thought. If possible, they had to do things better—but not too much better; then they would be even more popular. Thus, it did not seem necessary for Betty or her husband to set any standards for their children's conduct. If other children came home from a party at one, she would be considered unreasonable if she asked her children to be home at eleven. To make her children obey a different set of rules would not only make them "squares" and unpopular, but would infringe on their rights as individuals. To Betty, who had gone to a progressive college, it was unthinkable that she should supervise her children in such a way.

Shortly after the Greens were married, while they were still living in a Midwest college town, they attended a pot party. Both were offered joints to smoke, and Betty did not have the slightest hesitancy about trying one. She got a mild high and thoroughly enjoyed it. However, she led a busy, happy life then, and the incident rarely crossed her mind afterward. Again, after they moved to the East, she and her husband attended a party where pot was smoked, and although she was not really tempted this time, she took it once more—mostly to try to discover what all the fuss was about. The first time Betty had smoked pot, it was not the subject of such great controversy as it now seemed to be. She could not understand why such a harmless act could cause such a furor. Experts were always linking pot smoking with heroin addiction. To Betty, this was nonsense— she herself had no desire to smoke more pot, let alone try heroin, even though she enjoyed her second joint as much as she had the first try. However, like other parents, she felt differently about her children's smoking pot.

One rainy afternoon about two years ago, Betty's son was playing in his room with three older boys from school. When the weather cleared, the boys raced out to play ball. Her son ran back and yelled for Betty to throw down his baseball mitt. She had to rummage through several shelves of his bookcase before she found it. After throwing him the mitt, she went back to straighten up the shelves, and came upon an envelope with three joints of pot in it. Her own experience with pot made her recognize the joints. Upset at the thought that her twelve-year-old son might be smoking marijuana, she took the envelope to her own room until she could decide what to do.

By the time all the members of the family returned from their various activities, Betty had still not decided what to do about her son. But she had done one thing: she had smoked a joint. She smoked it in the bathroom and sprayed furiously afterward to get the smell out. She was still a little high at dinnertime, and everyone remarked that she was happier than usual, not her somewhat solemn self. Pleased that her family noticed her relaxed manner, Betty doubly enjoyed herself, knowing how stunned they would be if they knew the cause of it.

The next day, Betty smoked another joint before the family came home. She still had not told her husband about finding the pot nor said anything to her son, but she realized that she must. After dinner, she sat down with her husband to talk about the situation. He was furious at first, and wanted to rush upstairs and beat some sense into the boy. Betty pleaded and argued until she convinced him that a beating would serve no purpose and probably would make things worse. They resolved to tell the boy what his mother had found, ask him where he got the stuff, how he had paid for it, and how often he smoked pot. From his answers, they would decide how to proceed. As for the pot itself, Betty told her husband she had flushed it down the toilet.

They called Larry downstairs. The discussion went well, though Larry was frightened and a little defiant. He told them where he had bought the pot, that it was the first time he had bought any, and that he had not yet smoked any. The boy was relieved that no punishment was forthcoming, and Betty and her husband were relieved at stopping the problem before it got started and at Larry's apparent willingness to listen to their arguments.

The next day, Betty smoked the one remaining joint before going out to find the boy Larry had bought the pot from—not to trap him, but to buy more pot from him. A few weeks later, she bought some heroin from him, feeling she was ready to try something different.

It may seem inconsistent for parents to be terrified of having their child do something they themselves are doing. It *is* inconsistent, but it is also very human. Most parents who smoke cigarettes plead with their children not to start. The same is true of many parents who drink and drive recklessly. "Do as I say, not as I do," is a family motto in many American homes.

Betty had no trouble buying a dollar bag of heroin and some cocaine. Her reading and her viewing of films on drug addiction at PTA meetings had told her what she needed to know about snorting cocaine and heroin three or four times every day. Since her family was gone most of the time, it was only in the evening that she had to worry about anyone's seeing her. Even then it was not difficult. She used the bathroom at home, or a restroom if she and her husband were out. If they were at a friend's house for dinner, she excused herself and used the bathroom.

In the beginning, Betty had no set of works to hide—only the drugs, which she kept in an extra compact. All she had to do was go into a bathroom, fold a matchbook cover in half, put a little of the heroin and cocaine in the cover, and sniff a few times with each nostril. The high was always a little slow in coming with this method, but that was fine with her. That way, she could toy with her drink and say that lately she seemed to get high on one or two drinks. Since she obviously never had more than one or two, and obviously got high, there was no reason to question her behavior. A number of their friends got high from alcohol, and so she was not at all conspicuous.

Betty went on snorting heroin for several months until the pusher talked her into skin-popping. Up to then, she had been using leftover household money for her drugs, but skin-popping was more expensive, and she began to be anxious about money. Before she had solved that problem, however, she found out how to relieve the anxiety—the pusher talked her into mainlining. Drugs were now a habit she could not break. They took away all her worries, and her long days became a drugged haze in which time meant nothing.

Today, this suburban housewife who has everything also has a heroin habit— she mainlines five times a day. So far, no one has found her works. Her husband has just become aware of the fact that the various lamps and pieces of fine china Betty claims she broke have actually been taken out and sold to get money for drugs. He has not yet noticed the missing jewelry or begun to wonder about the household money, and so he does not realize the full extent of her habit.

[Barbara Millbauer, *Drug Abuse and Addiction*]

CAUSE–EFFECT

Almost everything we do or feel has some effect or result on our lives. In the preceding readings, the different feelings people experienced all produced the same result—the use of drugs.

The relationship between an action or feeling and the reason for it is often referred to as a cause–effect relationship.

On the lines below, write some of the causes for drug use that you found in the preceding readings. One is provided for you.

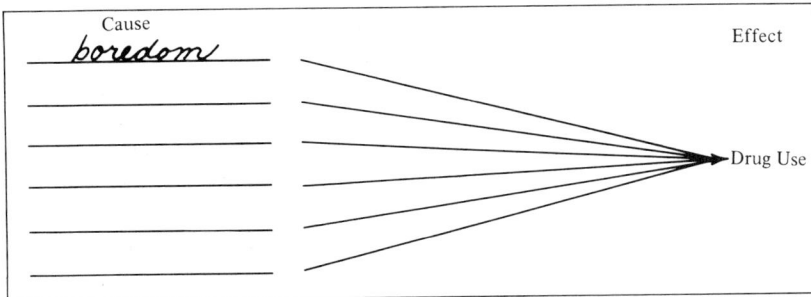

Cause

boredom

Effect

Drug Use

In this diagram, supply the causes which would result in someone choosing to attend college.

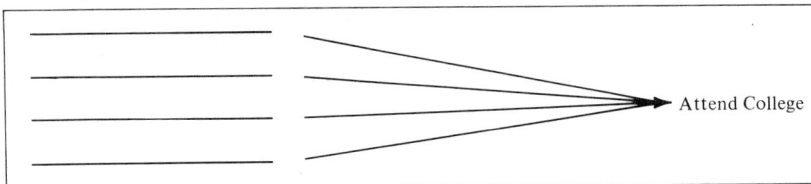

Attend College

Now write the possible effect of the causes given.

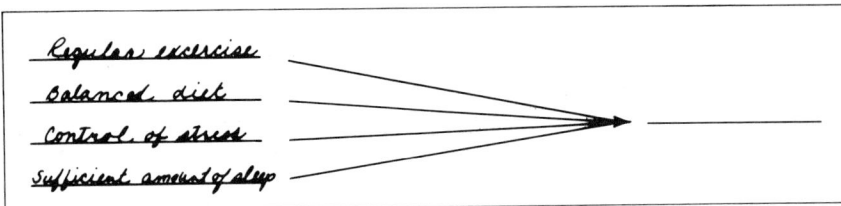

Regular exercise

Balanced diet

Control of stress

Sufficient amount of sleep

In the next reading, the author gives his point of view concerning the primary cause of drug use in our society.

Our society sets . . . many of our goals, and sometimes these goals are in conflict with personal goals. At this point, frustration or anxiety begins to be felt, and an individual must choose between societal goals and his own. Maslow, a well-known psychologist, proposed that man's end goal is one of self-actualization in which he meets his own goals, becomes what he thinks he can become, within a societal framework. The major drawback of this is that it takes time—

time to learn how to think, analyze, synthesize; time to learn how different people act and react; time to learn which things are deeply rewarding and which are only superficial; time to learn how to differentiate between truth and untruth and between goals set for an individual by society and those set by himself. Throughout this process one is continually bombarded with set rules, advertising, and other conditioning factors that will lead one toward the "good life"—as defined by the society. But the goals that are set up by the society appear to be ones of material wealth, ever greater affluence, and power over others, while self-worth, integrity, and self-fulfillment seem to be deemphasized. How many commercials does one see on television that push these personal commodites? Integrity is not the way to win friends; the best way is a new brand of mouth-wash or the newest model car. Creative work and play is not the way to set one's mind at rest or reverse personal disaster; commercials claim that the solution is various pills, miracle foods, or some other kind of "wonder" product. It is not difficult to understand the confusion that grows in the mind of a maturing child in this society. If he does not have a chance to work and play creatively, does not learn to analyze, and does not see working examples of the personal traits he is told about, his confusion grows and his maturing process is one of frustration.

What does this have to do with drug use? Simply that society sets the stage for drug taking: it imposes demands that are not always meaningful; it creates an atmosphere of "quick cure" for every problem; it pushes one toward material wealth; and it gives great lip service to desirable personal traits while giving little opportunity for its youth to see these traits in action.

Is there no way to avoid drug use? Must drugs be taken to pad the mind from society's stresses until the society changes? Obviously the answer is "no," because there are those who find life pleasing without the use of chemical agents. One will most often find that these are the individuals who have reached some degree of self-fulfillment in their lives. In order to reach this basic goal of man (self-fulfillment), one must conscientiously work toward it.

To find real self-fulfillment one must give, from his real self, efforts which are honest and which he feels will make him comfortable within the society in which he lives.

To find self-worth one must put forth creative effort. A wife cannot feel real accomplishment from the business achievements of her husband, but can derive satisfaction only from her own creative efforts. Again, drugs cannot give the lasting satisfaction that creative effort brings.

The perfect drug for relieving man's unhappiness . . . has not been found, and it is safe to assume it never will. Different drugs may temporarily alter one's perception of the problem, but none will solve it. There are no pills to make us intelligent, no beverages to make us strong or to ensure our accomplishments. The most efficient mode of accomplishment is a clear evaluation of one's abilities, desire, and a clear, well-functioning, honest mind.

[Girdano, *Drug Education*]

Below are six statements from the preceding selection and some related sayings. Indicate which statements you believe are most closely connected with which sayings. There may be more than one correct answer. Compare your responses and your reasons with other students.

1. Because society's goals are often in disagreement with personal goals, many people feel anxious and confused about what they want out of life.
2. Society sets the stage for drug taking: it imposes demands that are not always meaningful.
3. One must work conscientiously to achieve self-fulfillment.
4. To find self-worth one must put forth creative effort.
5. Drugs won't solve problems.
6. The most efficient mode of accomplishment is a clear evaluation of one's abilities, desire, and a clear well-functioning, honest mind.

_____ a. "I am the master of my fate/I am the captain of my soul." (Henley, *Invictus*)

_____ b. Even though you are careful when you make important decisions, you may still feel anxiety.

_____ c. If you're going to spend time, spend it on something important.

_____ d. It is useful to know what you want to know.

_____ e. One is better off not thinking about life's purposes and meaning.

_____ f. Life is unavailable to those who don't have the key.

_____ g. Expectation creates reality out of imagination.

1. Make a list of the five most important goals in your life. Do you think society has influenced you in any of these choices? Explain in what ways you have been influenced.

_____

_____

_____

_____

_____

_____

_____

_____

_____

2. Do you think there is any difference for Mrs. Green and Hector Rodriguez in attaining self-actualization? Explain.

_____

_____

_____

_____

_____

_____

3. Do you know someone you would consider a self-fulfilled person? What is it about this person that makes you believe he or she is self-fulfilled?

_____

_____

_____

_____

_____

_____

Write a few words about each heading in the next section (Marijuana) in the appropriate column below. This preview of the material will give you an idea of what to expect before you begin reading.

Background	Emotional effects	Physical effects

MARIJUANA

A Short History

Marijuana has been in use in many parts of the world for thousands of years. As early as 2500 B.C., the Chinese were using marijuana for medical purposes, such as treating gout, rheumatism, malaria, beriberi, constipation, and absentmindedness. Even at that time there was disagreement among the people as to its use. The drug was also used by the ancient Greeks and by tribes in South Africa. The Hindus in India use marijuana in many of their religious ceremonies to enhance mystical trances and meditation.

Marijuana has been used for a long time in Mexico and Latin America and was introduced in the United States in the early 1900s by Mexican workers. During that time its use was concentrated in New Orleans, where jazz musicians and artists indulged in the drug. The use of marijuana slowly spread through the urban centers of the country.

During the 1960s marijuana gained wide popularity among the middle class youth of America. Its use became a symbol of independence and protest and was prevalent at rock concerts and political demonstrations.

What Exactly Is Marijuana?

Marijuana (also called pot, grass, reefer, or weed) comes from a plant, with the botanical name of *Cannabis sativa*, that grows wild and is cultivated in many parts of the world. Containing over 400 chemicals, this plant has the ability to intoxicate its users, primarily because of the psychoactive or mind-altering ingredient called delta-9-tetrahydrocannabinol, or THC. It is the THC content, found at various concentrations in different parts of the plant, which determines the potency. And the THC content is controlled by plant strain, climate, soil conditions, and harvesting.

["*For Parents Only*"]

About 60% of the marijuana used in the United States is grown here and it is of a very weak variety; it is usually olive-green in color. Jamaican and Columbian marijuana is dark brown, Panama Red is a claylike red, and Acapulco Gold is dull yellow in color. All of these foreign types are stronger than the marijuana grown in the United States.

[Girdano, *Drug Education*]

Typically, the marijuana used in cigarettes (joints) is made from dried particles of the whole plant except the main stem and roots. In 1975, the average confiscated sample of marijuana contained 0.4 percent THC; in 1979, the average THC content was about 4 percent—a tenfold increase. Sinsemilla, a cultivated form of marijuana which is becoming more frequently available in this country, may contain as much as 7 percent THC.

Hashish (hash) is a green, dark brown, or black resin extracted from the *Cannabis sativa* plant and smoked to produce a high. In the past, hashish, which averages about 2 percent THC, contained more THC than marijuana. However, with the increased potency of marijuana on the streets, it now frequently is stronger than hashish.

Hash oil is an extract of the *Cannabis sativa* plant. It may contain up to 30 percent THC, many times the amount found in marijuana. Hash oil is a tarlike substance usually smoked in small amounts on tobacco or marijuana cigarettes or in small glass pipes.

["*For Parents Only*"]

How Do People Feel When They Smoke Marijuana?

Physically, users experience an increase in heart and pulse rate, a reddening of the eyes, a dryness in the mouth and throat, a mild decrease in body temperature, and, on occasion, a sudden appetite and intense thirst.

Studies of marijuana's mental effects have shown that the drug impairs short-term memory, alters the sense of time, and reduces the ability to perform tasks requiring concentration, swift reactions, and coordination. High doses may result in image distortions and hallucinations. Many users claim that marijuana enhances their hearing, vision, and skin sensitivity, but these reports have not been confirmed by researchers.

["*For Parents Only*"]

1. Since marijuana temporarily impairs short-term memory, one should not

smoke it before _____

_____ .

2. _____

_____ should not be done while under
the influence of marijuana because smoking reduces one's reactions and
coordination.

3. Smokers of marijuana often report enhanced hearing. Therefore, _____

_____

_____ might be a more pleasant experience
while smoking marijuana.

Do People Ever React Badly to Marijuana?

Yes. The most common adverse reaction to marijuana is a state of anxiety, sometimes accompanied by paranoid thoughts; these can range from general suspicion
to a fear of losing control and going crazy. Acute anxiety reactions are usually
experienced by novice users, and the symptoms generally disappear in a few
hours as the drug's effects wear off. While anxiety reactions can usually be
quieted by simple reassurance, some marijuana users may need professional
help.

[*"For Parents Only"*]

4. A bad reaction to marijuana might include _____

_____ .

What Happens if You Drive After Smoking Marijuana?

Marijuana delays a person's response to sights and sounds—so that it takes a
driver longer to react to a dangerous situation. The ability to perform sequential
tasks can also be affected by smoking marijuana. As a result, a marijuana smoker's
biggest driving problems occur when faced with unexpected events, such as a
car approaching from a side street or a child running out from between parked
cars. The greater the demands of a driving situation, the less able the marijuana
user will be to cope. The driver who doesn't feel high may still be under the
influence of marijuana since its effects may last for several hours after the high
has passed.

[*"For Parents Only"*]

5. Write the main idea of the paragraph above in your own words.

_____

_____

_____

How Long Does Marijuana Stay in the Body After It Is Smoked?

When marijuana is smoked, THC, its active ingredient, is absorbed by many tissues and organs in the body. The body, in its attempt to rid itself of the foreign chemical, chemically transforms the THC into metabolites. Human tests on blood and urine can detect THC metabolites up to a week after marijuana is smoked. Tests involving radioactively labeled THC have traced these metabolites in animals for up to a month.

[*"For Parents Only"*]

6. True or false: A blood test would show whether or not someone has smoked marijuana in the last several days.

Can Marijuana Cause Brain Damage?

To date, no definitive neurological study of humans has turned up evidence of marijuana-related permanent brain damage. However, in a recent study of rhesus monkeys, the animals were trained to smoke a marijuana cigarette 5 days a week for 6 months. The researcher reported that persistent changes in the structure of the monkeys' brain cells followed.

    This and other studies have led researchers to conclude that the possibility of subtle and lasting changes in brain function from heavy and continuous marijuana use cannot be ruled out.

[*"For Parents Only"*]

7. Researchers have not ruled out the possibility of permanent damage in

the human brain because _____

_____ .

How Does Marijuana Affect the Heart?

Marijuana use increases the heart rate as much as 50 percent and can bring on chest pain in people already experiencing a poor blood supply to the heart. For this reason, doctors believe that people with heart conditions, or those who are at high risk for heart ailments, should not use marijuana.

[*"For Parents Only"*]

8. Marijuana increases the smoker's heart rate. Therefore, _____

_____

_____ .

How Does Marijuana Affect the Lungs?

Scientists believe that marijuana can be particularly harmful to the lungs because some users inhale the unfiltered smoke deeply and hold it in their lungs as long as possible, thereby keeping the smoke in contact with lung tissue for prolonged periods. Repeated inhalation of smoke, whether marijuana or tobacco, inflames the lungs and affects pulmonary functions. In one study on humans, it was found that smoking five joints a week over time is more irritating to the air passages and impairs the lungs' ability to exhale air than smoking almost six packs of cigarettes a week. Another study on animals using THC levels similar to daily human use found that extensive lung inflammation developed after 3 months to a year of use.

["*For Parents Only*"]

9. True or false: It appears that smoking tobacco is more harmful to the lungs than smoking marijuana.

Can Marijuana Cause Cancer?

While marijuana smoke has been found to contain more cancer-causing agents than tobacco smoke, there is no direct evidence so far that marijuana can cause cancer in humans. However, biopsies of human lung tissue chronically exposed to marijuana smoke in a laboratory showed cellular changes called metaplasia that are considered precancerous. In laboratory tests, the tars from marijuana smoke have produced tumors when applied to animal skin.

["*For Parents Only*"]

10. True or false: Animal experiments suggest that marijuana smoke may cause cancer.

How Does Marijuana Affect the Hormonal and Reproductive Systems?

Men: A few studies of adult males have found that chronic marijuana users had lower levels of testosterone (the principal male sex hormone) than nonusers, and that abstention from marijuana after heavy use produced a reversal of this condition. Other research has shown that the sperm count in young adult males diminishes as marijuana use increases. Still other studies have shown that some of the sperm of chronic marijuana users are defective and nonfunctional. On the basis of these findings, scientists feel that those with marginal fertility or endocrine functioning should avoid marijuana. In addition, marijuana has been shown to affect the growth hormone from the pituitary. These findings indicate that marijuana may be particularly harmful during adolescence, a period of rapid physical and sexual development.

["*For Parents Only*"]

11. Circle the clue words in the paragraph above which introduce an effect.

12. The hormonal system of men is affected in the following ways by the use of marijuana:

a. _____

b. _____

c. _____

d. _____

13. Because of the hormonal effects on men, _____

_____ .

Women: Information about the reproductive effects of marijuana on women is scarce; marijuana research on women of childbearing age is not permitted because of possible reproductive risks. But one recent study of marijuana use and human female endocrine functioning with 26 women using street marijuana for 6 months or more found they had defective menstrual cycles three times more frequently than a similar group of nonusers. These defective cycles involved either a failure to ovulate or a shortened period of fertility—findings which suggest that regular marijuana use may reduce fertility in women. Many female animal studies have been completed and show that marijuana influences levels of estrogen, the principal female sex hormone, and progesterone, another reproductive hormone, as well as the growth hormone from the pituitary. These studies suggest that heavy use should be avoided by the physically and sexually developing adolescent girl.

["*For Parents Only*"]

14. List three effects of marijuana on the female reproductive system.

_____

_____

_____

Is It OK To Smoke Marijuana if You Are Pregnant?

Definitely not. As stated earlier, research on women is limited because of possible risks to the unborn child. Laboratory animal tests, however, have shown that THC-treated female monkeys were four times more likely than untreated monkeys to abort or have stillborn infants. And males born of the THC-treated monkeys were lighter than usual in birth weight. Scientists believe that marijuana, which crosses the placental barrier in the pregnant mother's womb, may have a toxic effect on embryos and fetuses. Use of marijuana or any other drug during pregnancy is an unnecessary risk.

["For Parents Only"]

15. Scientists believe that pregnant women should not smoke marijuana

because _____

_____ .

What About Breast Feeding?

Animal studies have shown that THC from marijuana can be transmitted to a baby through the mother's milk and that traces of THC have been found in the baby's urine and feces after nursing. Scientists have no doubt that THC is also transmitted in human milk, but because of possible risks to the mother and child, human research has not been done.

["For Parents Only"]

16. Human research on the effects of marijuana on a newborn baby during

breast feeding have not been done because _____

_____

_____ .

Are There Any Medical Uses of the Chemicals in Marijuana?

Research on marijuana has led to findings which indicate that some of the plant's chemicals, particularly THC, may have medical value. The following summarizes those areas currently being investigated.

Open-Angle Glaucoma

One of the first potential medical uses of marijuana to be explored was the treatment of open-angle glaucoma. This disease, which often leads to blindness, is caused by pressure within the eye. Marijuana cigarettes, often in combination with standard eye medication, have sometimes reduced this pressure. Synthetically made THC eye drops are also being tested on patients. However, mounting evidence suggests that tolerance (the need to increase amounts to achieve the effects produced by initial doses) develops and that ultimately little or no effect may be realized from the drug.

Use of marijuana does not prevent glaucoma or any other eye disorder, or improve vision.

Nausea

One of the more promising uses of THC is as a means of controlling the overwhelming nausea and vomiting which cancer patients experience during chemotherapy. These side effects sometimes force patients to discontinue necessary treatment. Because the available substances that control these symptoms are not effective for all patients, several research projects are now being sponsored by the Federal Government and a number of States and independent researchers to further investigate THC's anti-nausea effects.

But marijuana does not prevent cancer. As discussed earlier, marijuana smoke contains more cancer-causing agents than tobacco smoke.

Multiple Sclerosis

Some small studies are being conducted to test whether THC has any effect on reducing spasticity or involuntary muscle contractions in patients with multiple sclerosis. While the results are not conclusive, some patients have shown lowered spasticity after taking the drug. Whether this reduction will make any difference in the patients' ability to function is not yet known.

Epilepsy

A number of human and animal studies have been done to determine if marijuana or any of its ingredients has an effect on epileptic seizures. Some research on THC has shown that it may actually trigger convulsions in epileptics. Scientists hypothesize that this occurs when the drug stimulates high voltage brain waves, and that the likelihood of its happening is determined by the amount of THC in marijuana and the amount inhaled.

Another marijuana ingredient, cannabidiol, has been shown in limited studies to reduce or control seizures. It should be pointed out, however, that cannabidiol is dominant in only one strain of marijuana and that this particular "fiber" strain contains little of the mind-altering THC. This means that the marijuana available for sale on the street contains only trace amounts of cannabidiol. Cannabidiol has been synthesized and is administered orally or by injection to patients involved in studies.

["*For Parents Only*"]

17. Which of the medical uses discussed seems to be *least* beneficial to the patient? _____

_____ .

Does Marijuana Lead to the Use of Other Drugs?

There are a multitude of reasons why people use marijuana. One is the seeking of a solution to problems through chemical means. The individuals who do this may not find satisfaction in marijuana and so they move on to try another chemical, perhaps heroin. The fact that they happened to try marijuana as a solution somewhere along the way is of no greater importance than the alcohol they have consumed or (as some have quipped) the milk they drank as children—nearly every heroin addict in our society drank milk as a child, so perhaps milk is the factor that causes heroin addiction!

[Girdano, *Drug Education*]

However, there may be a link between marijuana and the use of harder drugs. If the person from whom one buys marijuana also sells heroin, and if in the process of using marijuana one is placed in contact with other persons who use heroin, then obviously the use of marijuana increases the opportunity for initiation to heroin. Several years ago, when marijuana use was limited mostly to lower socioeconomic groups, being a marijuana user often afforded the opportunity to obtain and use heroin. Now, of course, many young persons use marijuana fairly frequently without ever having seen heroin. On the other hand, heavy involvement in the current drug subculture will often provide access to heroin along with a variety of other drugs.

[Margaret O. Hyde, *Mind Drugs*]

18. Does the author believe that the use of marijuana always leads to the use of heroin? _____

19. What is the author's purpose in saying that "perhaps milk is the factor that causes heroin addiction!"?

_____

_____

20. Underline the main idea of the second paragraph.

DRUG USE, DEPENDENCE, AND ADDICTION

There are different kinds of drug users. Experimental users are those people who may try various drugs once or twice out of curiosity about their effects. Recreational users are people who use drugs to get high with friends or at parties, to be sociable, or to get into the mood of things. People who use drugs constantly to achieve or maintain a desired state, but continue to attempt normal activity (work, school, housework, etc.) are considered regular users. Finally, dependent users can't relate to anything but drug seeking and drug taking.

["*Drug Abuse Prevention For Your Family*"]

If people have become psychologically dependent on a substance, they will show concern or anxiety over doing without it. Many of the characteristics of anxiety—shakiness, rapid pulse, sweating, and so on—are similar to the symptoms of withdrawal from a physical addiction. Thus people may believe that they are addicted to a substance when they may only be psychologically dependent.

Addiction is defined as physiological dependence on a drug and refers to the changes that take place in the body as an individual uses the drug over prolonged periods of time. One characteristic of addiction is *tolerance:* The body becomes habituated to the drug, so that increasingly larger doses are required in order to achieve similar effects. But the central feature of addiction is the presence of withdrawal symptoms when the level of usage of the substance is suddenly decreased.

[Spencer Rathus, *Psychology*]

Most experts speak in terms of psychological "dependence" rather than addiction, when discussing marijuana. The body does not require continuing use of the drug, but many scientists have concluded that marijuana can cause psychological dependence in users who smoke it regularly.

[Whitney North Seymour, *The Young Die Quietly*]

1. Underline the different kinds of drug users described in the first paragraph.

2. What are the differences between psychological dependence and addiction?

Psychological dependence   *Addiction*

_____   _____

_____   _____

_____   _____

_____   _____

_____   _____

_____   _____

_____   _____

3. What is one thing you believe that you are psychologically dependent upon and explain why you believe you are.

_____

_____

_____

MARIJUANA AND AMOTIVATIONAL SYNDROME

Some have feared that marijuana could lead to *amotivational syndrome*, a lack of interest in achievement, a sort of generalized melting away of ambition. These fears have been fueled by evidence that regular, heavy marijuana smokers in the college ranks did not strive to succeed as much as their nonsmoking or infrequently smoking classmates. . . . Other studies have suggested that the type of person who will choose to use marijuana regularly may differ from the person who will choose not to smoke or to smoke rarely. For instance, the regular smoker may be more concerned about experiencing life emotionally than about excelling in intellectual performance. This different approach to life could lead to both relative lack of ambition and regular marijuana smoking.

[Spencer Rathus, *Psychology*]

1. Underline the definition of amotivational syndrome.

2. The author presents two explanations for the amotivational syndrome. What are they?

_____

_____

_____

_____

In Your Opinion

Which explanation seems to make more sense? Why?

_____

_____

_____

_____

_____

_____

_____

The following selection is a summary of the information you have read in this chapter. Every tenth word has been omited. Try to complete the sentences with words you think are appropriate to the meaning. If you are able to do this correctly about seventy percent of the time, it shows a good understanding of the materials you have read. This *cloze* procedure is often used by instructors to determine comprehension. After you have finished, your instructor will ask for your responses. This will enable you to see other possibilities and then determine whether or not these make sense.

Summary

Marijuana is generally smoked, although it may be taken _____ mouth as an ingredient in food or drink. It _____ a mild alteration in consciousness consisting of a sense _____ well-being, relaxation, and euphoria. Senses are often subjectively heightened, _____ performance of most physical and mental tasks is impaired. _____ large doses of marijuana, pronounced distortions of perception and _____ may be produced.

With the possible exception of bronchitis _____ heavy use, marijuana use is not known to cause _____ damage to the body or brain; however, there is _____ enough evidence to rule out this possibility for prolonged _____ use. Marijuana will occasionally produce panic reactions, especially with _____ doses, inexperienced users, or when used in a threatening _____. On rare occasions these have developed into temporary psychotic _____.

Marijuana is not physiologically addicting; however, a small proportion _____ users do become psychologically dependent on the drug, in _____ sense that it plays an integral part of their

_____. In these cases, its use can contribute to a _____

_____ of undesirable consequences. This type of heavy user often

_____ largely on his immediate needs and impulses, adopting

an _____ attitude toward the future and toward his environ-

ment. As _____ result, he frequently ignores basic health

requirements as well _____ economic responsibility, fails to

develop a discipline for self-expression, _____ adopts a pattern

of naive magical thinking, as opposed _____ rationality and

common sense.

Among the present population of _____, marijuana rarely

leads to the use of addictive drugs _____ as heroin. On the

other hand, the use of _____ does sometimes serve as an intro-

duction to LSD, amphetamines, _____ other dangerous drugs.

[Margaret O. Hyde, *Mind Drugs*]

Following are two opposing arguments presented before the Select
Committee on Narcotics Abuse and Control of the U.S. House of Representative in March 1977. The first argument was presented by Keith Stroup, the
National Director of NORML, an organization which favors the legalization
of marijuana. The second argument was presented by Edward M. Davis, the
president of the International Association of Chiefs of Police.

In Column A, check any of the following statements with which you
agree. After reading the next argument in favor of the legalization of marijuana, check in Column B those statements with which the author would
agree.

Column A   *Column B*

_____   _____   1. The government encourages the use of
                        alcohol and tobacco.

_____   _____   2. To make laws that men cannot and will
                        not obey serves to bring all law into
                        contempt.

_____   _____   3. "There are not enough jails, not enough policemen, not enough courts to enforce a law not supported by the people" (Hubert Humphrey).

_____   _____   4. This is a free country.

_____   _____   5. People should be forced to do things that are good for them.

Argument For the Reform of Marijuana Laws

[1] I am pleased to appear today in support of the concept of marihuana decriminalization. I am here as spokesperson for NORML, the National Organization for the Reform of Marijuana Laws, a non-profit, citizen action lobby whose only purpose is to decriminalize the marihuana smoker. Our organization does not advocate the use of marihuana, and we support a discouragement policy toward the recreational use of all drugs, including alcohol and tobacco as well as marihuana. But we distinguish between discouragement and coercion, and we oppose the use of the criminal sanction against otherwise law-abiding individuals who choose to smoke marihuana.

1. What is the difference between "discouragement" and "coercion"?

_____

_____

_____

[2] NORML attempts to represent the perspective of the consumer; that is, the marihuana smoker. We believe the thirteen to fifteen million regular marihuana smokers in this country are a legitimate political constituency and have a right to participate in the decision making processes, including especially the shaping of drug policy which affects their lives. Most basic to our overall position, we do not believe that an otherwise law-abiding individual who smokes marihuana is a criminal.

[3] Many Americans today hold exaggerated views concerning marihuana's potential harmfulness. This is the result primarily of 35 years of government-inspired propaganda, during which time marihuana smoking was said to be criminogenic and its regular use to lead to insanity. Based on what we now know about the effects of marihuana, the absurdity of those early claims is apparent. But in the 1930s, reinforced and encouraged by the Federal Bureau of Narcotics, they were widely believed and formed the basis of state and federal legislation outlawing marihuana smoking.

[4] Those affected by this policy during the early years were mostly Mexican-American migrant workers in the Southwest and blacks in the South—two groups that exercised little political power. They could not effectively fight back.

Whenever, periodically, claims would be made that marihuana smoking was on an increase, the penalties would be increased.

[5] In the 1960s marihuana smoking found its way to the college campuses. For the first time large numbers of middle-class whites began smoking marihuana, and finding out personally that the old claims were ridiculous, that it was pretty much like alcohol, without the hangover.

[6] To many it became a symbol. Alcohol was seen as the drug of the older generation, those that led us into an unpopular war in Vietnam. Marihuana became the counterculture's alternative to alcohol. Marihuana smoking became a social statement in itself. To smoke marihuana was to protest against the war, against the establishment.

2. Explain how marijuana use can be interpreted as a "social statement."

_____

_____

_____

_____

[7] The illegality of it merely added to its symbolic value, underscoring the hypocrisy of the establishment. It was only fitting that a government that seems to encourage 100 million alcohol drinkers and 60 million tobacco smokers would choose to treat those who smoke marihuana as criminals. To some degree marihuana smoking became the common thread that united the counterculture, its social cohesive. It was a shared risk, the basis for instant trust.

[8] Ironically, the Vietnam war itself was a major factor in the expanding popularity of marihuana during the 1960s. Hundreds of thousands of draftees— not college kids with deferments, but largely working class kids—were sent to Vietnam where they promptly were introduced to Southeast Asian marihuana, among the best in the world. As these military personnel began to return to the States, many naturally retained their marihuana smoking inclinations, greatly expanding the popularity of marihuana.

[9] This symbolism was not lost on the more traditional culture. From their perspective marihuana smoking became synonymous with radical politics, opposition to the war, and hippies. Just as smoking marihuana had become a symbol of protest, opposing its use became synonymous with patriotism, a belief in traditional values, and a repudiation of the excesses of the youth culture.

[10] As a result, enforcing the marihuana laws became a high priority— permitting marihuana smoking would be perceived as giving in to radicalism. Marihuana was feared as a symbol, a threat to the established value system.

[11] The result was a war against drug users, and those of whom smoke marihuana comprised the bulk of the casualties. From a mere 18,000 marihuana arrests nationwide in 1965, the total rose to 416,000 in 1975, according to the FBI Crime Reports. In fact, 69 percent of all drug users in the entire country in that year involved marihuana.

[12] I'm here today basically to make the point that we are not the enemy. Those of us who smoke marihuana do not deserve to be treated like criminals.

The vast majority of us are neither radical nor criminal. We are otherwise law-abiding citizens who happen to enjoy smoking marihuana. We span all socio-economic and age subgroups. To continue to confuse marihuana smokers as criminals is indefensible.

[13] We're your neighbors, your co-workers, often your children. Most of us are responsible citizens, who care about our community, and we share the same anxieties and aspirations as do other Americans.

[14] In fact, though marihuana smoking remains most popular among young adults, you will see from the statistics gathered by the National Institute on Drug Abuse that smoking is becoming more popular among older Americans as well. Millions of people now prefer marihuana to alcohol. Like the 60 million Americans who currently smoke tobacco, or the 100 million who currently drink alcohol, marihuana smokers are simply recreational drug users. None should feel superior to the others.

[15] But there is one major difference. Those who drink alcohol or smoke tobacco are discouraged from doing so, but not arrested for it. Those who smoke marihuana are not only discouraged, they play a game of roulette with the law-enforcement community.

[16] We recognize that in most jurisdictions today, the police do not go looking for marihuana smokers. Nonetheless, more than 400,000 citizens were arrested in this country last year on marihuana charges. The vast majority of those people were simply consumers—fewer than 10 percent were commercial traffickers.

[17] Some of them received long prison terms. These absurdly harsh marihuana sentences are less common today, but they still occur, mostly in rural areas where the misinformation about marihuana remains greatest.

[18] The great majority of marihuana offenders today do not spend long periods of time in jail. The prosecutors and judges have often instituted diversion programs to avoid the harshest consequences of the laws.

[19] Yet the individual is still arrested and run through the criminal justice system at a great cost, though the end result is usually a small fine and possibly a suspended sentence.

[20] I would ask that you consider for a moment the experience of someone who is arrested, taken to the station, finger-printed, booked, and in all other manners treated like a criminal on a minor marihuana charge. It makes a mockery of our criminal justice system and of our concepts of privacy and freedom of choice. Meanwhile the result to the offender is to brand him a criminal, unsuitable for higher levels of education, training, or employment opportunities. He receives, in most respects, very much the same treatment as someone who has committed a minor burglary.

[21] The cost of all this in terms of wasted law-enforcement resources is enormous. The best estimates available are that $600 million a year is currently being spent arresting and prosecuting marihuana smokers in this country. It seems rather obvious that this extraordinary drain on law-enforcement resources has a negative impact on our ability to detect and prosecute serious crimes.

[22] Also, the ineffectiveness of the criminal law as a deterrent is a factor which must be recognized. Despite harsh criminal penalties for 40 years, marihuana is more popular today than ever before. Even those who continue to strongly oppose the use of marihuana must concede the futility of attempting to prohibit the use of a drug already used regularly by 15 million Americans.

[23] One of the continuing tactics of those who attempt to hold back reform of the marihuana laws is to exaggerate the potential harm to an individual's health from marihuana smoking. No one is claiming that marihuana is harmless, nor that it is good for people, other than in particular therapeutic situations. But prestigious groups have reviewed the medical claims, and found that when used in moderation, marihuana does not appear to present any major medical problems.

[24] Even if marihuana were eventually shown to be as dangerous as alcohol or tobacco, we should nonetheless decriminalize it. If marihuana is harmful, then it is a potential health problem, not a criminal justice problem. We are not addressing the potential health risk to the user by subjecting him to arrest and jail. Any potential harm should be communicated effectively to the consumer, not used to justify arresting him.

[25] We believe the individual's constitutionally protected right to privacy should preclude any penalty, either state or federal, for the private possession and cultivation of marihuana for personal use.

[26] We believe the right to possess marihuana for personal use should also include the right to cultivate small amounts of marihuana for personal consumption. This would provide a legal source of marihuana for the millions who smoke, without the need to establish a legal distribution system. The potential for abuse from the private cultivation is far less than from the illicit market.

[27] We also favor decriminalizing the transfer of small amounts of marihuana. Small transactions, even where a small profit may be involved, are generally accommodation sales, not commercial selling. Since most marihuana smokers do in fact buy marihuana at times in greater quantities than they may personally smoke, and share it among friends, the law should recognize this custom and permit it without penalty.

[28] NORML opposes arbitrary quantity limitations on the amount of marihuana which a consumer can possess legally. The possession, cultivation, or not-for-profit transfer of any amount for personal use should be decriminalized. Just as an alcohol drinker often has several fifths of liquor in his cabinet without being confused with a liquor store, a marihuana smoker should be permitted to have a few ounces of marihuana on hand without being confused with a commercial trafficker.

[*The Congressional Digest*]

In Column A, check any of the following statements which you agree. After reading the next argument opposed to the legalization of marijuana, check in Column B those statements with which the author would agree.

Column A   *Column B*

———   ———   1. An individual should be permitted to do anything as long as it doesn't harm anyone else.

		2.	"When people are free to do as they please, they usually imitate each other" (Eric Hoffer).
		3.	"The law is reason free from passion." (Aristotle)
		4.	"Disobedience is the worst of evils. This it is that ruins a nation" (Jean Anouilh).

Argument Against the Reform of Marijuana Laws

In the intense campaign that has been waged over the past ten years to change our marihuana laws, three major points have been proposed:

1. That marihuana and its derivatives are essentially harmless;

2. That once it was legally available only a small minority would become marihuana users; and

3. That for legislation and law enforcement to curb drug abuse is a fruitless exercise and a waste of the taxpayers' money.

1. What specific arguments would you expect the author to discuss?

_____

_____

_____

First, it must be made clear that the preponderance of research conducted with regard to marihuana use has found that it *is* harmful to the user. The most recent research has only corroborated what earlier researchers had predicted, but were unable to verify.

Medical science tells us how communication within the brain and nervous system is based on a complex and delicate balance carried on by electrochemical processes. Research has further shown how the use of marihuana and other drugs disrupts these processes. Marihuana distorts both the sensory information received and the emotional responses of the user. In this state of distortion, the marihuana user's critical judgment is impaired and he may become more vulnerable to external evaluations and suggestions. He experiences a loss of will and conscious control. These effects are often pronounced during a marihuana high, and research has shown that the effects also persist after a period of acute intoxication and accumulate with chronic use. This is one factor which accounts for the amotivational state of the habitual user. Studies of chronic users, who were observed for periods of six to nine years, have documented that this type of user suffers from diminished drive, lessened ambition, decreased motivation, and apathy. The user, himself, ordinarily does not perceive the amotivational effect of his use until a sense of motivation returns subsequent to his giving up marihuana.

What might be termed moderate use (once or twice weekly) has also been found to have enduring and debilitating effects. Regular users show evidence of a continuing low grade intoxication manifested by mood swings, memory impairment, sleep disturbances and a generally lessened level of functioning.

Additionally, researchers have known that some of the more persistent effects of marihuana use are defective motor coordination and poor perceptions of time, distance, and speed. These symptoms become especially hazardous when the marihuana user attempts to drive an automobile.

It was noted by researchers that all accidental deaths increased approximately 30 percent during the 1960s among the category of those 15 to 35 years of age and that the automobile accidental death rate increased more than 30 percent during the same time. That increase was reflected first among college age persons and later in the younger and older groups. I think it is no coincidence that this corresponded very closely with the ages affected by the drug movement in the United States.

Prolonged exposure to marihuana results in significant increases in chromosome breakage. Although broken chromosomes are seldom a genetic hazard to offspring, researchers are concerned that the conditions causing broken chromosomes may also damage the genes in unbroken chromosomes. Due to nature's pairing of genes, a defective gene would not produce a specific genetic disease, but rather a general decline in the vigor of the offspring.

It is certainly time that all the latest research regarding marihuana use and its effects be brought to light and dispassionately examined—not just by legislators, but by the public. The Shafer Commission report has been criticized by many experts in the field of drug abuse. This report ambiguously recommended that private use of marihuana be made legal while public sale, use, and possession remained illegal and yet it also recommended that use of marihuana be discouraged. Although acknowledging that heavy use was dangerous, the Shafer Commission reported that the experience of most Americans was with low doses of weak preparations of the drug. While the Commission did recognize the dangers of heavy use, it failed to realize that users in this country would escalate to higher doses and stronger preparations if they were available. This type of escalation occurred among our servicemen in Germany and Vietnam and has occurred in other countries where marihuana has been used for centuries.

2. Underline some of the harmful physical effects mentioned in the preceding material.

This leads to the second myth in the pro-marihuana argument—that once marihuana is legally available only a small minority would become marihuana users.

History shows us that when drugs are readily available, their use increases. It's a known fact! I have already made mention of the experience of our servicemen in Germany and Vietnam where supplies of marihuana and other drugs were plentiful and cheap. The experience of Japan with amphetamines is another case in point. Prior to World War II, Japan had never had a serious drug problem. But when amphetamines, used during the war to counteract drowsiness and fatigue, were made available to the civilian population, through the black market and liberal prescription policies, the use of this drug increased to where in 1954, about 500,000 young Japanese were using amphetamines and half of these were injecting it intravenously. Government control and strict law enforcement, however, reversed this trend and essentially eliminated Japan's amphetamine abuse by 1968.

It should not go unnoted that the demand for legalizing marihuana has been most vociferous in those countries which have had the shortest experience and the weakest forms of the drug. In countries throughout the world where cannabis use is endemic, responsible individuals are both surprised and disheartened to hear of attempts in the United States to legalize marihuana. In countries like Greece, Turkey, and Egypt where cannabis had long been used, it is considered a scourge and a stupefying drug that is especially harmful to the young. Many consider it a factor in underdeveloped countries for keeping the poor impoverished.

3. What examples does the author use to support his argument that "when drugs are readily available, their use increases"?

_____

_____

_____

Congressmen and the general public should not remain naive to the "big business enterprise" represented by those trafficking in drugs. I intensely feel that the ability to "make a buck" off marihuana if it is legitimized, regardless of its social consequences, will lead to an ever expanding market for this drug.

It should be kept in mind that the experience of other countries, as well as our own recent experience, shows that those most vulnerable to marihuana use are the youth and young adults of this nation. The most recent polls have shown that 55 percent of the 1976 high school graduating seniors have experimented with marihuana. This percentage has been growing yearly, aided no doubt by the normal impressionability and rebelliousness of adolescence, but abetted also by the ambivalence of some law makers and responsible adults who recognize the consequences, but are afraid or unwilling to take a stand.

This brings me to the third myth—that for legislation and law enforcement to curb drug abuse is a fruitless exercise and a waste of the taxpayers' money.

Law has many functions in a society. It is partly a control mechanism used to restrict the behavior of citizens from unhealthy, unacceptable expressions and direct them toward healthy and productive ones. Law serves as a teacher of what is healthy, productive, and acceptable and what isn't. The fact that any law isn't perfectly kept does not mean that it is ineffectual. I have not heard, as yet, that God has retracted the Ten Commandments merely because mankind often fails to live up to them. The fact of the matter is strong, clear laws recognizing the dire effects of marihuana use are necessary as the stated policy of this nation and of its member states.

Law enforcement also sees this decriminalization as but a part of a whole process. They have seen from experience that the users of marihuana are first introduced into a drug oriented environment and mentality. With reduced powers of judgment and will, the user now functions in an environment where other pleasure drugs are available. He becomes more susceptible both to peer pressure and to the enticing possibility of greater pleasure. It is all too easy, almost natural, to slide into experiencing the variety of sensations which multiple drug use produces. Marihuana has proven to be the doorway to other, even more dangerous drugs. It is the most common initiator to the escapism of the drug subculture.

4. Underline the main idea of the paragraph above.

This step-by-step process of decriminalization brings us to the reality that decriminalization is but the first step—and marihuana the first drug—in a formula to legitimize the use of other pleasure drugs, such as cocaine. Already the arguments for legalizing cocaine are being heard. They begin by saying that cocaine is really harmless.

If the cultural and historical currents of this nation were presently flowing strong in the direction of individual self-reliance, personal responsibility, and emotional maturity, then the direction of decriminalization legislation would be less alarming. But in an age that is not only experiencing confusion about its goals and purposes, but is also being deluged by media advertising to relieve every ache, pain, or discomfort through some drug or other, I do not believe that the elected leaders of the public should legitimize yet another pleasure drug. Is this what the men and women responsible for the health and welfare of this great nation intend to do?

[*The Congressional Digest*]

In Your Opinion

Knowing that alcohol and tobacco are very harmful drugs which are legal in our society, should marijuana be legalized? Why?

_____

_____

_____

_____

_____

_____

_____

_____

Now that you have read this chapter, you probably have a better understanding of what marijuana is and some of the reasons why people use drugs. Perhaps you have also given some thought to the alternatives to drug use. The arguments for and against the legalization of marijuana may have helped you decide what *you* think is the right way to go on this question.

You had the opportunity to explore cause–effect relationships, in addition to using other important reading skills introduced earlier in the book.

A Further Reading

MARIJUANA

As soon as we were alone he [a jockey named Patrick] pulled out a gang of cigarettes and handed them to me. They were as fat as ordinary cigarettes but were rolled in brown wheatstraw paper. We both lit up and I got halfway through mine, hoping they would break the news to mother gently, before he stopped me. "Hey," he said, "take it easy, kid. You want to knock yourself out?"

I didn't feel a thing and I told him so. "Do you know one thing?" he said. "You ain't even smokin' it right. You got to hold that muggle so that it barely touches your lips, see, then draw in air around it. Say *tfff*, *tfff*, only breathe in when you say it. Then don't blow it out right away, you got to give the stuff a chance." He had a tricky look in his eye that I didn't go for at all. The last time I saw that kind of look it was on a district attorney's mug, and it caused me a lot of inconvenience.

After I finished the weed I went back to the bandstand. Everything seemed normal and I began to play as usual. I passed a stick of gauge around for the other boys to smoke, and we started a set.

The first thing I noticed was that I began to hear my saxophone as though it was inside my head, but I couldn't hear much of the band in back of me, although I knew they were there. All the other instruments sounded like they were way off in the distance; I got the same sensation you'd get if you stuffed your ears with cotton and talked out loud. Then I began to feel the vibrations of the reed much more pronounced against my lip, and my head buzzed like a loud-speaker. I found I was slurring much better and putting just the right feeling into my phrases—I was really coming on. All the notes came easing out of my horn like they'd already been made up, greased and stuffed into the bell, so all I had to do was blow a little and send them on their way, one right after the other, never missing, never behind time, all without an ounce of effort. The phrases seemed to have more continuity to them and I was sticking to the theme without ever going tangent. I felt I could go on playing for years without running out of ideas and energy. There wasn't any struggle; it was all made-to-order and suddenly there wasn't a sour note or a discord in the world that could bother me. I began to feel very happy and sure of myself. With my loaded horn I could take all the fist-swinging, evil things in the world and bring them together in perfect harmony, spreading peace and joy and relaxation to all the keyed-up and punchy people everywhere. I began to preach my millenniums on my horn, leading all the sinners on to glory. . . .

It's a funny thing about marijuana—when you first begin smoking it you see things in a wonderful soothing, easy-going new light. All of a sudden the world is stripped of its dirty gray shrouds and becomes one big bellyful of giggles, a spherical laugh, bathed in brilliant, sparkling colors that hit you like a heatwave. Nothing leaves you cold any more; there's a humorous tickle and great meaning in the least little thing, the twitch of somebody's little finger or the click of a beer glass. All your pores open like funnels, your nerve-ends stretch their mouths wide, hungry and thirsty for new sights and sounds and sensations; and every sensation, when it comes, is the most exciting one you've ever had. You can't get enough of anything—you want to gobble up the whole goddamned universe just for an appetizer. Them first kicks are a killer, Jim.

Suppose you're the critical and analytical type, always ripping things to pieces, tearing the covers off and being disgusted by what you find under the sheet. Well, under the influence of muta [marijuana] you don't lose your surgical touch exactly, but you don't come up evil and grimy about it. You still see what you saw before but in a different, more tolerant way, through rose-colored glasses, and things that would have irritated you before just tickle you. Everything is good for a laugh; the wrinkles get ironed out of your face and you forget what a frown is, you just want to hold on to your belly and roar till the tears come. . . .

Tea puts a musician in a real masterly sphere, and that's why so many jazzmen have used it. You look down on the other members of the band like an old mother hen surveying her brood of chicks; if one of them hits a sour note or comes up with a bad modulation, you just smile tolerantly and figure, oh well, he'll learn, it'll be better next time, give the guy a chance. Pretty soon you find yourself helping him out, trying to put him on the right track. The most terrific thing is this, that all the while you're playing, really getting off, your own accompaniment keeps flashing through your head, just like you were a one-man band. You hear the basic tones of the theme and keep up your pattern of improvisation without ever getting tangled up, giving out with a uniform sequence all the way. Nothing can mess you up. You hear everything at once and you hear it right. When you get that feeling of power and sureness, you're in a solid groove.

You know how jittery, got-to-be-moving people in the city always get up in the subway train two minutes before they arrive at the station? Their nerves are on edge; they're watching the clock, thinking about schedules, full of that high-powered mile-a-minute jive. Well, when you've picked up on some gauge that clock just stretches its arms, yawns, and dozes off. The whole world slows down and gets drowsy. You wait until the train stops dead and the doors slide open, then you get up and stroll out in slow motion, like a sleep-walker with a long night ahead of him and no appointments to keep. You've got all the time in the world. What's the rush, buddy? Take-it-easy, that's the play, it's bound to sweeten it all the way. . . .

The bandstand was only a foot high but when I went to step down it took me a year to find the floor, it seemed so far away. I was sailing through the clouds, flapping my free-wheeling wings, and leaving the stand was like stepping off into space. Twelve months later my foot struck solid ground with a jolt, but the other one stayed up there on those lovely soft clouds, and I almost fell flat on my face. There was a roar of laughter from Patrick's table and I began to feel self-conscious and nauseous at the same time. I flew to the men's room and got there just in time. Patrick came in and started to laugh at me.

"What's the matter, kid?" he said. "You not feeling so good?" At that moment I was up in a plane, soaring around the sky, with a buzz-saw in my head. Up and around we went, saying nuts to Newton and all his fancy laws of gravitation, but suddenly we went into a nosedive and I came down to earth, sock. Ouch. My head went spattering off in more directions than a hand grenade. Patrick put a cold towel on my temples and I snapped out of it. After sitting down for a while I was all right.

When I went back to the stand I still heard all my music amplified, as though my ear was built right into the horn. The evening rolled away before I knew it. When the entertainers sang I accompanied them on the piano, and from the way they kept glancing up at me I could tell they felt the harmonies I was inventing behind them without any effort at all. The notes kept sliding out of my horn like bubbles in seltzer water. My control over the vibrations of my tones was perfect, and I got a terrific lift from the richness of the music, the bigness of it. The notes eased out like lava running down a mountain slow and sure and steaming. It was good.

[Mezzrow and Wolfe, *Really the Blues*]

Suggested Readings

Alcoholics Anonymous. New York: Al Anon Publishers, 1955.

The story of how many thousands of men and women have recovered from alcoholism.

Bagley, Desmond. *The Spoilers.* New York: Doubleday & Co., Inc., 1970.

A young English girl dies of an overdose of heroin. Her wealthy father convinces a doctor who works with addicts to seek out and smash the dope ring.

Berry, James. *Heroin Was My Best Friend.* New York: Macmillan Publishing Co., 1971.

This book reveals actual conversations the author had with seven young ex-addicts who began using drugs in their teens, and with an addict's mother. Each ex-addict explains why he took drugs as well as the reasons for quitting. Some smoked pot. Others popped pills. But Donny took heroin—up to twenty bags a day.

Flender, Harold. *We Were Hooked.* Fawcett World, 1973.

The author interviewed hundreds of young people in twenty-five drug treatment centers from California to Connecticut. He selected thirteen of them, ages fifteen to twenty-seven, to tell their stories of how and why they got into drugs, the problems related to drugs, and how they kicked the addiction.

Howard, Marion. *Did I Have a Good Time? Teenage Drinking.* New York: Continuim, 1980.

Teenage Drinking follows the lives of three young people with typical problems, whose encounters with alcohol change their lives.

Kastle, Albert J., and Lena Kasth. *Journey Back, Escaping the Drug Trap.* Chicago: Nelson-Hall Company, 1975.

A series of interviews with fifteen people who have devoted their lives to solving the drug problem.

Moscow, Alvin. *Merchants of Heroin.* New York: Dial Press, Inc., 1968.

The story of organized crime and its connections with narcotics.

Motley, Willard. *Let No Man Write My Epitaph.* New York: Random House Inc., 1958.

This novel, set in the Chicago slums, is the story of the brutal education of young Nick Romano and Nellie Watkins, a dope addict. There is little hope for the boy until a group of concerned friends urge him to give up narcotics. How long Nick can stay away from them will be anyone's guess.

Stricker, George, and Fred Weiss. *Kicking It.* Benwood, West Virginia: Pyramid Press Pub. Co., 1971.

Through words and pictures this book conveys the setbacks, struggles, and victories of young people who find hope and help in Topic House.

U.S. Dept. of Health, Education and Welfare. *The Whole College Catalog About Drinking.* Rockville, Maryland: Alcohol, Drug Abuse and Mental Health Administration, 1976.

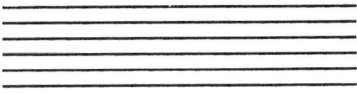

CHAPTER 6

"Why don't you work/Like other men do?"
"How the hell can I work/When there's no work to do?"

WELFARE-WORKFARE

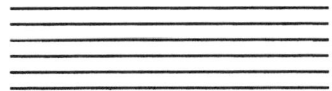

Most people have strong feelings about welfare, a government-funded program to assist the poor. Various programs which require welfare recipients to engage in assigned jobs have been proposed. These work programs, referred to as workfare, are in effect in some states.

Some of the questions addressed in this chapter include: Are workfare programs practical? Do they help people reach a point where they do not need to receive welfare benefits? Who pays the cost of such programs? You will read what welfare recipients have to say about being dependent on the government for support.

You will also consider the difference between facts and opinions by exploring your own ideas about welfare.

1. What do you believe are some of the causes of poverty?

_____

_____

_____

_____

2. Do you think people are entitled to receive welfare? Why?

_____

_____

_____

_____

3. What are some specific circumstances which make it necessary for people to receive welfare?

_____

_____

_____

_____

4. Do you think any of the circumstances you listed above should *not* entitle a person to receive welfare? Which ones, and why?

_____

_____

_____

_____

5. What kinds of feelings might welfare recipients have about receiving welfare?

_____

_____

_____

_____

6. Where does money paid to welfare recipients come from?

_____

_____

DISTINGUISHING BETWEEN FACTS AND OPINIONS

In the spaces provided, write the letter "F" is you believe the statement is a fact, and "O" if you believe the statement is an opinion.

_____ 1. Most people on welfare are unable to work.

_____ 2. Poverty exists because of the greed of others.

_____ 3. There will always be poor people.

_____ 4. Many people who are now unemployed are having difficulties finding jobs.

_____ 5. There are only two families in the world, the Haves and the Have Nots.

_____ 6. Poverty is created by our society.

_____ 7. Most people on welfare know how to "use" the system.

_____ 8. You can't trust the poor.

_____ 9. The poorest paid job should pay more than a welfare subsidy.

_____ 10. Work gives meaning to one's life.

_____ 11. Social services such as welfare, unemployment insurance, and Medicaid are items in our national budget.

_____ 12. Food stamps are supposed to be used for food items only.

_____ 13. Some people receive welfare checks even though they are not entitled to them.

Facts are usually defined as truths which can be proven. If you read that "x number of people are receiving welfare," it is possible to verify that statement by obtaining information from several reliable sources (such as government statistics, a current almanac, etc.). On the other hand, the statement "All people on welfare don't want to work" expresses an opinion. Although you may agree with the statement, there is no way to check the validity of it.

Sometimes what seems to be a fact is really not. The statement "The average number of children in families receiving welfare is six" appears to be a fact—after all, you could check this statement in the library. If it turns out that the average number of children in these families is actually three, the original sentence is an incorrect statement. Therefore, just because you can check the accuracy of a statement does not make it a fact. A fact is a true statement.

Sometimes writers try to convince you to agree with their points of view (or biases) by distorting facts, or by presenting personal opinions as _though_ they were facts. You as a reader must be alert to recognize the author's intent to avoid accepting opinions as facts. Bias is most commonly used in advertising, editorials, and political writing. It is also important that you be aware of your _own_ opinions, not only the author's, when reading.

Now look back at the list of statements. Are your responses correct? You may want to discuss your ideas with other students.

In the next section, a welfare recipient tells of his feelings about being on welfare.

Speaking as a member of the black race and not from books, newspapers, radio, T.V., or any other sources, these are my thoughts and feelings on the welfare system.

1. Welfare mentality. To me welfare mentality is the state of mind of a person having to depend on welfare to survive.

2. What does welfare do to a person?. . . I do know that it takes something away from your pride. Not everyone wishes to be on welfare, but there comes a time (or a point in time) in one's life where there is no other choice.

To the male, or I would like to think to most of them, it's a lowering of self-esteem. They seem to feel or fear a lack of respect from family and loved ones.

To the female, it means a way of survival for their children when there's no father, and jobs are a rarity for untrained persons. . . .

3. How does welfare help financially? To be sure the amount of monies that is doled out is not sufficient for one person (not speaking of two or three) in a household. . . .

4. Education. Another sore spot because the family on welfare usually cannot afford decent clothing, lunches, books, and other material things that a child should have in order not to feel ashamed or embarrassed to be seen in school. Therefore, many young children decides [sic] to heck with school, take to the streets and start them a hustle. . . . Does welfare have any good points? Welfare does have some self-defending points in that there are scores of people who are physically as well as mentally unable to work, and without the little dole could not make it at all. But the bad part of it is that people have to go through so much hell to even get that meager handout.

[Ken Auletta, *The Underclass*]

1. What does the author mean by "the hell" that people who receive welfare go through?

_____

_____

_____

_____

In the following selection, a working mother expresses *her* feelings about welfare recipients. ("American Pie" is an expression that refers to the luxuries in life that every American feels he or she is entitled to.)

AMERICAN PIE, IN SOME SKY

There's something disconcerting about standing in line at the checkout counter behind someone using food stamps. Especially when one is paying for one's own order with the family's mortgage money.

Breathes there a soul so liberal that comparisons do not arise upon watching such purchases? My thought processes work this way: "Hamburger, I'm buying hamburger. She's buying a roast. Potato chips, candy—will food stamps really pay for those?" Then I watch as the cashier rings them through with nary a word.

My basket is full of generic no-names with their depressingly obvious black-and-white labels. Hers, my God, rivals the rainbow—not a cheapie to be found in that order.

I find myself thinking that there must be something terribly wrong with a system which causes me to, even for a moment, consider the advantages of being a food-stamp recipient.

"God help me" (says my conscience), "the poor soul probably needs them." "God help me" (says the rest of me), "so do I!"

The rumors fly fast. And I ignore them. I really do. Third-party stories are just that—stories. It is personal experience that rankles me. A friend who delivers takeout dinners assured me unabashedly that his best customers pay him with food stamps. I was aghast, but he seemed to take it for granted; according to him, it's legal.

While window-shopping at a lobster pound and bemoaning the astronomical prices, I spoke to the owner: "See this?" he said while fanning food stamps, "The only lobster sales I've had today were paid for by these. Sad commentary, huh?"

Huh, indeed. I left, half-heartedly clutching a small package of frozen fish. All the way home, I wondered: "Where did I go wrong? Does this really bother me? Should it bother me? Does it bother anyone else?" It was a long way home, believe me.

It's not that I begrudge the needy. It's just that I begrudge living less well than they do. Three doctors in a week have refused to process my insurance forms. "Sorry," said one receptionist, "pay now. We no longer submit insurance forms." I had to pay $90 for my daughter's ears, $50 for mine, $30 for bronchitis—all out-of-pocket. "I don't carry that kind of money around," I said. "What would you do if I had Medicaid, or Medicare?"

"Many of our patients do," came the reply. "We'd have to submit them for you then. Those are the only forms we do process."

Great. Tell that to the bank when my mortgage payment is due.

As I looked about the waiting room I tried to single out even one Medicaid patient. No luck. They look like everyone else. And they get treated like everyone else—better, when it comes to payment forms. Ah, then I saw a man fingering a Medicaid card. Mesmerized, I watched the receptionist who had not kept her voice down when we were talking about my paying my bill. She was suddenly transformed into an understanding protector of the Medicaid patient's privacy, of his sense of dignity. My jealously knew no bounds. Indignation gave way to something else. Longing. Longing to own such a magic card, to be one of the accepted, to be one of the true participators in society, to, for once, be a taker instead of a giver.

"Oh," a friend once said, "you're too proud to withstand the humiliation of public assistance, of food stamps, of Medicaid. It's degrading."

That may have been so at one time. But what could be more degrading than struggling to move to a nicer home, a better neighborhood, trying "to keep up with the Joneses" who just happen to be setting the pace with your tax money? And where is the incentive for the Joneses to get off welfare, to "live the good life"? They already live it.

Sure, he's employed. So is she. They are not married, but it seems that one or the other of them qualifies for Section 8 housing, Medicaid, low-interest farmers' loans, free college tuition (plus expenses), free child care, as well as food stamps.

Another neighbor summed it up for many of us when she said: "Why should my husband and I have to work 70-odd hours a week to earn $30,000 a year, to live equal to, or substandard to, a welfare family? Ridiculous!"

What could I say to that?

I couldn't argue with it. After all, while I was feeding a wood stove and living in one room of my house all winter, the Joneses lived it up in warmth and applied for fuel assistance.

Where is my piece of the American pie? I finally figured it out. Yup, it seems the system has placed it on someone else's table.

Kathleen Kroll

1. In what ways do the authors of the two articles you just read differ in their perceptions of welfare recipients?

_____

_____

_____

_____

_____

_____

_____

The author of "American Pie, In Some Sky" is one of the many people in our society, not on welfare, who has strongly held views about the welfare system. The following article reflects another of these points of view. Can you tell, from the title, what this author's opinion is?

_____

_____

_____

The following article is reprinted from *U.S. News & World Report.*

LIFE IS NOT A FREE LUNCH

There was no question that the old man was blind. His head was cocked to one side, as if watching a distant vision. But after a quick glance, passers-by didn't notice his eyes—instead, they heard his music.

The saxophone he cradled was old and tarnished. His hands, chipped and gnarled by time and labor, rippled over the keys and his cheeks tensed with every note.

There was no plea from the man for help or charity, but hanging from the bell of his horn was a small plastic cup. As the melodies—spirituals, marches, camp songs—flowed smoothly from that battered horn, coins rattled one after another into the cup. The old man shuffled on, paying his way with music.

A few yards up the street, as if stalking the blind horn player, came a young man in jeans, a T-shirt and a careless manner. He sauntered along, his eyes darting hopefully from person to person.

Occasionally, he would stop someone, and each time his story was the same: "Could you spare a quarter?"

Once, twice, a dozen times he was turned down, often just ignored. But he was untroubled and continued to beg, his palm outstretched, as if seeking what was owed him.

Both the old man and the young man sought the same thing—the pocket change of passing strangers. But examine the philosophical difference. The old man was offering all that he had—a fading talent and a dying strength—in return for the silver. The young man offered only his need and the expectation that the need would be, and should be, met.

1. What were both the blind man and the young man doing?

_____

_____

2. What difference does the author see between the blind man and the young man?

_____

_____

_____

So we ask: Is it the young man's thinking that has become dominant in this country? Is there a growing belief that life does, in fact, provide a free lunch and that all one needs to receive it is to expect it? Is the idea of the work ethic gone forever?

Marvin Stone

3. What is meant by "work ethic"?

_____

_____

_____

_____

4. Do you agree that only one of the two people described was asking for a "free lunch"? Why?

_____

_____

_____

_____

In the next article, John Tropman writes about the organization of our society into classes and how many people view the members of "the lowest class" and "the second lowest class."

COPPING OUT OR CHIPPING IN

American society is contradictory in its attitude toward those in need. On the one hand, we often express dislike, aversion, and even hatred toward the people who have not made it, who are disadvantaged in some way. On occasion, we go further than that and blame the victim. As William Ryan stated, "The poor person is blamed for being poor, the rape victim is blamed for causing the rape, and even recently the cancer victim is blamed for having a 'cancer personality.'"

On the other hand, let someone's plight be published in the paper or other media, and Americans are a very generous group, contributing cash and other essentials to the person who is in that instance in need. An article in *The New York Times* titled "Hundred Neediest Cases" provides an ample illustration of our generosity, as do the various telethons for a myriad of appropriate causes. The question becomes: Why are we so hateful on the one hand and so generous on the other? An extension of that question occurs within the context of modern society: as Americans become wealthier, there does not seem to be any particular increase in the sense of social obligation; rather the dislike seems as strong and vigorous as ever. If anything, wealth increases dislike over generosity. Even religion, as measured by religious attendance, does not contribute to social compassion.

The Lowest Class

Some perspective on this question is provided in an analysis of the attitude Americans have toward the "lowest class" and the "next-to-the-lowest class" as revealed in a survey undertaken in Boston and Kansas City in 1972. The respondents were asked to make a distinction between the lowest class and the next-to-the-lowest class. Their answers and the nature of the distinctions they made help us to understand why Americans feel as they do.

For the lowest class, the respondents mentioned first that it was the welfare class. The Aid to Families with Dependent Children program (AFDC) was specifically mentioned, as well as terms like *on the dole, on relief,* and *handout.* Not only was the specific program disesteemed but the character of the responses was of a very negative moral evaluation. A substantial proportion (18 percent) commented that the lowest class does not try.

Why is the lowest class the "welfare class"? Is it because it is comprised of blacks, women with families, or the elderly? Not according to these respondents. In reality, of course, race, sex, and age are importantly related to poverty states, but in the perception of the Boston and Kansas City people, lack of education was the most likely villain. Forty-four percent of the respondents mentioned lack of education as a reason for "welfarism," while only 3 percent mentioned race, ethnicity, or gender and 2 percent mentioned age. Clearly, the image of the poor is different from the real circumstances surrounding poverty.

The Second-Lowest Class

When the respondents began to mention their views toward the second-lowest class, however, some differences began to creep in. Rather than the negative, hostile cast that had characterized their view of the lowest class, a more supportive, more understanding tone emerged from the response. Welfare was not mentioned by name. Rather, the language itself shifted and phrases like *government aid* or *a little help now and then* or *some help to make ends meet* became the language. Rather than perceived as not trying, many respondents (21 percent) specifically saw those in the second-lowest class as trying. Sixty-five percent of the respondents saw those in the second-lowest class as working, but having a job which was not adequate to make ends meet for them. The respondents saw the second-lowest class of persons as entitled to a more enhanced life-style than their economic level permitted; somehow, the respondents felt, the second-lowest-class person was cheated out of his just due, rather than enjoying illegitimate goods and services.

Indeed, this sense of legitimacy, as opposed to illegitimacy, is the cutting edge of difference between the image of the two classes. Clearly it is not the receipt of benefits themselves—both classes are reported as receiving some benefits. Rather, one group is seen as having legitimate benefits, while the other is seen as having benefits which are somehow improper. The reason for this distinction between the "worthy" and the "unworthy" poor lies in the perception, it seems, of the extent to which the recipients are "copping out" or "chipping in" to the society in which they live. If they are seen as chipping in, then they are entitled to supplementary benefits to help them over the rough spots. But to deserve this approval, they need to be making some kind of effort on their own behalf.

The Reciprocal Society

American Society might be called the "reciprocal society" because of the importance of sharing and trading within the context of our history—a sort of social economy with credits, debits, interest, investments, and so forth. While there has been, to be sure, an emphasis upon individualism and doing it yourself, one is also aware of the extent to which the efforts of the individual are supplemented by the shared efforts of others. The barn raising, the mutual help in harvesting, the famous borrowed cup of sugar—these interconnected elements represent the communal aspect of American society. . . . The making of a contribution enhances both the individual and the collective elements within American society. As long as someone is chipping in, then that person is entitled to draw on the resources of the society. It is seen that the individual is continuing to make a contribution, and it is anticipated that the individual will continue to do so. If he runs up a little debit on his social account, it is not regarded as serious.

If, however, the person is not making a contribution, is not chipping in, then the society feels that that individual does not deserve to make any claims upon the society itself even if, in some objective sense, he *needs* help. In a sense, society sees that there is always something you can contribute. If you are paralyzed from the neck down, then you can contribute by painting holiday cards by holding the brush in your mouth!

Perhaps the most striking example of this is the Nicholas plan, developed by an executive of Oklahoma Utilities during the depression. "By the Nicholas plan, restaurants were asked to dump food left on plates into five-gallon containers; the unemployed could then qualify for these scraps by chopping wood donated by farmers. We expect a little trouble now and then from those who are not worthy of the support of the citizens," wrote Nicholas philosophically, "but we must contend with such cases in order to take care of those who are worthy." Even garbage cannot be provided to the poor without them making some kind of contribution. One wonders whom Nicholas would deem unworthy of these slops.

The high and the low in society apparently feel similarly about the poor. Perhaps one illustration comes from a man in prison for armed robbery: "I wonder at them coming all the way up here from the South and getting welfare and just having babies. They ain't worth nothing. . . . I'm worth more than them; I got skills. I'm a dedicated stick-up man." Even a robber feels he is making a contribution; after all, he is not just sitting around watching television and drinking beer.

Why should "contribution" be so important, and why do we attribute such negative images to people using a program set up to help them?

John E. Tropman

Listed below are the headings from "Copping out or Chipping in," followed by 8 statements. Write the number of the heading which contains the information given in each statement.

1. The lowest class.
2. The second-lowest class.
3. The reciprocal society.

_____ a. You have to give something to get something.

_____ b. Many people think that welfare recipients don't try hard enough.

_____ c. Receiving financial aid is no disgrace.

_____ d. Anything is better than nothing.

_____ e. Race, sex, and age are related to poverty.

_____ f. People who have should help people who have not.

_____ g. Some people who work also receive government aid.

_____ h. There is a feeling among people in the United States that welfare recipients are of low moral character.

In the article "Life is Not a Free Lunch" which man would be considered "worthy"?

_____

The author of the next article argues against the use of labeling the nation's poor.

POVERTY'S VOGUISH STIGMA

Homeless men and women, young and sometimes violent street criminals, unwed teenaged mothers, longterm welfare recipients—all represent serious social problems. What, besides poverty, do they all have in common?

If you believe the latest vogue word making the rounds of the news media, all these people are members of a single group—the "underclass."

"Underclass" is a misleading and destructive label that lumps together distinct people with distinct problems. Although it sounds precise and scientific, the term confounds analysis and social policy by shifting the debate away from the real problems—bad jobs and racial discrimination.

Policymakers working with the distorting "underclass" notion are like marksmen who cannot clearly see the target and therefore can't hit it accurately.

"Underclass" is the latest in a long line of labels that stigmatize poor people for their poverty by focusing exclusively on individual characteristics. Older terms include the "undeserving poor," the "_lumpenproletariat_," and the "culture of poverty."

Today, "underclass" is often seen as synonymous with "unemployable." But even people with serious physical and mental handicaps can no longer be unambiguously described as "unemployable," as recent supported-work programs for blind and for mentally retarded persons have shown.

Most poor people can and do work. For instance, women on welfare and street criminals are often thought of as people who don't work. Yet Bennett Harrison, an economist at the Massachusetts Institute of Technology, found that in a sample of families receiving some welfare over a five-year period, 92 percent also received some money from legal jobs. And a survey by the Vera Institute of Justice found that only 4 percent of a random sample of people arrested for felonies in Brooklyn never worked.

When the poor work, they work at jobs that are dead-end, sporadic, and low-paying—what labor economists call "secondary" jobs in a divided labor market, where "primary" jobs are the only ones that promise advancement, stability, and reasonable pay and benefits.

These secondary jobs are expanding faster than primary jobs. It is a commonplace to note that McDonald's employs about two and a half times as many people as U.S. Steel. The number of people seeking even these secondary jobs has outstripped recent growth in jobs. With the current recession, the prospects for an increasing number of any kind are dismal. This shift in the economic structure is covered up by reference to a growing "underclass" of "unemployables."

The "underclass" analysis also fails in not connecting racial discrimination to the structural economic problem. Nonwhites are more likely to be found in secondary jobs; the sporadic nature of these jobs results in higher unemployment and lower family income for them.

Specific policies must pierce the fog of the "underclass" label and confront the widely divergent realities of diverse groups of the poor. Those who are actually unemployable require social services that are appropriate to their particular handicaps, and adequate income. Young women who head households alone need decent child care to allow them to work or adequate income subsidies to bring up their children without working. Young people need programs to encourage school attendance, while older, chronically unemployed persons need better experience in primary jobs, not make-work and dead-end programs that continue to blame them for their poverty.

Richard McGahey

1. What two reasons does the author give for the widespread existence of an underclass?

---

2. What are the two job categories described in this article?

---

3. Using the chart that follows, write the words the author uses to describe each kind of work. Think of some examples to illustrate each type.

	Primary	*Secondary*
Description		
Examples		

4. Is the author in favor of welfare?

_____

5. What suggestions does the author make for treating some of the problems of the poor?

_____

_____

_____

_____

_____

THE FUNCTIONS OF POVERTY

Poverty and the poor may well satisfy a number of positive functions for many nonpoor groups in American society.

First, the existence of poverty ensures that society's "dirty work" will be done. Every society has such work: physically dirty or dangerous, temporary, dead-end and underpaid, undignified and menial jobs. Society can fill these jobs by paying higher wages than for "clean" work, or it can force people who have no other choice to do the dirty work—and at low wages. In America, poverty functions to provide a low-wage labor pool that is willing—or, rather, unable to be *un-*willing—to perform dirty work at low cost. Indeed, this function of the poor is so important that in some Southern states, welfare payments have been cut off during the summer months when the poor are needed to work in the fields. . . . Many economic activities that involve dirty work depend on the poor for their existence: restaurants, hospitals, parts of the garment industry, and "truck farming," among others, could not persist in their present form without the poor.

Second, because the poor are required to work at low wages, they subsidize a variety of economic acitivities that benefit the affluent. For example, domestics subsidize the upper middle and upper classes, making life easier for their employers and freeing affluent women for a variety of professional, cultural, civic, and partying activities. Similarly, because the poor pay a higher proportion of their income in property and sales taxes, among others, they subsidize many state and local governmental services that benefit more affluent groups. . . .

Third, the poor can be identified and punished as alleged or real deviants in order to uphold the legitimacy of conventional norms. To justify the desirability of hard work, thrift, honesty, and monogamy, for example, the defenders of these norms must be able to find people who can be accused of being lazy, spendthrift, dishonest, and promiscuous. Although there is some evidence that the poor are about as moral and law-abiding as anyone else, they are more likely than middle-class transgressors to be caught and punished when they participate in deviant acts. Moreover, they lack the political and cultural power to correct the stereotypes that other people hold of them and thus continue to be thought of as lazy, spendthrift, etc., by those who need living proof that moral deviance does not pay. . . .

Fourth, poverty helps to guarantee the status of those who are not poor. In every hierarchical society someone has to be at the bottom; but in American society, in which social mobility is an important goal for many and people need to know where they stand, the poor function as a reliable and relatively permanent measuring rod for status comparisons. This is particularly true for the working class, whose politics is influenced by the need to maintain status distinctions between themselves and the poor.

[Herbert J. Gans, *"The Uses of Poverty"*]

Listed below are the four functions of poverty.

1. The poor do society's dirty work.
2. The poor help support many of the activities of the wealthy.
3. The poor become the scapegoats of the rich.
4. The rich are at the top of the ladder of success because the poor are at the bottom.

Each of the following statements is an example of one of these functions. In the space provided, write the number of the correct function.

_____   a. The Browns play tennis at the public courts twice a week.

_____   b. A majority of the prisoners in the city jails are of minority background.

_____   c. Even though Ted does not want to sweep the streets and he feels he is underpaid, he has worked at this job for the past two years.

_____   d. As Mr. Norman's income grew he had less to do with the men at the bowling alley.

WORKFARE

In the past several years an alternative to welfare, called workfare, has been tried in many states. Workfare is a program in which able-bodied welfare recipients take community public-service jobs, such as day-care supervisors, park attendants, school-crossing guards or teaching aides, to repay part of the value of their benefits. Those who refuse—with the exception of the elderly and mothers with preschool children—would risk losing their benefits.

In Your Opinion

Should people on welfare be required to work at public-service jobs to repay part of the value of their benefits? Why?

_____

_____

_____

_____

_____

_____

_____

_____

Newspapers express opinions about many issues in daily columns called editorials. Following are editorials taken from newspapers from different regions of the country. These editorials express a variety of views about workfare.

ST. LOUIS GLOBE–DEMOCRAT

Work for welfare? Some would think that this is an inhumane proposal. Able-bodied persons who receive federal aid without having to do anything more than go down to the mailbox to pick up the check have nothing to brag about.

Providing useful work for welfare recipients can achieve a number of desirable results. Those who earn their way can feel a sense of pride rather than guilt for receiving aid. It can offer those who have never had a job some work experience. And it can help taxpayers by discouraging those who don't really need the aid from getting welfare.

Rep. Paul Findley, R-Ill., who led a drive to set up a pilot workfare program in the late 1970s, is encouraged by the results of test projects at 13 sites.

It is interesting to note that during the first year two thirds of the eligible recipients dropped out of the food stamp program rather than go to work.

"When they applied for food stamps and were told they had to work, some of them just said, 'Forget it, I don't need stamps that badly,'" said Doug Thompson, an aide to the Illinois congressman.

Results of the test program in such places as San Diego County, Calif., indicate it would work well nationally. San Diego officials reported this pattern:

Of 2,787 food stamp recipients referred for job interviews under the workfare program, only 277 completed the work assignments. Another 1,076 failed to complete the program for justifiable cause, and more than 1,500 were removed from the food stamp rolls for failure to comply with the program requirements.

The work load on the recipients doesn't appear to have been excessive because some 84 percent of the program participants had to work 22 hours or less a month.

It is a fact of life that some people will take advantage of federal aid programs if the prospect of getting something for nothing is held forth. Workfare does a good job of discouraging the free loaders and getting the aid to those who really need and deserve it.

1. What is the opinion about workfare expressed in this editorial?

_____

_____

_____

2. List the arguments presented to support this point of view.

(a) _____

_____

(b) _____

_____

(c) _____

_____

HOUSTON CHRONICLE

President Reagan has announced plans to link welfare with a work requirement, creating what is known as workfare. Workfare is not a new idea; it is an idea that has had mixed success; it is an idea that is becoming more widespread; it is an idea that deserves more support.

Requiring work where possible from a welfare recipient is not a penalty but a boost upwards. . . .

Various forms of workfare have been tried. The federal government has been edging that way, first urging registration for jobs by welfare recipients, except for those with dependents or those aged and ill, then requiring registration in a work incentive program. . . .

Generally, requiring work of those able to work and without young children to care for has resulted in a decrease in the number on welfare. Those who do participate benefit in several ways. One experimental program found that many female heads of households in the Aid to Families with Dependent Children category were willing to work for small financial gains in order to avoid the social opprobrium of continuing on welfare and having governmental interference in their lives. Those who participated also found having current employment made it easier to find better jobs in the private sector.

Presidents Nixon and Carter backed extensive welfare reform programs that created controversy and never made their way through Congress. There is a "welfare constituency" that tends to keep existing laws on the books. Whether workfare will win congressional approval is problematical. But a program that stresses work as part of welfare is certain to have a large measure of public approval.

1. What is the opinion expressed in this editorial?

_____

_____

2. What are some of the benefits mentioned which support the opinion?

_____

_____

_____

3. Is the "welfare constituency" for or against workfare? Explain.

_____

_____

THE MIAMI HERALD: 'WORKFARE' IS A CRUEL MIRAGE

Hiding among the Administration's many budget slashes at Federal social programs is a nasty little proposal that has nothing to do with saving Federal dollars and everything to do with a punitive attitude toward the poor. It is euphemistically called "workfare."

President Reagan would require about 800,000 recipients of Federal welfare funds to work without wages at such community jobs as park attendants, school-lunchroom aides, and babysitters. Workfare should not be considered an economy measure; it is a wholly social program that does not save tax dollars.

To the contrary: Past experience indicates that workfare plans can be exorbitant to administer. The only leverage the Government has to force such unpaid work is the threat to cut off welfare payments. Because those benefits are mandated by law for all eligible persons, there are appeals procedures and due-process requirements attached to terminating them. Recipients must be warned. Their arguments about lack of transportation, illness, or unreliable babysitters must be investigated. These are costly steps, not economy measures.

If the Administration wants to put welfare clients to work, it should offer wages for those community-service jobs under the existing work-incentive program. If the goal is to drive away any free-loading childless adults who are physically and mentally able to work, those persons can simply be ruled ineligible. Healthy, childless adults in Florida and many other states never have been eligible for welfare.

Workfare is a dead end, expensive to supervise. Instead of workfare, why not schoolfare? Instead of herding semi-literate welfare parents in work gangs, why not require them to attend adult-education classes? Upward mobility should be the goal, not permanent dependence.

There are, of course, many Americans who can never fend for themselves in a competitive labor market. They are retarded, permanently and totally disabled, or are the sole caretakers for afflicted spouses or children. It makes no sense, economic or social, to force a parent to put a retarded or disabled child into a state institution in order to participate in workfare.

No one suggests that able-bodied adults should be supported in mere laziness by the taxpayers. But millions of Americans rightly question the motives of an Administration that would rather coerce the poor into unpaid, dead-end labor than enroll them in basic education or vocational training that can make them productive and self-sufficient.

1. Why does this editorial refer to the workfare program as punitive?

_____

_____

_____

2. What alternatives are suggested?

_____

_____

_____

_____

_____

DETROIT FREE PRESS

In theory, the Reagan administration's proposal that welfare recipients work 20 hours a week sounds fine: If nothing else, it might at least keep people in the habit of working. In practice, though, "workfare" seldom works, usually creating such a confused tangle of labor and administrative problems that nobody benefits.

The administration claims the proposal would help meet community needs and provide welfare recipients with "valuable training and self-esteem." Up to 800,000 adults, mostly women, in the Aid for Dependent Children (ADC) program could be involved. Among those exempt from the Reagan revisions would be the elderly, the ill, parents of a child under the age of three and parents of a child under age six if daycare is unavailable

Reasonable as all of this may look on paper, is it an approach fraught with potential problems. Recipients probably would work without pay as park sweepers, lunchroom and bus aides and in other low-skill and public service jobs. Unfortunately, such jobs do very little to improve either training or self-esteem and may heighten a recipient's perception that work is a game. . . .

Labor unions are another barrier to putting unpaid welfare recipients on jobs. In Ohio's Cuyahoga County, officials who tried to put general relief recipients on productive jobs kept running into roadblocks. In one instance, they discovered they couldn't have the recipients wash walls because wall washing is a union job.

Even when workfare recipients are able to evade union barriers, administrative difficulties abound. As governor of California, Mr. Reagan launched a "work for welfare" program in 1971. A state report on the three-year project called it a failure. No money was allocated for administration, tools or participants' job-related expenses. State officials were either apathetic or hostile toward the program and made only 9,627 job assignments. Moreover, civil service tests and other entrance requirements kept most participants from making the leap from workfare to regular jobs.

If not handled with care, workfare quickly degenerates into meaningless make-work. In Louisiana, welfare recipients once had to earn their benefits by beating snakes to death. Making mothers with young children sweep parks isn't quite as bad as that. But before the administration moves ahead with its workfare proposal, it must clearly define "work" and make sure it can be provided for welfare clients. Otherwise, workfare will do little to help recipients break out of the welfare trap and little to make the program more than another welfare reform sham.

1. This editorial describes six problems associated with workfare. List as many as you can find.

_____

_____

_____

_____

_____

_____

_____

_____

Think About This

Refer back to your earlier responses on pages 178–179. Now that you have read several editorials arguing for and against workfare, have you changed any of your ideas? Explain.

_____

_____

_____

_____

_____

_____

_____

Now your instructor will organize the class into several small groups, depending on your point of view. As a group, organize your ideas, write a clear statement of your group's position, and be prepared to debate with your classmates who hold the opposite point of view.

Are You For or Against Workfare?

_____

_____

_____

_____

_____

_____

_____

_____

_____

_____

_____

_____

_____

_____

_____

_____

"In slavery, everyone had a job—but no one had dignity." What would the person who said this think of workfare?

_____

_____

_____

_____

_____

_____

_____

The preceding quote was made by the Rev. Jesse Jackson, whose Chicago-based Operation Push stresses hard work and self-help as the road to minority success. Jackson, quoted in *Time*'s March 23, 1981 issue, calls workfare "psychological warfare against poor people. It's fueling the meanness mania in this country. It suggests something negative about the character of poor people." Because there are so few jobs around, *Time* says, some critics fear that workfare will force welfare recipients to labor for low pay in substandard conditions.

In this chapter you have read arguments for and against workfare programs. Newspaper editorials have given you some idea of the differing points of view represented throughout the country.

After reading about the difference between facts and opinions, you had an opportunity to organize a coherent argument expressing your personal opinion on this issue.

A Further Reading

WEAK ON WELFARE

In 30 years, my husband and I never had a serious argument about money. Then we, together with several other Congressional families, were "invited" by the National Welfare Rights Organization to live for a week on the equivalent of the welfare allotment in our home state.

I was sitting at the kitchen table with cookbooks and newspaper advertisements, trying to figure to the penny the cost of 21 low-income meals, when my husband called from the next room, "Be sure to leave enough for a beer."

"Beer?" I shouted. "You can't have a beer."

His face in the doorway would have chilled the beer. "I'd like to know why I can't have one can of beer."

"We can't afford it."

"Don't be silly."

"I'm not silly: 28 cents is silly. I can't make 28 cents cover our food, let alone soap, toilet tissue, deodorant . . ."

"Where did you get that figure of 28 cents?"

"It's New York's allotment per person per meal."

"Oh no it isn't."

"What are you talking about?"

"It's been cut."

"*Cut*? It can't be cut. It has to be bigger. 28 doesn't give us meat or fish even every second day."

He sighed. "Sorry, but you'll have to figure on 22."

"I can't!"

"Listen. People in Washington, D.C. have only 17 cents. People in Arkansas have only 8 cents; people in Mississippi have only 4 cents."

I put my hands over my ears.

He turned and left the room.

"And prices are going *up*," I wailed.

"Hurry, then," he called back. "You might still fit in one can of . . ."

"No beer," I shouted. And there was a new taste of venom on my tongue.

As the day approached for Welfare Budget Week to start, we confessed to each other that we are dreading it more than we had thought. Mutual reassurance helped but little; it was true that we had previously lived for weeks in the Far East on little more than rice and condiments, bread and tea. But that was different; there, we had been in tune with the majority; here, we would be out of tune with it. Also, we began to understand the ferocity with which people in the low-income areas have often resisted any enforced scientific improvement in their food habits. Like a person's handwriting, his characteristic diet feels to him like a hallmark of the self, a component of his identity. When it is threatened from the outside, a surprisingly basic form of anxiety seems to be mobilized.

At the briefing for the participants in Welfare Budget Week, a staff representative of NWRO had mentioned the wide variety of excuses offered by invitees who not only did not wish to take part in the experiment but also, apparently, did not wish to say so directly. Perhaps one reason for their reluctance, so variously rationalized, was precisely the discomfort of this anxiety. I found myself haunted by the statement of a student leader on the *Generations Apart* television program: "Comfortability is a very dangerous god." On the other hand, in many countries of Europe, I consoled myself by thinking, a comparable group of people would have responded to such an invitation with disbelief or disdain.

Like prisoners on Death Row my husband and I had a ceremonial "last meal." It cost almost as much as the $9.24 (66 cents per person per day) that would cover all food and sundries for the following week. Unlike the prisoners, we enjoyed every bite of the steak and broccoli hollandaise, the fresh peaches with cream, the bottle of wine. Not only did we disregard cost and calorie count, but also cholesterol. For, as I had discovered through my menu-making, one backhanded advantage of a low-cost diet is that the high cholesterol foods, such as eggs and butter, "marbled" beef and shell fish, are out of the question, while low cholesterol foods, such as the legumes (including vegetarian baked beans) and canned fish must, for the reason of price, be the chief source of protein.

Our first breakfast was typical (except for Sunday when we had pancakes and syrup), a small glass of grapefruit juice (large can 41 cents), oatmeal with reconstituted milk, and coffee with the same milk (15 cents a quart and good).

Since my husband could no longer afford lunch at one of the Capitol restaurants, I gave him sandwiches, together with a raw carrot and a bruised banana (4 cents, reduced). In return, he promised to bring home all baggies and pieces of Saran wrap to be washed and re-used, although I resented devoting any of our precious detergent for this purpose; finally I learned to leave a pot of soapy water in the sink all day.

The welfare mothers at the NWRO briefing had offered various suggestions. One was to buy day-old bread at half price. But the markets within walking distance of our house do not carry it. Instead, a bakery truck comes daily and picks it up to be resold at a discount store miles away. The saving on bread, for a family of two, would not have been sufficient to pay my carfare. Bread, therefore, was too expensive ($1\frac{1}{2}$ cents per slice) to use for *my* lunch. In its place I baked biscuits (using the self-rising flour recommended by the welfare mothers) and tried to make the sandwich filling stay between their halves. For the first two days this filling was peanut butter and jelly, a high carbohydrate taste-thrill that we do not ordinarily permit ourselves. But it "held" us less well than did the subsequent tunafish salad. After the weekend, we had for sandwiches slices of meatloaf (stretched with oatmeal) which tasted so grim when cold that I blew 40 cents from my dollar emergency fund for half a pound of American cheese and 8 cents for a bruised tomato with which to dress these up. The tastelessness and monotomy of the foods available on welfare became depressing even though we were on it merely for one week.

A further item of advice given by a welfare mother, to buy luncheon meats and hot dogs, I decided to disregard because of their relative expense and dearth of protein. Our meatloaf came cheap because we waited until late Saturday afternoon, shortly before the market closed for the weekend, to buy hamburger at half price (50 cents). We also received free from the butcher a soup bone he would otherwise have thrown away. Previously I had procured from the man who prepares fresh vegetables for display the lettuce, cabbage, and celery "trimmings" that would otherwise have rotted in the garbage can. With two beef bouillon cubes (two cents apiece) I boiled the washed, ungritted outer lettuce leaves. They were delicious. The celery and cabbage, on the other hand, were almost too tough to eat, even after having been boiled. I was able, however, to salvage enough celery for the tuna salad sandwich filling and enough cabbage to serve once as hot vegetable. Potatoes were tempting to buy, but too expensive, as compared with the spaghetti and rice on which we filled ourselves—for a couple of hours at least.

The main trouble with a diet made up mostly of starch is that one is subject to flash-hungers between meals. Without warning, one is not merely hungry; one is ravenous, hurting, unable to concentrate on anything except getting something into the stomach. We both drank more water than usual, sometimes mixed with Kool Aid (five cents for several quarts). We also kept an emergency supply of biscuits in pocket or pocketbook or even, on Sunday, in our golf bags.

This type of hunger appears, moreover, to be cumulative. The first day we felt it not at all. Indeed, there was a slight euphoria that stemmed perhaps from at last being engaged in meeting the challenge, rather than merely dreading it. We got through the morning nicely on our oatmeal, and enjoyed our peanut butter and jelly for lunch. That night we had California Limas (baked with Worcestershire sauce, tomato juice, and onion—a total of 18 cents) and some of our "braised" lettuce. But at bedtime we discovered we were too hungry to sleep. Having long outgrown the habit of a midnight snack, we found ourselves deep into dishes of Jello ($2\frac{1}{2}$ cents apiece), and biscuits. Psychologically, those biscuits were as important as physically because, like the lettuce, they were something of which we could have all we wanted.

By the third day, however, we were not getting through the morning without hunger pangs. Yet we could not afford whole milk or cream or eggs for breakfast. The ration of six small eggs for the week was needed for cooking. A 29-cent can of mackerel, for example, can be mixed with egg and flour, the egg serving to bind the fish together; this can then be made into patties and sauteed as a good main dish for supper. Belatedly, we realized that our comparative comfort that first day could be credited less to the welfare breakfast than to the carry-over from our pre-welfare "last supper."

During the latter half of the week, despite added quantities of oatmeal for breakfast, I found myself frequently empty, as against consciously hungry, and too lethargic to force myself to the typewriter. Even when I gave up my quarter-century routine of morning hours at the desk and instead tried to read some of the serious books necessary to the career of a free-lance writer, my mind wandered off, not "wool"-gathering, but food-gathering.

Accompanying the loss of concentration was a loss of physical energy. In place of an afternoon swim or tennis game, I stayed flat on the bed, partly because walking the requisite distance (two blocks) seemed like too much work, partly because exercise would whet my already too great appetite, and partly because I did not feel up to the effort of casual conversation, especially since some people were so antagonistic to our Welfare Week experiment. One upper-income acquaintance termed our participation "a cheap political trick." One lower-income acquaintance told of a neighbor who cheats on welfare.

My eschewing company, nonetheless, was a mistake. While I was undergoing an unpleasant combination of loneliness and fear of people, my husband, on Capitol Hill, was constantly stimulated by his contacts with constituents, office staff, and fellow legislators, even when they disagreed with him. At the end of the day he was hungry and tired but fulfilled, while I was debilitated and frustrated. How on earth, we asked each other, can people be expected to get off welfare when they cannot afford to buy the proteins and vitamins, the so-called "brain foods," that energize? We began to understand better the report that some children on welfare fell asleep in class, or mooned out the window.

Besides thinking far more than usual about food by day, I dreamed of it by night. During the first part of the week my dreams featured roast beef (rare); by the latter part, they were down to biscuits.

I learned the hard way that the best time to prepare supper is right after breakfast; otherwise the cook is too tempted to "taste" the dish half to death. (The kinds of foods demanded by welfare also tend to take longer to cook than the more expensive kinds). Probably because I so much wanted to cheat, I became compulsive about keeping a scrupulous fairness in regard to our food supplies. Anything I nibbled during the day had its counterpart saved for my husband. And the evening he casually reported he had bought a five cent box of raisins, I carried on as if he had had a beer. (One form of cheating we did indulge in was to pretend that we had given our dog away while actually keeping her at home and dispensing her usual canned dog food; it was all I could do not to cadge a bit: all that lovely meat and fat! Later, we found out that the sale of pet food in some ghetto areas far outruns the supply of pets.)

What would I be doing, I wondered, if our four children were still small or teenage, forever rifling the refrigerator? What would I say (or scream?) if they spilled their milk or absentmindedly drank up the juice for the next day's breakfast? What would I offer (besides biscuits and Kool Aid) if they arrived from school with the usual parched and starving friends? How could I deafen them to the pied piper of the Good Humor bell without making myself into a witch straight out of Endor? I began to appreciate how much of family harmony is dependent on middle-class privileges (shared by farmers of lesser means) such as room enough for one's near and dear not to be too near when they are not very dear, and a certain spontaneity about food. Is this not one more maddening example of "to him who hath, it shall be given?"

As I bargain-hunted in the market, I found a balefulness growing within myself toward those well-dressed, well exercised women who were idly plopping a big chunk of meat, a pile of frozen vegetables, and a veritable still-life of fresh fruits into their baskets. How dared they be so unthinking in regard to their affluence? The fact that, a week before, I had been among their number, made me more, not less, critical of their apparent smugness. I was on a "trip," not psychedelically or geographically, but socio-economically, and I began to identify with my new colleagues, not only the welfare poor and the working poor, but the youthful rebels. If the occupational hazard of lifelong poverty is a chip on the shoulder, the occupational hazard of lifelong affluence is insensitivity.

Our grown son phoned one evening. "Are you gaining in spiritual insight?" he asked.

"No," I said. "I'm deep in the sin of pride. Now that I recognize the soft underbelly of American life, I look down on the fat-cats who don't."

"I see what you mean," he said.

"And I'm furious. Here is our country, capable of growing enough food for everyone, and yet we still have hunger. Hunger must be stopped!"

The following day, the rage which I thought had reached its peak took another surge upward. In the daily newspaper which I scrounged from a neighbor's pile of discarded printed matter (thus saving ten cents), the following item revived the nightmare horror of the Great Depression:

Farmers in Oregon, Idaho and Washington have begun plowing under part of their potato crops in an effort to reverse a decline in prices.

Glen Eppich, chairman of the Adams County, Washington, unit of the National Farmers Organization, said potato prices dropped $15 a ton after the Department of Agriculture reported that about 3 per cent of the nation's potato crop is surplus.

The department's report was followed by a National Farmer's Organization call for a 4 per cent cutback. In Oregon, an estimated 1,000 acres of potatoes were destroyed, and officials in the Columbia basin of Washington estimated that 400 to 500 acres were ploughed under at a cost to farmers of about $350,000. Idaho reported crop destruction in several counties.

Intellectually, I know that the parity problem is a complex and difficult one. But then, so was putting men on the moon. When I can't buy potatoes because they are too expensive, and farmers are paid to plow them under, so as to make them more expensive, something is wrong, not only economically but humanly. If the astronauts have taught us anything, it is that we no longer have an excuse to leave our human problems unsolved.

As my husband ascertained, there were surplus foods available to welfare families in New York. But the distribution center for our area was a considerable distance from our house, was open only a few days a month, and provided a package for two which weighed 73 pounds. I, with a fused spine, cannot carry 73 pounds on a subway or bus (or anywhere else), nor can the majority (95 per cent) of people on welfare who comprise the aged, the infirm, the mothers of small children, and the children themselves. They, moreover, unlike me, do not have ready access to a car.

In most parts of the U.S. there is either a surplus commodity distribution program or a food stamp program, but not both. New York's surplus food allotment has recently been somewhat, though inadequately, improved. Where food stamps are available the family has been compelled to turn its entire "food" allotment into them. Not a penny can be saved out for emergency supplies that are not on the stamp-redeemable list, such as aspirin.

MENUS

Seven breakfasts	Seven lunches	Seven suppers
6 days –grapefruit juice, oatmeal, powdered milk, coffee Sunday–tomato juice, pancakes with syrup, coffee	Thurs. (7/17)–peanut butter with jelly sandwich (1 each) –1 tuna salad sandwich –1 banana for husband Fri. (7/18) –1 egg salad sandwich (husband) –1 french toast (myself) –1 raw carrot (husband) –1 parboiled celery (myself) Sat. (7/19) –chicken wings with rice braised lettuce Sun. (7/20) –meat loaf with oatmeal raw carrots Mon. (7/21) –2 meat loaf sandwiches (1 for each of us) raw carrots biscuits with jelly banana for husband Tues. (7/22) –2 tuna salad sandwiches (1 for each) Wed. (7/23) –2 tomato and cheese and meatloaf sandwiches (1 for each)	Thurs. (7/17)–baked California lima beans–with tomato juice and onion, celery and carrot braised lettuce –snack before bed–Jello and biscuits Fri. (7/18) –veal kidney with soup scraps spaghetti cooked lettuce Sat. (7/19) –baked beans raw carrot (lunch was larger than usual) banana and orange Sun. (7/20) –soup with rest of rice and lettuce (lunch large) biscuit –moon feast–cheese and biscuits; cold meat loaf; Kool Aid Mon. (7/21) –mackerel cakes cabbage cooked in chicken bouillon biscuit Tues. (7/22) –rest of kidney rice and rest of beans gelatin vegetable salad Wed. (7/23) –pepper stuffed with rest of meat loaf plus gravy from soup fat.

And aspirin, I found, was being eaten by me almost like peanuts, although ordinarily my average is less than one a month. Daily, starting the fourth day of welfare, I was suffering sharp, uncharacteristic headaches. After the week –and the headaches—were safely past, I phoned the family doctor to ask what might have caused the pain. "Two things " he said. One was the culture shock of a radically changed diet, particularly since the new one was high in starches. This culture shock, presumably, would not be suffered by most people on welfare. The second item was one which they might well share, namely, the self-rising flour in the biscuits which increases the sodium in the body and thus encourages the retention of fluids. Further evidence for his hypothesis was the fact, the unkindest cut of all, that after living with hunger for a week I had *gained* a pound!

After I had lost my pound and regained my composure, I phoned to report to the welfare adviser whose acquaintance I had made at the NWRO meeting. She was particularly interested in the free soup bones and the vegetable trimmings and set about checking the supermarkets in the ghetto to find out if this mutually beneficial arrangement could be duplicated. When last heard from, the two big chain stores said they would not only give away these items but would advertise the fact. So perhaps in a small way, some of the terrible wastefulness that goes on in the United States at the human level as well as the material one, may be mitigated as a result of our short experiment.

The first morning after Welfare Week I had an egg, a whole egg, a large egg, for breakfast.

It gave me indigestion.

I think, perhaps it always will. . .

June Rossbach Bingham

Suggested Readings

Caldwell, Erskine. *Tobacco Road*. Cambridge, Massachusetts: Robert Bentley, Inc., 1978.

Story of a degraded poor-white Georgia family living in a tumbledown shack on worn out land which had once been a prosperous tobacco plantation. The story carries this family through the steps of their progressive degeneration.

Horowitz, Julius. *The Diary of A. N.: The Story of the House on W. 104 St.* New York: Coward-McCann-Geoghegan, Inc., 1980.

This novel, based on the author's years of experience as a welfare caseworker, presents an account of a family living on welfare in Harlem.

Terkel, Studs. *Working*. New York: Pantheon Books, 1974.

This book is a series of interviews taped by the author, describing the lives of hardworking Americans.

Wright, Richard. *Native Son*. New York: Harper, Row and Co., 1969.

Bigger Thomas, an embittered young Negro, works hard for the barest subsistence, and lives in squalor in a single room with his mother, sister, and brother in Chicago's South Side. Through Home Relief, Bigger gets a job with a wealthy realtor. His meeting with the boss's daughter leads to murder and suspense.

Wright, Sarah E. *This Child's Gonna Live*. New York: Delacorte Press, 1980.

Tangiernick is a Maryland black ghetto in the 1930s. Its residents are destitute and powerless to alter their fate. The heroine of this novel is determined to escape from this environment with her children. But her strong faith and years of work are futile; two of her children die, stricken horribly by disease, and her hopes are finally extinguished in guilt and despair.

CHAPTER 7

Department of Defense

The Atomic Age is here to stay—
but are we?

—Bennett Cerf

NUCLEAR ARMS

HYPOTHETICAL REASONING

Although you may never have heard of "hypothetical reasoning," you engage in this kind of thinking frequently. In fact, you have done a great deal of it while answering questions in this book.

Hypothetical reasoning is a theory, or guess, you make about a certain situation or problem. If you ask yourself, "What if . . ." or "Suppose . . . ," you are thinking hypothetically. We often do this when trying to imagine the consequences of different actions.

For instance, think about the consequences of the following hypothetical situations:

1. Suppose there were twice as many people living in your house or apartment as there are at present. What would be some of the effects on your home life?

2. Suppose the water in your town were contaminated; if you used it for drinking or eating purposes you would die. How would this affect your life? What would you be unable to do? What would you do instead?


```
_____
_____
_____
_____
_____
```

In this chapter you will consider questions of the nuclear arms race and the consequences of a nuclear war. At the moment, the latter is merely a hypothetical situation. But the choices we make in this area of our lives will have far-reaching consequences in the future.

A Poll: The Nuclear Question*

1. Which one of these categories best describes you?

   —Frequently worry about the chances of a nuclear war
   —Concerned, but try to put nuclear war out of mind
   —Don't think nuclear war is likely—don't worry
   —Don't know

2. Those that propose a nuclear freeze argue that the U.S. and the U.S.S.R. already have more than enough weapons to destroy each other. They want both sides to ban all testing and production of nuclear weapons. How do you feel about the nuclear-freeze movement?

   —Strongly in favor
   —Opposed
   —Strongly opposed
   —Don't know

3. The ability to verify (check) whether the other side is complying with an agreement presents a major problem. Some people feel that a good system of checks is essential for the success of any agreement. Others feel that it is more important for the U.S. to stop the production of nuclear arms even if we are not sure the other side is doing the same. In your opinion, which is more important?

   —Verification
   —Stopping production, regardless of ability to verify
   —Don't know

4. If we were involved in a limited nuclear war, what do you think would be your chance of survival?

—Good
—Poor
—50–50
—Don't know

5. Do you think an increased civil-defense program would improve your chances of surviving a nuclear attack?

— A great deal
—Somewhat
—Not very much
—Not at all
—Don't know

Your teacher has polled the class concerning your feelings about the nuclear question. These questions are uppermost in the minds of many people because they are indeed issues of life and death.

The development of nuclear weapons began in the United States during the years of World War II. The following account describes the beginning of that era.

THE BEGINNING OF THE NUCLEAR AGE

World War II broke out in Europe in September, 1939. The month before, Einstein had written to U.S. President Franklin D. Roosevelt urging him to commit the United States to developing an atomic bomb. Einstein had fled to the United States from Germany to escape Nazi persecution. He warned Roosevelt that German scientists might already be working on a nuclear bomb.

Roosevelt acted on Einstein's urging.

[Excerpted From *The World Book Encyclopedia* © 1983 World Book, Inc.]

The "Atomic Age" was born. U.S. scientists were brought together with a few brilliant Europeans who fled Nazism. They began work under the aegis of the Manhattan District of the U.S. Army Corps of Engineers.

Hidden from public view by elaborate fronts and cover stories, the members of the so-called Manhattan Project huddled in laboratories scattered across the nation, struggling to unlock the secrets of fission. The project made it necessary for an entire new industry to be created covertly.

In only a matter of months, factories, laboratories and manufacturing plants sprung up in such varied locations as New York City; Hanford, Washington; Oak Ridge, Tennessee; St. Louis; Los Alamos, New Mexico; Washington, D.C.; and Chicago. Thousands of construction workers, assembly line laborers, physicists, metallurgists, chemists, engineers, administrators, managers, typists and clerks were needed for the effort.

Finally, at the closely guarded Los Alamos laboratory of physicist Dr. J. Robert Oppenheimer, a prototype bomb was assembled during the early summer months of 1945. In the years preceding, all the work and thought invested in the bomb had been only an intellectual exercise. Germany had already surrendered, and though the war appeared to be winding down that summer, the scientists felt compelled to prove their theories right or wrong.

At 5:30 A.M. on July 16, 1945, the theories were put to the test. While nervous scientists and skeptical military observers lay flat on the ground with their eyes protected by gray-lensed goggles, a 19-kiloton atomic bomb was electronically detonated 20 miles away on a 100-foot tower above the white sands of the desert near Alamogordo, New Mexico. The searing flash of the explosion was seen 180 miles away.

Questions about the bright, predawn light were avoided by government experts who explained the phenomenon away as the explosion of an ammunition dump. The existence of the atom bomb remained a tightly held secret— that is, until nearly three weeks later on August 5, 1945.

[Howard L. Rosenberg, *Atomic Soldiers*]

In an effort to hasten the end of the war the U.S. government decided to use the atomic bomb against Japan. From a B-29 bomber called the Enola Gay, the first bomb was exploded over a point near the center of Hiroshima at 8:15 A.M. on Aug. 6, 1945, destroying almost everything within a radius of 6,000 to 8,000 feet. The damage beyond this area was considerable, and over 71,000 people were killed. Many more later died of injuries and the effects of radiation. Survivors are still dying of leukemia, pernicious anemia, and other diseases induced by radiation.

Almost 98% of Hiroshima's buildings were destroyed or severely damaged.

[*Encyclopedia Americana*]

Four days later a 23-kiloton plutonium-fueled bomb devastated the Japanese industrial center of Nagasaki and the war quickly ended with Japan's unconditional surrender.

[Howard L. Rosenberg, *Atomic Soldiers*]

1. What might have caused Einstein to urge Roosevelt to develop an atomic bomb?

_____

_____

_____

_____

2. What is meant by the phrase "intellectual exercise"?

_____

_____

_____

3. What reasons might the government have had for keeping the development of the bomb and test explosion secret?

_____

_____

_____

_____

Imagine That

You were a scientist working on this project, aware of the fact that you
were developing a weapon capable of enormous destruction. What concerns
might you have?

_____

_____

_____

_____

_____

_____

_____

_____

_____

_____

In the next selection, you will read a true story of the experience of one
young physicist involved in the development of the bomb.

In the springtime of 1946, a young physicist risked his life by performing an
experiment called "tickling the dragon's tail." Louis Slotin used a screwdriver to

slide two hemispheres containing uranium toward each other, urging them along until they approached "the critical mass," the first step in a chain reaction. If he allowed them to remain together an instant too long, the mass would become supercritical and cause a nuclear explosion. He worked unprotected from the radiation that would fill the room if he were to tickle the tail too hard.

Slotin's Geiger counter measured the amount of radiation released by the hemispheres as he pushed them closer. As more material was used, and was pushed closer together, the radiation mounted. His neutron recorder counted the number of neutrons that emanated from the radioactive material inside the hemispheres. These measurements determined how much radioactive substance should be placed in the heart of an atomic bomb.

Slotin worked in a white, oblong room in the Omega Building, a restricted canyon site at the Los Alamos Scientific Laboratory in New Mexico, the birthplace of atomic weapons. He had worked in the Omega Building during World War II and throughout nearly a year of peacetime. He expected to leave Los Alamos soon to go to the Pacific, where he would see tests of some of the bombs he had helped to build. After that he wanted to go back to work at a university. In 1946, on a day late in May, he was tickling the dragon's tail for the last time.

Louis Slotin had performed the experiment many times. In spite of the danger, he had persisted cheerfully, christening each experiment with a name— Topsy, Jezebel, Little Eva. The names belied the risk he ran each time he pushed the radioactive pieces toward each other.

Louis Slotin stood at the demarcation line between the world of "conventional" weapons and the time of atomic ascendance. Slotin belonged to two eras: At the age of thirty-four, he was already a member of a generation of scientists who had learned their art in the "string and sealing wax" days, before the military and big business had taken over their laboratories, replacing quieter, slower work with money and machines. Slotin was a Canadian who, from an early age, had devoted his life to physics. He had received degrees from the University of Manitoba and from the University of London. In Chicago, he had worked, for no pay, for the pioneer atomic chemist William D. Harkins. When the United States had committed itself to build an atomic bomb, Slotin had gone willingly to Los Alamos to work on the Manhattan Project with other scientists from all over the world. Louis Slotin was an old-fashioned scientist who had become embroiled in a new business—atomic bombs. At the beginning of the era of remote control, Slotin still worked with his hands. His method of working, using his hands and a screwdriver, would soon be outdated. Until then his was the most efficient way to manipulate the lethal material.

Slotin was aware of the risk he and his colleagues ran when they worked with radioactive substances. A friend had warned him that if he persisted in his experiments, he would not live another year, but he disregarded the advice.

On this day in late May of 1946, he had agreed to demonstrate the experiment for seven other scientists. One of them, Alvin Graves, stood at his shoulder, watching intently as Slotin's screwdriver teased the hemispheres toward each other. Graves was going to take over after Slotin had left. He needed to observe carefully, to see just how Slotin's hands moved, steadily, slowly, never too fast or too far. Six other men stood farther away from Slotin's metal table. They watched the short, stocky physicist, dressed in cowboy boots, blue jeans, a cotton shirt, and a belt with a large and gleaming silver buckle. They were still; only the staccato clicking of the Geiger counter broke the silence in the room.

In an instant everything changed. The light seemed to turn blue, the air intensified. Slotin lunged across the table and pulled the hemispheres apart with his bare hands, saving the other men from more radiation than had already been unleashed. His screwdriver had slipped, and the material had gone critical. The Geiger counter chattered wildly, then stopped. The dial on the neutron counter ran off the scale and stopped recording at 3:20 P.M. The radiation was so intense that the monitor could not register it. The men in the room felt an odd sensation in their mouths, the kind of dry prickliness, or sharpness, that comes from electricity in the air. The fillings in their teeth became strangely noticeable and tasted metallic.

Silently, the men filed out of the room. Slotin calmly asked each man to record where he had been standing in the room. In that way it would be possible to determine how much radiation each had received. Then he telephoned the hospital.

At the hospital, he spoke softly to Alvin Graves, "I'm sorry I got you into this. I am afraid that I have less than a fifty-fifty chance of living. I hope you do better than that." Slotin had already begun to feel ill.

Every effort was made to assess the effects of the accident on the victims. Of all the observers, Graves received the worst injuries because he had been the closest to Slotin. He eventually developed radiation cataracts. Most of the other men seemed all right and soon were allowed to leave the hospital.

Louis Slotin's hands were badly burned by the radiation so they were wrapped in layers of towels and buried in ice-filled troughs. Anna May Dickey, the nurse assigned to him, stayed with him for as long as was humanly possible, helping him as his body rebelled against the violent invasion of radiation. He vomited again and again until he was left, exhausted, with the dry heaves. The pain had already begun in his arms; blisters grew on his hands.

Slotin understood exactly what had happened to him and he knew what symptoms to expect. His colleagues worked uninterruptedly to calculate the amount of radiation he had received, but it was extremely difficult to discover the exact figure. Everyone knew that it was very high, but there was still hope that his life might be saved.

The blisters on his hands ruptured, and a burn appeared on his abdomen, indicating that his internal organs also had been subjected to the atomic bombardment.

The U.S. Army flew in specialists; ten doctors were called to the case. General Leslie R. Groves, chief of the Manhattan Project, wrote to the patient: "I have nothing but admiration for your heroic actions . . . your quick reactions and disregard for the danger to yourself undoubtedly prevented a much more serious accident." People pored over radiation literature, but there was little available medical data on human radiation sickness.

Slotin's arms, packed in ice, turned a deathly blue. He knew that they would be slowly deadened by freezing. In his tranquil moments he wished that he could read. Anna May Dickey could not read to him all day, so some of his friends went to work to build a machine that could be propped in front of him and that would support and turn the pages of a book.

A sore appeared in Slotin's mouth. The gold in a filling had retained radioactivity; sooner or later its emanations would burn a hole in his tongue. His temperature had risen. It was no longer possible to take a blood-pressure reading because the cuff placed on his arm became too painful.

A telephone was installed in his room so that he could call his parents in

Canada. Then the Army paid their plane fare to Los Alamos. It was apparent to everyone that there wasn't much time. Five days after the accident, the final exposure estimate was in: Slotin had received at least 880 roentgens of radiation to his entire body—beyond any doubt a lethal dose.

On the same day, his blood count showed a sudden drop in white blood cells. The skin on his arms had begun to slough off. His temperature rose higher. His friends had completed the reading machine, but it was too late. The radiation had begun to gnaw at Slotin's brain, and his mind strayed, away from them, away from time, away from pain. He lived on for a while in a state of mindlessness, and then, nine days after the accident, he died in the Los Alamos hospital.

Alvin Graves wrote: "It is unquestionably true that I and perhaps others of those present owe our lives to his action. I do not know whether this is heroism or not. I suspect that Louis would have objected to such a term."

The Army gave the Slotins $10,000 in recompense for his death.

[Browne and Munroe, *Time Bomb*]

1. The author describes Louis Slotin as a man who "belonged to two eras." What does that mean?

_____

_____

_____

_____

2. List those words you would use to describe Louis Slotin.

_____

_____

_____

_____

3. After considering the words you have used to describe Slotin, do you believe that he would have described himself as "heroic"? Why?

_____

_____

_____

_____

_____

_____

_____

Many people do not have any idea of the enormous destructive power generated by one atomic bomb. The following selection is a description of what takes place when an atom bomb is dropped. This selection contains many specialized words that pertain to the topic of nuclear bombs. As you read, underline these words and their definitions.

DESTRUCTIVE POWER*

Atomic Blast. The release of huge amounts of explosive power from an atomic bomb in only a fraction of a second creates a powerful blast effect. The _blast wave_ moves through air at speeds greater than the speed of sound (about $12\frac{1}{2}$ miles . . . a minute). As the blast wave travels away from the point of the explosion, it creates high pressure in the atmosphere. The blast pressure knocks down buildings and produces great destruction.

As the blast wave travels away from _point zero_, the place at which the bomb explodes, it becomes progressively weaker. For example, the bomb exploded over Hiroshima demolished all buildings, except those of earthquake-resistant construction, out to a distance of $\frac{1}{2}$ mile . . . from ground zero.

Ground zero is the point on the ground directly above or below the point of detonation. Ground zero at Hiroshima was 1,800 feet . . . below point zero, because the bomb was exploded in the air. One mile . . . away from ground zero, the blast cracked brick walls 12 inches . . . thick. At a distance of $1\frac{1}{2}$ miles . . . all homes were severely damaged. Moderate damage extended out 2 miles. . . . Beyond that, the blast caused only light damage to frame structures.

Heat Effect. TNT explosions produce a temperature of a few thousand degrees. But atomic bombs produce a glowing ball of fire that may reach temperatures of millions of degrees. The radiant energy produced in the fireball travels out from point zero with the speed of light. It includes visible, ultraviolet, and infrared rays. Two effects combine to reduce the burning power of these rays as they travel away from point zero. First, the atmosphere absorbs some of the heat rays. Second, the energy shoots out in all directions. As the distance from point zero increases, the intensity of the radiation drops.

At Hiroshima, flash burns killed persons directly exposed to the heat as far as 1 mile . . . away from ground zero. Paper, wood, and foliage were scorched as far as $1\frac{1}{2}$ miles . . . from ground zero. Closer in, the intense heat ignited fires. These fires started other fires. The ultimate effect was a raging firestorm that burned out much of the city.

Nuclear Radiation. Atomic bombs emit penetrating radiations. Radiation released at the time of the explosion is called _prompt radiation_. Radiation that is not released until after the blast is called _delayed radiation_, or _fallout_. Prompt

*Adapted from _The World Book Encyclopedia._ Copyright © 1982 World Book-Childcraft International, Inc.

radiation issues from the bomb explosion in a great flash of *neutrons* and *gamma rays* (high-energy rays similar to X rays). The neutrons can penetrate concrete and solid substances. But the neutrons do not extend their lethal effect as far from ground zero as do the gamma rays. Gamma rays, like rays of visible light, drop sharply in intensity with increasing distance from the point of origin. At Hiroshima, the prompt penetrating radiation produced by the blast was lethal up to 1 mile . . . from ground zero.

The effect of gamma rays on human beings is measured in *roentgen* (r) units. A dose of about 450 roentgens of total body radiation produces death within a month in half of the persons exposed. Half of this dose will produce temporary sickness. The radiation dose from a Hiroshima-type bomb is about 3,000 r at $\frac{1}{2}$ mile . . . from point zero, and 100 r at 1 mile. At $1\frac{1}{2}$ miles . . . the dose falls to only a few roentgens.

Fallout from an atomic bomb may occur soon after the bomb explodes, or it may be delayed for weeks, months, or even years. When an atomic bomb explodes near the earth's surface, dirt is sucked into the fireball. This dirt becomes coated with radioactive fission fragments, and is carried aloft in the bomb cloud. The radioactive debris drifts back to earth after the explosion. Some atomic bombs are detonated in the air. In such cases, very little dust rises into the fireball. But the radioactive fission fragments are swept up into the bomb cloud. Depending on the size of the explosion and the height to which the cloud rises, the fission fragment might be scattered in the *troposphere*, the lower air, or in the *stratosphere*, the upper air. Debris scattered in the atmosphere descends to earth as fallout within a month after the blast. Stratospheric fallout may not fall to earth for years.

Now write the words you have underlined and their meanings in the following spaces.

Words   *Definitions*

a. _____   _____

b. _____   _____

c. _____   _____

d. _____   _____

e. _____   _____

f. _____   _____

g. _____   _____

h. _____   _____

i. _____   _____

Words	*Definitions*
j. _____	_____
k. _____	_____
l. _____	_____

The author of the next selection describes the series of emotions and thoughts experienced when imagining a nuclear holocaust. They are:

1. Revulsion at seeing so much suffering and death.
2. A sense of helplessness and defeat.
3. Recoil (or withdrawal).
4. A decision.

You will discover what the decision is, and the reason for it, as you read.

Anyone who inquires into the effects of a nuclear holocaust is bound to be assailed by powerful and conflicting emotions. Preeminent among these, almost certainly, will be an overwhelming revulsion at the tremendous scene of devastation, suffering, and death which is opened to view. And accompanying the revulsion there may be a sense of helplessness and defeat, brought about by an awareness of the incapacity of the human soul to take in so much horror. A nuclear holocaust, widely regarded as "unthinkable" but never as undoable, appears to confront us with an action that we can perform but cannot quite conceive. Following upon these first responses, there may come a recoil, and a decision, whether conscious or unconscious, not to think any longer about the possibility of a nuclear holocaust. . . . When one tries to face the nuclear predicament, one feels sick, whereas when one pushes it out of mind, as apparently one must do most of the time in order to carry on with life, one feels well again. But this feeling of well-being is based on a denial of the most important reality of our time, and therefore is itself a kind of sickness. A society that systematically shuts its eyes to an urgent peril to its physical survival and fails to take any steps to save itself cannot be called psychologically well. In effect, whether we think about nuclear weapons or avoid thinking about them, their presence among us makes us sick, and there seems to be little of a purely mental or emotional nature that we can do about it.

A part of our quandary may lie in the fact that even a denial of the reality stems from what is, in a sense, a refusal to accept nuclear annihilation. . . . As such, the denial may have intermixed in it something that is valuable and worthy of respect. Like active revulsion and protest against nuclear weapons, a denial of their reality may spring—in part, at least—from a love of life, and since a love of life may ultimately be all that we have to pit against our doom, we cannot afford thoughtlessly to tear aside any of its manifestations. Because denial is a form of self-protection, if only against anguishing thoughts and feelings, and because it contains something useful, and perhaps even, in its way, necessary to life, anyone who invites people to draw aside the veil and look at the peril face to face is at risk of trespassing on inhibitions that are a part of our humanity.

Looked at in its entirety, a nuclear holocaust can be said to assail human life at three levels: the level of individual life, the level of human society, and the level of the natural environment—including the environment of the earth as a whole. At none of these levels can the destructiveness of nuclear weapons be measured in terms of firepower alone. At each level, life has both considerable recuperative powers, which might restore it even after devastating injury, and points of exceptional vulnerability, which leave it open to sudden, wholesale, and permanent collapse, even when comparatively little violence has been applied. Just as a machine may break down if one small part is removed, and a person may die if a single artery or vein is blocked, a modern technological society may come to a standstill if its fuel supply is cut off, and an ecosystem may collapse if its ozone shield is depleted. Nuclear weapons thus do not only kill directly, with their tremendous violence, but also kill indirectly, by breaking down the man-made and the natural systems on which individual lives collectively depend. Human beings require constant provision and care, supplied both by their societies and by the natural environment, and if these are suddenly removed people will die just as surely as if they had been struck by a bullet. Nuclear weapons are unique in that they attack the support systems of life at every level. And these systems, of course, are not isolated from each other but are parts of a single whole: ecological collapse, if it goes far enough, will bring about social collapse, and social collapse will bring about individual deaths. Furthermore, the destructive consequences of a nuclear attack are immeasurably compounded by the likelihood that all or most of the bombs will be detonated within the space of a few hours, in a single huge concussion. Normally, a locality devastated by a catastrophe, whether natural or man-made, will sooner or later receive help from untouched outside areas, as Hiroshima and Nagasaki did after they were bombed; but a nuclear holocaust would devastate the "outside" areas as well, leaving the victims to fend for themselves in a shattered society and natural environment. And what is true for each city is also true for the earth as a whole: a devastated earth can hardly expect "outside" help. The earth is the largest of the support systems for life, and the impairment of the earth is the largest of the perils posed by nuclear weapons.

[Jonathan Schell, *The Fate of the Earth*]

The diagram below represents an illustration of Schell's theory of the interdependence of human life. Label each part.

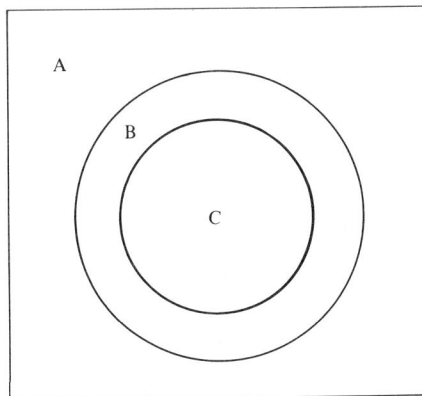

In the years since the end of World War II, many countries have developed the bomb. The United States and the U.S.S.R. are considered to be the two major nuclear powers. In the United States an important part of our nuclear preparedness is an attempt to organize civil defense plans, including the evacuation of heavily populated areas.

The following selections discuss some of the varying opinions on this subject.

DOES CIVIL DEFENSE MAKE SENSE?*

Our government now wants to devote billions of dollars over the next seven years to a plan for mass evacuation of cities and other "high risk" areas if attack ever seems imminent.

This new policy has rekindled an old debate. One side, alarmed by what it regards as an ominous improvement in the Soviet Union's ability to protect its civilian population, argues that civil defense is not only a lifesaver of last resort, but also an essential element of nuclear deterrence. The other side says, in the words of Sen. Alan Cranston of California, that civil defense is "a cruel and dangerous hoax that encourages the false notion that nuclear war is . . . tolerable and perhaps even winnable."

1. What two arguments are presented in favor of a civil defense plan?

_____

_____

_____

2. How would such a plan act as a deterrent?

_____

_____

_____

3. Does Senator Cranston believe that a nuclear war can be won?

_____

4. How can a civil defense plan encourage the nation to believe that a nuclear war is winnable?

_____

_____

_____

_____

_____

The plan designates nearly 450 cities and strategically important areas like missile sites and airfields as likely targets for Soviet war-heads. In all, about 145 million Americans live in such places, and they would be removed to "host communities" in rural areas throughout the countryside. The Federal Emergency Management Agency (FEMA), which is in charge of the program, estimates that an orderly evacuation even of a metropolis like New York could be managed within a few days—just about the amount of time that would be available, assuming that a previous evacuation of Russian cities had signaled the Soviet Union's intention to attack. The result, according to advocates of the plan: the death toll would be cut from perhaps 140 million to fewer than 50 million Americans.

Critics say that for relocation to work, every one of a series of optimistic assumptions must pan out. There must be not only adequate warning time but also decent weather, docile evacuees and hospitable hosts. The plan for Texas calls for residents of high-risk areas to drive to host counties, then calmly surrender their cars to authorities for impoundment. The goals are obvious—traffic control and fuel conservation—but cooperation is uncertain, at best. Similarly, the ban on taking firearms and alcoholic beverages along in an evacuation would doubtless be ignored. Even with the best will imaginable among evacuees, the process seems likely to degenerate into congestion and often panic. Many important American cities—San Francisco, for example—have overwater escape routes that are clogged enough during normal rush hours. Perhaps mindful of the problem, Marin County at the other end of the Golden Gate Bridge recently voted not to plan for civil defense. "The bottom line," says Marin supervisor Barbara Boxer, "is that there's no way we can evacuate skeletons."

5. What explanation is given for the fact that there would be a few days to evacuate a large city before a nuclear attack?

_____

_____

_____

In the following chart list the four requirements critics claim are necessary for successful relocation, and give examples of some of the problems that might arise.

Four requirements for successful relocation	*Possible problems*
1. _____	_____
_____	_____
_____	_____
_____	_____
2. _____	_____
_____	_____
_____	_____
_____	_____
3. _____	_____
_____	_____
_____	_____
_____	_____
4. _____	_____
_____	_____
_____	_____
_____	_____

The Federal Emergency Management Agency (FEMA) has published a booklet with advice for surviving a nuclear attack. This booklet is described in the following selection.

"Protection in the Nuclear Age" is a bright-orange-and-yellow, sixty-eight-page booklet with the flavor of a newspaper "style" section. It has a chapter entitled "Shelter Living," and another on private shelters which suggests that one option might be a "snack bar shelter" that could be converted quickly into a fallout shelter. The tone is breezy and understated. "In a nationwide nuclear attack, people close to a nuclear explosion in the area of heavy destruction probably would be killed or seriously injured by the blast, or by the heat of initial nuclear radiation of the nuclear fireball. People a few miles away—in the light damage area of the explosion—would be endangered by the blast and heat, and by fires that the explosion might start."

What is to be done? "People in the areas of heavy destruction would likely need protection from various combinations of blast, initial radiation, heat, fire and radioactive fallout. . . . Therefore, people living in or near likely target or high risk areas may wish to relocate to safer areas and take fallout shelter there. This would be a serious option for many to consider if a period of international tension permitting time for such relocation should precede a nationwide nuclear attack."

The booklet concludes with a discussion of radiation sickness and notes the early symptoms are lack of appetite, nausea, vomiting, fatigue, weakness, and headache. "Later the patient may have sore mouth, loss of hair, bleeding gums, bleeding under the skin, and diarrhea." It cautions, however, that these same symptoms can "be caused by other diseases. . . . If the patient has headache or general discomfort, give him one or two aspirins every 3 or 4 hours (half a tablet for a child under 12)."

[Peter Stone, *"The Bomb: The Last Epidemic"*]

1. What is your reaction to FEMA's proposal?

_____

_____

_____

_____

_____

_____

What life would be like when evacuation was complete is another imponderable. In some places the refugees would be less than welcome, even though they would be housed exclusively in public buildings rather than private homes. Both they and their hosts might well have to spend time together in fallout shelters, adding social and possibly racial tensions to the already formidable difficulties of life in a cramped underground space. The Federal plan envisions the eventual training of 20,000 shelter-management instructors who would teach 2 million others how to keep peace under pressure—but that is years away. "I won't . . . say that there's not going to be [confusion] at all," says Thad Zale, planning manager for the Nuclear Protection Division of the Michigan state police. "Obviously, there's going to be some. But in every disaster we've seen, the crisis period is probably the only time that we pull together as a people in this country."

Even so, law and order may turn out to be the critical problem for a post-attack United States.

The government hopes to provide civil defense for the economy, too, on the theory that—as a Federal Reserve System booklet puts it—"Victory in a nuclear war will belong to the country that recovers first." Nine of twelve Federal Reserve banks maintain emergency quarters underground, and records are updated every day. The system will try to clear all checks—"including those drawn on destroyed banks," according to the National Plan for Emergency Preparedness—but just in case, the Fed's main relocation center in a hillside bunker in Culpeper, Va., also has a large stockpile of currency. Credit cards will also be honored in a post-attack economy, the government advises; evacuees should not leave home without them. Skeptics, however, envision a reversion to a primitive barter economy. The most valuable items for trading purposes, says survivalist Duncan Long, will be penicillin, candy and .22-caliber bullets.

The extent to which industry survives would depend, of course, on the magnitude of the attack. Oil refineries would be a prime target in almost any conceivable Soviet strategy, even one for "limited" nuclear war. They cannot be protected. Heavy industries would also be at risk. But sheltering some equipment is at least within the realm of possibility; Boeing, the aircraft manufacturer, has gotten encouraging test results by packing sand, polyurethane foam and earth around machinery, then detonating high explosives nearby. One critical industry, communications, would probably survive in some form. The American Telephone and Telegraph Co. has already "hardened" a nationwide network of cables against the effects of nuclear weapons. Many companies, including AT&T and Exxon, have plans of their own for relocating top executives to underground refuges.*

2. Using one of the points mentioned, draw a cartoon or write an advertisement which would be appropriate in a society which was in the process of recovering from a nuclear attack.

3. Underline the three industries mentioned, and their plans for survival in case of a nuclear attack. How do you think these industries finance these operations?

*Copyright © 1982 by Newsweek, Inc. All Rights Reserved. Reprinted by Permission.

_____

_____

_____

_____

_____

_____

_____

Neither snow, nor rain, nor heat, nor gloom of night used to prevent the postal couriers from delivering the mail, and now the Postal Service says it will not be deterred on its appointed rounds by a nuclear war, either.

According to Mr. Jusell [civil defense coordinator for the Postal Service] and James K. Jones, general manager of the Postal Service's Prevention and Planning Division, the goals of the contingency plans are to deliver mail in an emergency "to the extent possible under the circumstances" and to protect postal employees as much as possible.

The officials described an elaborate chain of command under which one of the five regional postmasters general would assume control if Washington was destroyed. The headquarters would shift first to Memphis and then, if Memphis was devastated, to San Bruno, Calif.

The officials said that they did not know how much money the Postal Service had spent on the plans. Mr. Jusell said about $18,000 to $20,000 worth of food and medical supplies had been purchased for the five centers where emergency postal personnel would stay.

The officials also said about 2,000 emergency change-of-address forms had been stocked in each post office except very small ones.

[Judith Miller, "_Postal Service Plan_"]

4. The postal service plan has been described by a congressman as "long on wishful thinking and short on reality." What is your reaction to this statement?

_____

_____

_____

_____

_____

If, in fact, we could accomplish a successful evacuation and people did survive, what kind of government would exist?

A year or so ago a Pentagon spokesman, reporting on an internal study, said that the United States, in the aftermath of a nuclear exchange, could sustain a "medieval" standard of living. The statement was apt—perhaps more apt than the spokesman imagined. Under medieval economic conditions, men and women grubbed a living from the soil over a short and recurrently disease-ridden life. They had what was made with their hands; there was no manufacturing, little trade. There was nothing that could be called capitalism or free enterprise—or freedom. It was not that these had yet to be invented; it was rather that they belong to a far later and higher stage of economic development. They were born not out of ideological invention or preference but out of historical change.

There was little personal freedom in the medieval system, because it could not be afforded. Men and women were tied to the land. . . . Property rights and values were of little consequence; property is of significance only when it has value in production or in use. So it all would be in the post-nuclear world. Everything that is now known as free enterprise or the free economy would be gone. So likewise socialism. As capitalism and communism would be indistinguishable in the ashes of the target areas, they would be wholly irrelevant for those who survived.

[From *The Bulletin of the Atomic Scientists*]

1. What kinds of personal freedoms do you have?

_____

_____

_____

_____

2. What is meant by "personal freedom could not be afforded"?

_____

_____

_____

_____

3. Why would capitalism and communism be irrelevant after a nuclear attack?

_____

_____

_____

_____

Imagine That

Fifteen persons are in an atomic bomb shelter. An atomic attack has occurred, and these people are the only known human beings left alive in the totally destroyed world. It will take two weeks for the external radiation level to drop to a safe survival level, but the food and oxygen supplies can just barely sustain seven persons for two weeks. Thus a maximum of seven persons can survive to start a new society.

Each of the thirteen people will be assigned a role to play. You will be one of the people on the list that follows (nobody will play Bobby Dane or Jean Garcia, but you are to assume they are present) and must speak for this person as you interpret how he or she would think and speak, if this were a real-life situation.

You must discuss the problem and decide whom you will allow to live. If you do not determine quickly which seven persons will remain inside, you will all perish!

1. Dr. Dane: Ph.D. in history; college professor; good health; married; one child (Bobby); active and enjoys politics.
2. Mrs. Dane: A.B. and M.A. in psychology; counselor in mental health clinic; good health; one child (Bobby); active in community.
3. Bobby Dane: age 10; special education classes for four years; mentally retarded; good health; enjoys his pets.
4. Mrs. Garcia: age 33; ninth grade education; cocktail waitress; good health; married at sixteen, divorced at eighteen; abandoned as a child; in a foster home as a youth; ran away from home; returned to reformatory; stayed until 16; one child (Jean).
5. Jean Garcia: age three weeks; good health.
6. Mrs. Evans: age 32; A.B. and M.A. in elementary education; teacher; good health; divorced; one child (Mary); cited as outstanding teacher; enjoys working with children.
7. Mary Evans: age 8; third grade; excellent student; good health.
8. John Jacobs: age 13; eighth grade; honor student; good health; very active; broad interests; father is a minister.
9. Mr. Newton: age 25; starting last year of medical school; good health; antisocial; enjoys gardening.
10. Mrs. Claret: age 28; college graduate in electrical engineering; good health; married; no children; enjoys outdoor sports and stereo equipment; grew up in ghetto.

11. Sister Mary Kathleen: age 27; nun; college graduate; English major; good health; from a middle-class upbringing; father is a businessman.
12. Mr. Blake: age 51; high school graduate; mechanic; Mr. Fixit; good health; enjoys outdoor sports; likes people.
13. Father Smith: age 37; Catholic priest; college plus seminary; good health; active in civil rights; former college athlete.
14. Dr. Gonzalez: age 66; Medical Doctor; general practitioner; has had two heart attacks in the past five years but continues to practice.
15. Billy Romannini: age 20; starting third year of college; Math major; good health; active in sports; likes people.

[Arthur Diagon (Ed.), *Tomorrows*]

In response to the continued development of nuclear weapons and the government's civil defense plans, many groups of professionals have begun to organize and to present alternative views to those of our government. One of the most active of these professional groups is an organization of doctors known as Physicians for Social Responsibility. The following selection presents some of this group's views.

THE BOMB: THE LAST EPIDEMIC

In the past few years, a group of American doctors has been moved by the lack of medical information about nuclear war to examine in detail what the effects of such a war would be and whether "survival" is really possible. Like physicists before them, including Albert Einstein, Robert Oppenheimer, and Leo Szilard, who spoke bluntly about the dangers of nuclear war, these physicians have felt a professional responsibility to warn other members of their profession and the public about what they believe could well be "the last epidemic" for mankind. They call themselves Physicians for Social Responsibility (PSR), and they have had a significant impact nationwide.

PSR take seriously the words of Albert Einstein, who said, "The unleashed power of the atom has changed everything except our way of thinking. Thus we are drifting toward a catastrophe beyond comparison. We shall require a substantially new manner of thinking if mankind is to survive." Robert Jay Lifton, a Yale psychiatrist who has written extensively on the survivors of Hiroshima, shares this view. "Nuclear numbing," in Lifton's view, affects millions of people, creating a state of overwhelming fear and anxiety that leads to feelings of helplessness and passivity about halting the nuclear-arms race. He stresses that PSR must address a double illusion about nuclear war: that doctors can "patch you up after nuclear war, and that devices like shelters can help." Both of these notions are "part of a campaign of psychological preparation for nuclear war," he says.

PSR actually began in 1961, when a group of physicians in the Boston area decided to investigate the consequences of a nuclear war. The doctors, recalls Dr. H. Jack Geiger, now at City College of New York, were disturbed at how lightly politicians were taking the dangers of a nuclear conflict. During the 1960 campaign, all the talk of a missile gap between the United States and the Soviet Union, of the need for a large-scale fallout-shelter program in the U.S., and of the casual atmospheric testing of nuclear weapons had heightened their fears.

In their projection, the doctors estimated that 1,052,000 people out of Boston's 3 million would die immediately, as a result of the initial blast and of the devastating heat accompanying it. Temperatures in some places would reach as high as 800° centigrade. The force of the blast combined with the heat would first cause trauma and burns; shortly thereafter, vomiting, nausea, diarrhea, and other symptoms of radiation sickness would ensue. The doctors calculated that in the weeks right after an attack another one million people would perish, as a result of fatal injuries sustained during the explosion. Hundreds of thousands of survivors would suffer simple and compound fractures; severe wounds of the skull, thorax, and abdomen: and multiple lacerations with extensive hemorrhaging. Third-degree burns would be an overwhelming problem for physicians, because treatment requires specialized burn-care facilities, sophisticated laboratory equipment and enormous supplies of blood and plasma, as well as a wide variety of drugs. These would simply not exist after a nuclear attack, because the area's hospitals would be largely destroyed. On top of all this, the doctors noted that since most physicians are concentrated in areas that would suffer the greatest damage from a bomb, their profession would be decimated: out of the 6,560 physicians working in Boston (a 1960–1961 AMA estimate), only about 640 would survive, or one doctor for every 1,700 acutely injured people. They concluded that if the surviving doctors spent only ten minutes diagnosing and treating each patient, and worked twenty-hour days, it would take eight to fourteen days to see every severely injured person once. This assumes that every physician would be willing "to expose himself to high or lethal levels of radiation," and would "be able to identify the areas in which he is most needed" and get there and begin work immediately.

A host of other medical problems would require special attention. Large numbers of people, for example, would be deaf, having suffered ruptured eardrums in the blast, and many others would be blind, since even a quick glance at the fireball from as far away as thirty-five miles would cause retinal burns of extreme severity. Acute radiation sickness would be widespread, and tens of thousands of survivors would suffer what Dr. Geiger refers to as "superficial burns produced by beta and low-energy gamma rays, and damage due to radionuclides in specific organs." All these injuries need intensive care, which would be virtually nonexistent, and large numbers of those so afflicted would die slowly and painfully. The psychological trauma from witnessing this catastrophe would be unprecedented, and would create shock and despair among the already sick and injured survivors.

A view of what nuclear war today would entail must take into account its broadest social effects and not simply how many people are still breathing after an attack. Society would be fundamentally disrupted by even a limited war, Geiger asserts. The systems of communication, transportation, and electricity on which we depend for medical care and food would cease to function effectively. Survival would thus be much more problematic for those who were seriously injured. For example, Geiger notes that it would be very difficult to bring food into an area directly hit, and extreme water shortages would occur almost at once. Most Americans today use about 50 to 150 gallons of water daily, but in the post-attack period, "a quart a day would be generous, and there would be no way to assure potability or freedom from radioactive contamination." Mass infection would be another critical problem. Geiger estimates that a twenty-megaton attack on San Francisco today would leave at least

300,000 decomposing corpses, even if the firestorm burned up another 500,000. With no safe water supply or sanitation, "the vectors of disease—flies, mosquitoes, and other insects—will enjoy preferential survival and growth in the post-attack period because their radiation resistance is many times that of mammals." Conditions would be ripe for the outbreak of epidemic diseases. Food production, too, would be profoundly disrupted, and vast changes in weather, caused by a reduction of the atmospheric ozone, could precipitate major alterations in human beings, animals, and plants. Under these circumstances, says Geiger, "simply to tally those who are still alive, or alive and uninjured, is to make a biological body count that has little social meaning."

Just how many people would die in a full-scale exchange of nuclear weapons between the Soviet Union and the U.S. is uncertain, but physicians agree generally that deaths would run well into the tens of millions, and millions more, exposed to the blast and to radiation in the days and weeks following, would develop leukemia and a wide spectrum of malignant tumors. As Professor Sidney Drell, of Stanford University, has written, "No matter how small its yield, a nuclear weapon [unlike a conventional one] has a long memory—a deadly, radioactive memory," which means, of course, that genetic defects like those widespread in Japan would occur in children who had been exposed as fetuses to powerful radiation doses.

Peter Stone

1. What is "the last epidemic" referred to in the title of this article?

2. What does Lifton mean by "psychological preparation for nuclear war"?

3. Describe a time in your life when psychological preparation was necessary.

_____

_____

_____

_____

_____

4. List three problems which would make it difficult for doctors to work following a nuclear attack.

_____

_____

_____

_____

_____

5. In what other areas does the author foresee problems?

_____

_____

_____

_____

At present our national defense budget includes $180 billion for strategic nuclear arms for the next five years—a sum that is difficult to imagine. To give you some idea of what such an amount of money represents, consider the following.

How much money per year do you expect to earn at your job? _____

How many years do you expect to work? _____

Multiply the number of years you expect to work by the amount of money you expect to earn annually. That is the amount you will earn as a working adult in your lifetime.

Does that seem like a lot of money? _____

The following letter to a "Dear Abby" column gives you an idea of the enormity of our national defense budget for nuclear arms.

Dear Abby

Dear Abby: Our politicians toss the term "billions of dollars" around so casually that it might interest your readers to know how much a billion dollars really is. To illustrate:

A man gave his wife a million dollars and told her to spend $1,000 every day and come back when she ran out of money. She did so, and returned, broke, after about three years.

He then gave her a billion dollars. After spending $1,000 a day, she returned— after about 2,740 years!—FELIX IN L.A.

In this chapter you have read differing viewpoints about the question of nuclear arms. The following exercise presents six statements reflecting some of these differences.

Which quotations belong in which boxes?

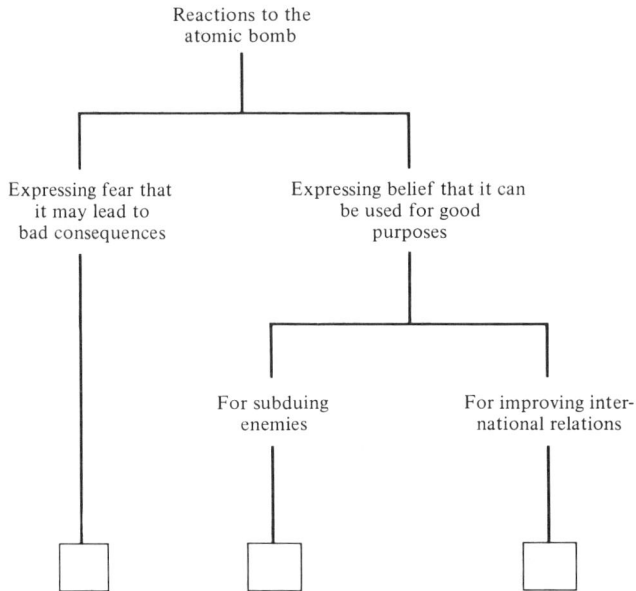

A. "Since I do not foresee that atomic energy is to be a great boon for a long time, I have to say that for the present it is a menace."
    Albert Einstein, "Einstein on the Atomic Bomb,"
    Atlantic Monthly (November, 1945)

B. "The bomb that fell on Hiroshima fell on America too. It fell on no city, no munition plants, no docks. It erased no church, vaporized no public buildings, reduced no man to his atomic elements. But it fell, it fell. It burst. It shook the land. God, have mercy on our children. God have mercy on America."
    Hermann Hagedorn, *The Bomb That Fell on America*

C. "We turned the switch, we saw the flashes, we watched them for about ten minutes—and then we switched everything off and went home. That night I knew that the world was headed for sorrow."

Leo Szilard, Speech at 80th anniversary of *The Nation*

D. "Sixteen hours ago an American airplane dropped one bomb on Hiroshima. . . . It is a harnessing of the basic power of the universe. The force from which the sun draws its powers has been loosed against those who brought war to the Far East."

Harry S. Truman, First announcement of the dropping of the atomic bomb, August 6, 1945

E. "Nothing could have been more obvious to the people of the early twentieth century than the rapidity with which war was becoming impossible. And as certainly they did not see it. They did not see it until the atomic bombs burst in their fumbling hands."

H. G. Wells, *The World Set Free*

F. "It [the atomic bomb] may intimidate the human race into bringing order into its international affairs, which, without the pressure of fear, it would not do."

Albert Einstein, "Einstein on the Atomic Bomb," *Atlantic Monthly* (November, 1945)

[Richard W. Samson, *Thinking Skills*]

As you read the following story, try to determine the author's opinion about nuclear weapons.

THE WEAPON

The room was quiet in the dimness of early evening. Dr. James Graham, key scientist of a very important project, sat in his favorite chair, thinking. It was so still that he could hear the turning of pages in the next room as his son leafed through a picture book.

Often Graham did his best work, his most creative thinking, under these circumstances, sitting alone in an unlighted room in his own apartment after the day's regular work. But tonight his mind would not work constructively. Mostly he thought about his son—his only son—in the next room. The thoughts were loving thoughts, not the bitter anguish he had felt years ago when he had first learned of the boy's condition. The boy was happy; wasn't that the main thing? And to how many men is given a child who will always be a child, who will not grow up to leave him? Certainly that was rationalization, but what is wrong with rationalization when. . . . The doorbell rang.

Graham rose and turned on lights in the almost-dark room before he went through the hallway to the door. He was not annoyed; tonight, at this moment, almost any interruption to his thoughts was welcome.

He opened the door. A stranger stood there; she said, "Dr. Graham? My name is Niemand; I'd like to talk to you. May I come in a moment?"

Graham looked at her. She was a small woman, nondescript, obviously harmless—possibly a reporter or an insurance agent.

But it didn't matter what she was. Graham found himself saying, "Of course. Come in, Ms. Niemand." A few minutes of conversation, he justified himself by thinking, might divert his thoughts and clear his mind.

"Sit down," he said, in the living room. "Care for a drink?"

Niemand said, "No, thank you." She sat in the chair; Graham sat on the sofa.

The small woman interlocked her fingers; she leaned forward. She said, "Dr. Graham, you are the man whose scientific work is more likely than that of any other man to end the human race's chance for survival."

A crackpot, Graham thought. Too late now he realized that he should have asked the woman's business before admitting her. It would be an embarrassing interview—he disliked being rude, yet only rudeness was effective.

"Dr. Graham, the weapon on which you are working—"

The visitor stopped and turned her head as the door that led to a bedroom opened and a boy of fifteen came in. The boy didn't notice Niemand; he ran to Graham.

"Daddy, will you read to me now?" The boy of fifteen laughed the sweet laughter of a child of four.

Graham put an arm around the boy. He looked at his visitor, wondering whether she had known about the boy. From the lack of surprise on Niemand's face, Graham felt sure she had known.

"Harry"—Graham's voice was warm with affection—"Daddy's busy. Just for a little while. Go back to your room; I'll come and read to you soon."

"*Chicken Little?* You'll read me *Chicken Little?*"

"If you wish. Now run along. Wait. Harry, this is Ms. Niemand."

The boy smiled bashfully at the visitor. Niemand said, "Hi, Harry," and smiled back at him, holding out her hand. Graham, watching, was sure now that Niemand had known: the smile and the gesture were for the boy's mental age, not his physical one.

The boy took Niemand's hand. For a moment it seemed that he was going to climb into Niemand's lap, and Graham pulled him back gently. He said, "Go to your room now, Harry."

The boy skipped back into his bedroom, not closing the door.

Niemand's eyes met Graham's and she said, "I like him," with obvious sincerity. She added, "I hope that what you're going to read to him will always be true."

Graham didn't understand. Niemand said, "*Chicken Little*, I mean. It's a fine story—but may *Chicken Little* always be wrong about the sky falling down."

Graham suddenly had liked Niemand when Niemand had shown liking for the boy. Now he remembered that he must close the interview quickly. He rose, in dismissal.

He said, "I fear you're wasting your time and mine, Ms. Niemand. I know all the arguments, everything you can say I've heard a thousand times. Possibly there is truth in what you believe, but it does not concern me. I'm a scientist, and only a scientist. Yes, it is public knowledge that I am working on a weapon, a rather ultimate one. But, for me personally, that is only a by-product of the fact that I am advancing science. I have thought it through, and I have found that that is my only concern."

"But, Dr. Graham, is humanity *ready* for an ultimate weapon?"

Graham frowned. "I have told you my point of view, Ms. Niemand."

Niemand rose slowly from the chair. She said, "Very well, if you do not choose to discuss it, I'll say no more." She passed a hand across her forehead. "I'll leave, Dr. Graham. I wonder, though . . . may I change my mind about the drink you offered me?"

Graham's irritation faded. He said, "Certainly. Will water do?"

"Admirably."

Graham excused himself and went into the kitchen. He got the decanter of water, ice cubes, glasses.

When he returned to the living room Niemand was just leaving the boy's bedroom. He heard Niemand's "Good night, Harry," and Harry's happy "Night, Ms. Niemand."

Graham poured the drinks. A little later, Niemand declined a second one and started to leave.

Niemand said, "I took the liberty of bringing a small gift to your son, doctor. I gave it to him while you were getting the drinks for us. I hope you'll forgive me."

"Of course. Thank you. Good night."

Graham closed the door; he walked through the living room into Harry's room. He said, "All right, Harry. Now I'll read to—"

There was sudden sweat on his forehead, but he forced his face and his voice to be calm as he stepped to the side of the bed. "May I see that, Harry?" When he had it safely, his hands shook as he examined it.

He thought, *only a madwoman would give a loaded revolver to a retarded child.*

Frederic Brown

1. What kind of work does Dr. James Graham do?

_____

2. What do you know about Dr. Graham's son?

_____

3. Why has Niemand come to visit Dr. Graham with a loaded gun?

_____

_____

_____

4. Why does Niemand give the gun to the boy?

_____

_____

5. What do you think is the author's opinion about "the ultimate weapon"?

_____

_____

_____

In this chapter you have used many of the reading and reasoning skills introduced throughout the book. These include:

1. Making inferences.
2. Awareness of the author's point of view.
3. Finding main ideas.
4. Identifying examples.
5. Hypothetical reasoning.

Perhaps you would like to reconsider your answers to the questions at the beginning of this chapter. Have any of your ideas on this subject changed? If so, why have they changed?

A Further Reading

CHILDREN OF HIROSHIMA

We could not have been expected to hear that engine drone just after the all-clear that morning. The air-raid alarm had been on all night long. It was superb timing for that extra-high flying B-29. The sky over Hiroshima was perfectly clear. There could have been no better conditions for dropping the first atom bomb. Came 8:15.

Nobody had any idea that it was an atom bomb. 'Don't know what was dropped. Probably some new kind of bomb,' was what the people in the suburbs, who were spared the disaster of the direct hit, said that evening. But at that time, the conflagration was at its height in the city. Pitifully disfigured bodies of men and women, young and old, were floating in its seven rivers. The few who found themselves alive fled the city they had known for a place of refuge, leaving their names scratched on the water tanks provided for coping with fires from air raids, but which had proved to be useless for the purpose. Some had left their families behind, inside burning houses. Some had gone without heeding the cries for help that they heard coming from the wreckage of their neighbors' houses. They went, carrying with them their grief at being able to do nothing. But those cries for help are branded on our hearts, and will never leave us. After the flames of that day and night went out, Hiroshima was of a city of death. What was left there was hell. Dying people lay down with their heads on train tracks. There were rows of white skeletons inside the steel frame of a streetcar. There were bones of the legs of the people who had tried to escape, sticking out of the doors.

There were junior high school children of twelve or thirteen, who had been mobilized for the Building Clearance Program, who were still barely alive, and calling out for their mothers, fathers, brothers and sisters in faint voices, without knowing that they would soon be dead. Yet others went to the rivers to cool their bodies that had been burned by the radiation of the bomb, and they died there.

For days after, smoke from the burning of the bodies drifted in the sky of Hiroshima. The sight of smoke wafting up from here and there along the river banks was enough to cause one's spirits to sink to the depths of hell. People who had forgotten even their sense of sorrow stood, watching the smoke rise, as if in a daze. And as it faded into the August sky, new grief would burst forth from their hearts. The tears they shed fell on the burned soil of Hiroshima, and were absorbed by it.

Following this period of grief, a new terror came over the people who had narrowly escaped death: radiation sickness. The radioactivity of the uranium of the bomb had penetrated the bodies of those who appeared to be uninjured, even to the marrows of their bones. Their hair fell out, their gums bled, eventually purple spots showed up all over their bodies, and they died one after the other.

The atom bomb brought death to Hiroshima. The city became a desert of white ashes. The priceless lives of three hundred thousand innocent people were claimed by heaven. That day will come again this year. Six years have gone by. The sky over Hiroshima is clear. When I look at it, I am reminded of that day. The blue of the sky seems to be reflecting the endless pain of those of us who were in Hiroshima that August 6.

There was a time when the words democracy and liberty, and also peace, were on the lips of everyone. Is it possible to call the 'peace' of Japan today, real peace? To be more specific what about that of Hiroshima? Is there true peace in Hiroshima?

There are peace campaigns, peace exhibitions, and there is that festival called Peace Day every August 6 that exploits the three hundred thousand atom bomb deaths. Who is behind them? Where were they on August 6, 1945?

As things are now, it is impossible to refute the charge that Hiroshima's title, that of "Peace Memorial City," was only meant to attract tourists. Should a "Peace Memorial City" be a mere sightseeing spot? Is it right that those pathetic keloid-stricken people be made exhibits in a show booth? Or guinea pigs in a laboratory? You visitors to the Peace Dome by the Motoyasu River! Remember that you are not looking at a side show.

The talk of dedicating Hiroshima as the Mecca of Peace died away as soon as that City Bill was passed, and has not been heard since. Perhaps it was just as well for the three hundred thousand dead and their families, since the intention behind the plan was all too clear. It showed the whole thing up for what it was. The surviving members of the families of those who were killed by the bomb lost fathers and mothers, or sons and daughters who would have supported them. Their health is poor. And they have been left alone, without aid, these six years.

There are people who say that those three hundred thousand were sacrificed to give us peace. Have we got anything worth such a high price in return? We sought true peace. Were we not given something false in its place? Now is the time for all of us to forge true peace. First, we must create true peace, little by little, here in Hiroshima.

Six years have passed. The seventh anniversary of those killed by the atom bomb is coming. Let us meet his day solemnly and reverently. Let us pray to those three hundred thousand souls that we will achieve true peace in Hiroshima. Let us build the real City of Peace, Hiroshima, not the side-show attraction, Hiroshima, the City Destroyed by the Atom Bomb.

Once that is done, Hiroshima will have taken her first step toward becoming the Mecca of Peace.

Tohru Hara
12th Grade Boy (6th Grade at the Time)

In an instant, the atom bomb shattered the happiness of my family—it was when I was in the sixth grade of primary school.

I was safe because I had been moved away from my family to my grandmother's house in the country. We were told that my grandfather must have been trapped under the wreckage of the house in the city. Not even his bones were found. My brother was missing, too. We had no idea if he was alive or dead. And my dearest mother also died.

I stayed with my grandmother for a year, in the tiny house in the country where she had been living alone until then. There were three other families, all relatives of ours, living in the same house with us. Whenever I saw my cousins enjoying themselves with their parents, I would remember my dear mother and become very sad. To avoid seeing my cousins' family together, I would go off by myself, out of the back door, and into the hills behind the house. I would run around there as fast as I could. When my teacher took my class out for long walks, my friends were happy to go along but I told my grandmother that I did not want to go, and stayed inside alone. My cousins started avoiding me. But after that one hard year, I was able to live with my own family again. My father, who had escaped without injury, remarried, and so my brother and I were able to live together. I was able to smile again.

My father would tell us about the "hell on earth" after the bomb was dropped. There was a mother who was all bloody, with her dead baby in her arms. There were people whose skin had been stripped off their arms from the shoulders and was hanging from their finger tips. There were people on the ground that had been burned so badly it was impossible to tell whether they were lying on their stomachs or on their backs. There were school girls who were crying because they had pieces of glass stuck all over their backs. Everyone was trying to get out of the city to the suburbs. Those who could not walk further dropped by the side of the road or in the fields. Between gasps for breath, they screamed for water. Children with pale faces were looking for their parents and babies crying for milk clung to the dead bodies of their mothers or fathers.

Peace came at last: One evening after supper, my father, my new mother, my brother and I were listening to the radio. A preview of the movie, *The Beginning or the End?* came on. "The aircraft is approaching Hiroshima," the commentator said in a tense voice, to the sound of airplane engines. As the metallic roar of the engines got louder, the atmosphere in the room became stifling and our faces turned pale. "Stop!" my father suddenly shouted. His face was tense and white. I knew very well how my father felt then.

Now that the world is at peace, my heart feels as if it will break when I think of my mother, who died saying, "I hate America and England." We have had enough of wars.

Kumiko Tamesada
12th Grade Girl (6th Grade at the Time)

Up to six years ago, I had a happy and joyful life, with my whole family there—parents, brother, and sister. War shattered this happy family. And not only this home; it destroyed the happiness of uncountable houses, tens of thousands of homes. Around that time, my big brother was called up and had to leave our home. As for my father, a carbuncle had formed on his face and he had been going to the hospital every day for about the last five days. The memory of August 6 makes me shudder and sends a chill down my spine. My unsuspecting father and big sister set off in high spirits for Hiroshima. A few hours later, the fate of the people in Hiroshima had been completely changed. This was of course the result of the single atom bomb. My father and sister were able to get back home. But I would like to tell about the three weeks from the time my father was atom-bombed to when he died.

A little after eight o'clock on August 6, my father was waiting in the waiting room of Taruya Surgical Clinic at Dobashi in Hiroshima for his turn to be examined. Suddenly there was a flash and a great noise and the house began to break apart. It became so dark that you could not see even an inch in front of your face. He thought someone would come to rescue him, and so he was waiting quietly with his eyes closed, when he suddenly heard the people around him starting to call for help. As he peered around him, he saw it was gradually getting brighter in one direction. As he began to crawl toward this light to get out, he bumped into someone who was already dead. He climbed over the dead body and kept going toward the light. But what do you suppose the brightness was? It was a fire, furiously blazing.

Outside was a sea of flames. His way out was gone, and he just stood rooted to the spot, in a daze. Then a calm old man of about seventy came walking up, and Father regained his spirits and began to feel much more confident. The man told him that they would be all right if they went to the river bank, so together they made their way toward the Honkawa River. But when they reached the bank, they found it a sea of fire there, too. Not only that, flames were licking at the parapet of the bridge, and when they looked at the river, they saw fire there, too. Buildings and timbers and doors had been blown into the river and these were blazing with a crackling noise. There was nothing to do but to turn back toward Motohara, where they stopped for a while. But as the flames advanced toward them, the heat drove them on. As they were wandering around, they came out on some train tracks, but even some of the ties were burning. There was no place left to avoid the flames. Together with many other people, they began to walk along the tracks toward Koi; the flames of the burning houses on both sides of the tracks looked like the tongues of devils.

Afterward, Father said to us, "With that long procession of people, the scene was more horrifying than any picture of Hell."

It was after eleven when Father finally managed to reach home after wandering all over. And what a sight he was! We clung to him, crying. He was in bed for three days, but he had work to do. His external injuries were not so serious, so he got up. Saying how hard it all was, he kept working on the problem of providing food for the victims of the atom bomb, and put up with the pain and discomfort. But the horrible atomic radiation had already eaten deep into my father's body. On August 20, he finally collapsed. He had a constant high fever with no clear cause.

We tried every treatment, exchanging our precious food provisions for medicine and going without food but he only got worse. His temperature went up to about 107 degrees and would not come down, whatever we did. Patches appeared on his body and his white blood count steadily decreased. His gums bled and the bleeding wouldn't stop. The family provided blood transfusions, and he got many injections to stop the bleeding, but they had no effect.

What was for us the most tragic end was approaching. It happened on the night of the twenty-seventh. Father's bleeding, which we hadn't been able to stop before, now stopped by itself. About eleven hours later, he grasped each of our hands and, anxiously calling the name of my brother who was away at the front, over and over again, my father departed on the journey from which there is no return.

Akiko Ohga
10th Grade Girl (4th Grade at the Time)

Suggested Readings

Amrine, Michael. *Great Decision.* New York: Putnam and Sons, 1959.

The gripping story of the 100 days in World War II between the death of President Roosevelt and the atom bombing of Hiroshima.

Browne, Corinne, and Robert Munroe. *Time Bomb: Understanding the Threat of Nuclear Power.* New York: William Morrow and Company, 1981.

Buck, Pearl. *Command the Morning.* Toronto: Longmans, 1959.

Fictitious account of the scientists who worked on the atomic bomb—their private and professional lives burdened with awesome responsibility and gnawing guilt.

Clayton, Bruce D. *Life After Doomsday.* New York: Dial Press, 1980.

A survivalist guide to nuclear war and other major disasters.

Hersey, John Richard. *Hiroshima.* New York: Alfred A. Knopf, 1946.

This is a factual account of what happened in Hiroshima on the morning of August 6, 1945 and in the sad days that followed. Devoted to a story about the atomic bombing of Hiroshima, as it affected six people.

Lifton, Betty. *Return to Hiroshima.* New York: Atheneum, 1970.

This is an account in words and pictures of the lingering effects of the first atomic bomb on survivors and families of victims.

Lilienthal, David E. *Change, Hope, and the Bomb.* Princeton, N.J.: Princeton University Press, 1963.

In these essays based on a lecture series at Princeton University, a former chairman of the Atomic Energy Commission discusses the role of scientists in political life, and comments on then current atomic policy.

Masters, Dexter. *The Accident.* New York: Alfred A. Knopf, 1955.

Set in Los Alamos, New Mexico, a young scientist is exposed to atomic radiation. This is the story of the eight days before he died.

Pauling, Linus. *No More War.* New York: Dodd, Mead, and Co., 1958.

World renowned American scientist makes an impassioned plea for international agreements to end nuclear bomb testing.

Phillips, John Aristotle, and David Michaelis. *Mushroom.* New York: William Morrow and Co., Inc., 1978.

Phillips is the Princeton student who became famous when he designed an atomic bomb to demonstrate the dangers of nuclear weapons and also to fulfill his academic requirements.

Publishing Committee for Children of Hiroshima. *Children of Hiroshima.* Cambridge, Mass: Oelgeschlager, Gunn, and Hain Inc., 1980.

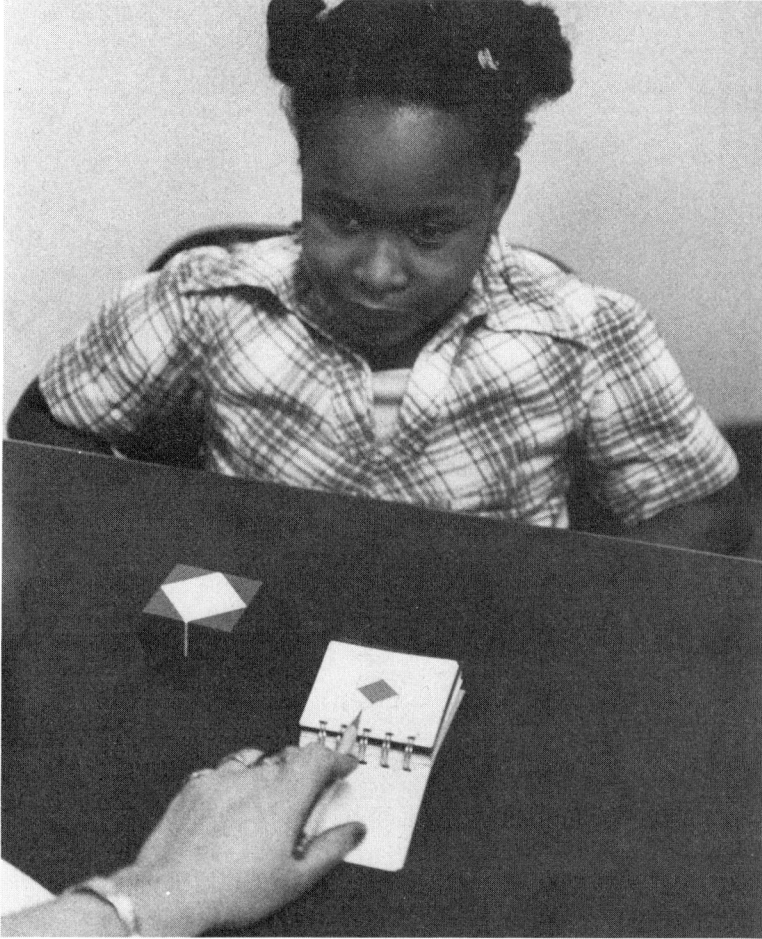

It matters not if you were born in a duck pond,
provided that you were born from a swan egg.
                    —Hans Christian Anderson

CHAPTER 8

INTELLIGENCE

This chapter contains a great deal of information about I.Q. tests, how they were developed, and some of the current controversies which surround them. The responsibility for finding and organizing some of this information rests with you. Therefore, we have provided you with the necessary aids to use the library well. This is a skill that will often be useful to you during the course of your college career.

Further, we have included some useful tips to help you succeed in taking tests, which, as you know, are an ever present part of a student's life.

1. Do you consider yourself an intelligent person? Why? _____

_____

_____

_____

_____

_____

2. Have you ever taken an intelligence test? _____

3. The score you achieve on an intelligence test is called your I.Q. (Intelligence Quotient). Do you know your I.Q.? _____

4. If you don't already know your IQ, would like to know it? Why?

_____

_____

_____

_____

_____

5. What advantages or disadvantages would there be in knowing your IQ? In having your teacher know you I.Q.? In having your parents know your

I.Q.? _____

_____

6. List as many questions as you can think of about I.Q.

In this chapter you are going to read about:

    1. A Definition of Intelligence

2. How To Compute an I.Q. Score

_____

_____

_____

_____

_____

3. I.Q. Score Distribution

_____

_____

_____

_____

_____

4. The History of the Development of I.Q. Tests

_____

_____

_____

_____

_____

5. The Meaning of I.Q. Scores

_____

_____

_____

_____

_____

6. Heredity–Environment

_____

_____

_____

_____

_____

7. Cultural Bias in I.Q. Tests

_____

_____

_____

_____

_____

8. How to Take Tests

_____

_____

_____

_____

_____

9. What I.Q. Scores Predict

_____

_____

_____

_____

_____

Look at the list of questions you constructed in question 6. Decide where each of them fits in the chapter outline above. Write your questions under the appropriate heading of the outline. Think of some questions to write below the headings you did not originally have questions for.

> Almost everyone likes to think that he or she pretty much knows what intelligence is and how to judge who has it and who doesn't. Indeed, people make informal judgments about others' intelligence all the time, and don't seem to need intelligence tests to do so. One could argue that the bulk of intelligence testing is not the kind that takes place in schoolrooms and psychologists' consulting rooms, but the kind that goes on in face-to-face encounters between people: in job and admission interviews, in classrooms, in meetings, at cocktail parties, during coffee breaks, and in initial encounters with strangers.

> [Robert J. Sternberg, "*Who's Intelligent?*"]

How do you judge someone's intelligence? Write a paragraph describing an imaginary person (or someone you know) whom you consider to be intelligent. You may want to describe the person in terms of some or all of the following categories: work, speech, social abilities, education, hobbies, and interests.

_____

_____

_____

_____

_____

_____

_____

_____

_____

_____

_____

_____

A DEFINITION OF INTELLIGENCE

Like so many important concepts in psychology, intelligence cannot be observed directly. It has no mass, occupies no space, and is invisible. Nevertheless, we feel certain it exists.

[Dennis Coon, *Introduction to Psychology*]

If intelligence is the ability to learn, who is more intelligent—a woodsman who knows every trail and tree and animal track or sound in the forest but cannot read; a musician who can play hundreds of songs from memory but cannot tell an oak from a pine tree; or a high-school math teacher who thinks all jazz music sounds alike?

A famous comedian, Will Rogers, once said, "We're all ignorant, only on different subjects." Most psychologists would agree, and it is just as true that everyone is intelligent in some areas but not in others.

Obviously, "the ability to learn" is not a complete definition of intelligence, because it makes it impossible to answer the question about the woodsman, the musician, and the teacher. All three are intelligent, because all three can learn. Who can say which has learned the most, or what kind of learning is most important?

So far, no one has been able to suggest a definition of intelligence that satisfies everyone. In fact, psychologists have had much more success in trying to measure intelligence than in trying to figure out what it really is.

[Gail K. Gains, *Brain Power*]

1. In your own words, explain the author's main idea. _____

_____

_____

2. In what areas would you consider yourself "ignorant"? _____

_____

_____

3. In what areas would you consider yourself "intelligent"? _____

_____

_____

HOW TO COMPUTE AN I.Q. SCORE

A formula is used to arrive at a numerical score which represents your I.Q. The formula for finding an I.Q. is:

$$I.Q. = \frac{MA}{CA} \times 100.$$

MA stands for mental age, and CA stands for chronological age.

An advantage of the I.Q. is that it allows comparison of intelligence among children with different combinations of chronological and mental ages. A ten-year-old child with a mental age of twelve has an I.Q. of 120:

$$\frac{(MA)\,12}{(CA)\,10} \times 100 = 120 \ (I.Q.)$$

A second child having a mental age of twelve but with a chronological age of twelve would have an I.Q. of 100:

$$\frac{(MA)\,12}{(CA)\,12} \times 100 = 100 \ (I.Q.)$$

The I.Q. shows that the younger child is brighter than his twelve-year-old friend, even though their intellectual skills are actually the same. Notice that I.Q. equals 100 when MA = CA. An I.Q. of 100 is therefore defined as average intelligence, and an I.Q. over 100 indicates above-average intelligence. I.Q. scores below 100 occur when age in years exceeds mental age, as would be the case for a fifteen-year-old with a MA of twelve:

$$\frac{12}{15} \times 100 = 80$$

[Dennis Coon, *Introduction to Psychology*]

1. What is the meaning of "chronological age"?

   _____

2. What is an average I.Q.?

   _____

3. Using the formula, indicate the I.Q. of two eighteen-year-olds, one being of average intelligence and one being above average. Explain the difference in the two formulas:

$$\frac{(MA)\ ?}{(CA)\ ?} \times 100 =$$

$$\frac{(MA)\ ?}{(CA)\ ?} \times 100 =$$

Explanation: _____

_____

_____

_____

_____

I.Q. SCORE DISTRIBUTION

Test-makers have predicted that the I.Q. scores from a large group of people would fit neatly into what statisticians call the normal distribution, or bell-shaped curve. To make the "bell" shape, most values must fall in the middle, with other values tapering off on each side.

The figure below shows the kind of I.Q. distribution found in the population in general, and gives an indication of the meaning of different I.Q.s.

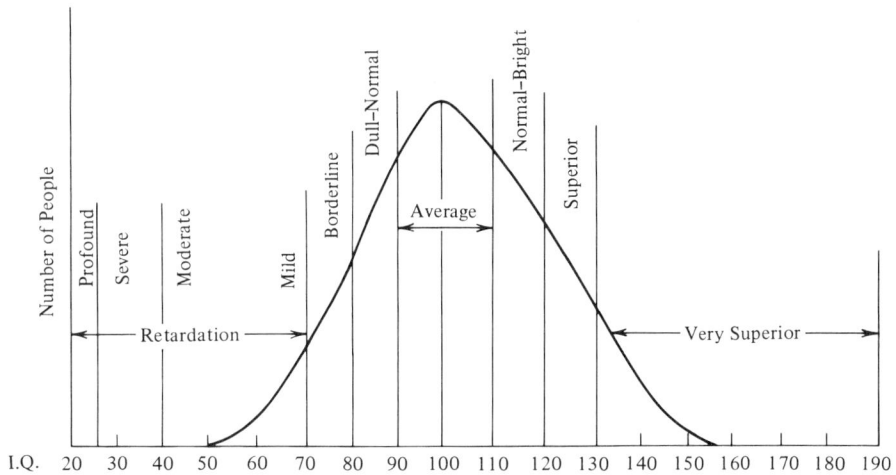

1. Why is the distribution shown in the graph called a bell-shaped curve?

_____

_____

_____

2. The average I.Q. falls between _____ and _____.

3. True or false:

_____ A person with an I.Q. of 80 is considered retarded.

_____ An I.Q. score of 115 is considered superior.

_____ No one can have an I.Q. of 30.

THE HISTORY OF THE DEVELOPMENT OF I.Q. TESTS

The most commonly used I.Q. tests are

- Binet-Simon
- The Revised Stanford Binet
- Wechsler Intelligence Scales (WISC)
- Army Alpha-Beta

These tests were developed at different times for different reasons.

In order to find out more about each of these tests, your instructor will divide the class into four groups, each responsible for the research on one test.

What questions would you like answered in order to be well-informed about each test? List those questions below.

_____

_____

_____

_____

_____

_____

_____

_____

_____

_____

If, in researching the topic, you answer the questions listed above, you should have a complete picture of the I.Q. test To get started, put the questions dealing with similar ideas into categories. Let each student in your group be responsible for one of these categories.

You can use the chart below to help you.

Student: _____   Responsible for: _____

_____

_____

_____

Student: _____   Responsible for: _____

_____

_____

_____

Student: _____   Responsible for: _____

_____

_____

_____

Student: _____   Responsible for: _____

_____

_____

_____

Student: _____   Responsible for: _____

_____

_____

_____

_____

To help you find the information for a research paper, you need to be familiar with the reference materials in the library.

The Card Catalog

In order to locate the books you want, the place to start is the card catalog. A card for every book is filed in a large cabinet, usually situated in a prominent place in your library. Books are filed in at least three different ways in the catalog: by title, by author, and by subject. The call number in the upper left-hand corner of each card is used to find that book on the shelf of the library.

Following are samples of each type of card for the same book. Can you tell which card would be found under the author's name, the subject, and the title? Indicate your answers on the lines provided.

```
153     Haines, Gail Kay
Ha            Brain power; understanding human intelligence.
        New York, Franklin Watts, 1979.

            117 p., illus., biblio., index.

            1. Intellect.    2. Brain.    I. Title.
```
_____

```
        Brain power

153     Haines, Gail Kay
Ha            Brain power; understanding human intelligence.
        New York, Franklin Watts, 1979.

            117 p., illus., biblio., index.

            1. Intellect.    2. Brain.    I. Title.
```
_____

```
        INTELLECT

153     Haines, Gail Kay
Ha            Brain power; understanding human intelligence.
        New York, Franklin Watts, 1979.

            117 p., illus., biblio., index.
```
_____

Dictionaries

You are probably already familiar with the dictionary. But did you know that there are special purpose dictionaries which may be helpful in your research? Some of these include the *Biographical Dictionary*, the *Dictionary of American History*, and the *Dictionary of Psychology*. The next time you are in the library, you might find it interesting to explore the large variety of dictionaries available.

Encyclopedias

Libraries usually contain different kinds of encyclopedias, ranging from one-volume, which may touch on a particular subject only briefly, to multivolume encyclopedias like the *World Book Encyclopedia,* the *Encyclopedia Americana,* and the *Encyclopaedia Britannica.* The multivolume encyclopedias usually deal with topics in greater detail and offer more scholarly information. The books are arranged alphabetically. Encyclopedias are basic references for the general fund of human knowledge.

Periodicals

Undoubtedly you know or have read at least a dozen different magazines. In the library you will discover that there are hundreds of magazines (or periodicals) which you may never have seen on the newstands. How is it possible to locate an article in a magazine which deals with the topic with which you are concerned? Every library has a publication called *The Reader's Guide to Periodical Literature.* Magazine articles are listed alphabetically by topic in the *Reader's Guide*, and a new guide is published monthly to keep the listing up to date.

Magazine articles often offer the most current information on a subject. You may find an entire book dealing with your subject, but it might have been written five or ten years ago. On the other hand, you probably can find a magazine article written within the past few months dealing with the same subject.

Page 256 shows a page from *The Reader's Guide to Periodical Literature.*

Topics are listed in alphabetical order. Look at the sample page and find the heading *Intelligence tests.* Notice there are five articles listed under this heading. Using the first entry as an example, the kinds of information provided are listed below. Can you fill in the correct information for the first entry?

1. Title _____

2. Author _____

3. Are there illustrations? _____

4. Magazine _____

Israel

CIA-Israeli collaboration [accusation of cooperation with Mossad] V. Bozhenkov. il World Press Rev 29:51 N '82

Intelligence tests

A biological basis for IQ. S. Begley. il Newsweek 100:112 O 18 '82

Hérédité v. environnement [social influences on IQ scores; study by Michel Schiff and others] Sci Am 247:77+ D '82

Intelligence test: sizing up a newcomer [Kaufman Assessment Battery for Children] W. Herbert. il Sci News 122:280-1 O 30 '82

IQ testing and the media. R. J. Herrnstein. il Atlantic 250:68-74 Ag '82; Discussion. 250: 6+ N; 6+ D '82

New intelligence test said to reduce bias. Phi Delta Kappan 64:221-2 N '82

Intense Pulsed Neutron Source. See Neutron sources

Intensive care units, Coronary. See Coronary care units

Inter-American relations

Reagan's dream: a united New World. il pors U S News World Rep 93:9 D 13 '82

Intercultural education

Isla Vista's Tower of Babel. il Newsweek 100:147 D 6 '82

Multicultural education and independent schools. G. N. Davis. Educ Dig 48:54-5 N '82

Aids and devices

Multicultural materials [UNICEF materials] Child Today 11:32 S/O '82

Interest (Economics)

Another boost from the Fed. S. Dentzer. il Newsweek 100:71-2 N 29 '82

At last, relief for the small borrower. il Newsweek 100:106-7 O 25 '82

A back door to fixed-rate loans [one borrower swaps floating-rate interest obligation for another's long-term fixed rate] il Bus Week p85-6 D 13 '82

Behind the market's wild ride. il Bus Week p98-100+ O 25 '82

Bulls are stampeding again. J. S. DeMott. il Time 120:88-9 O 18 '82

Drop in interest rates is not over yet. P. M. Scherschel. il U S News World Rep 93:89-90 N 22 '82

Easing the interest-rate pain. J. Hay. il Macleans 95:50 O 18 '82

Executives think bond rates are still too high [Business week/Harris poll] il Bus Week p 19 N 29 '82

The Fed stampedes the bulls. D. Pauly. il Newsweek 100:72+ O 18 '82

The Federal Reserve and interest rates. America 147:224 O 23 '82

Getting high yields despite low interest rates.

5. Volume _____

6. Page _____

7. Date _____

In order to save space, the names of many magazines are abbreviated. Look at the second entry. This article could be found in *Sci Am*. If you look at the front of the *Reader's Guide*, you will find that all the abbreviations for magazines are listed with their full titles. *Sci Am* is an abbreviation for *Scientific American*.

Once you have decided what magazine you need, give the information to the librarian and she/he will get the magazine for you.

The Librarian

The librarian can be of help if you have difficulty finding needed information. Most librarians are very happy to offer their assistance if asked. You should feel comfortable in utilizing their expertise.

Organizing the Material

Index cards (3″ × 5″) are useful for taking notes when researching a topic. Each card should contain a separate "chunk" of information. Using this method makes it possible to shuffle the cards and change the sequence in order to organize and reorganize the material into a sensible order.

There are certain principles that you should keep in mind as you research a topic and take notes:

1. Write a few words at the top of each index card to describe the information on that card.
2. Keep separate topics on separate cards. This makes it possible to put together information of the same topic from different sources.
3. Include on each card (a) the name of the source, (b) the author, and (c) the page numbers from which you have taken the information.
4. Direct quotations should be indicated as such by the use of quotation marks.

To share what you learned about the I.Q. test you researched, you should decide, with your instructor, on a method of presentation to the class. As students report on other I.Q. tests, take notes, using the pages that follow.

Binet-Simon Intelligence Test

_____

_____

_____

_____

_____

_____

_____

_____

_____

_____

_____

_____

_____

_____

_____

_____

_____

_____

_____

The Revised Stanford Binet Intelligence Test

_____

_____

_____

_____

_____

_____

_____

_____

_____

_____

_____

_____

_____

_____

_____

_____

_____

_____

_____

_____

_____

_____

Wechsler Intelligence Scales (WISC)

_____

_____

_____

_____

_____

_____

_____

_____

_____

_____

_____

_____

_____

_____

_____

_____

_____

_____

_____

_____

THE MEANING OF I.Q. SCORES

Many educators and psychologists today are critical of I.Q. tests. What do you think are some possible criticisms of I.Q. tests?

_____

_____

Evelyn Sharp, a writer on education and a severe critic of I.Q. testing, contends in her book *The I.Q. Cult* that the entire concept of "mental age" is outmoded.

> For one thing, it tends to give the impression that two children with the same mental age have the same kind of mind. This is not true. If a seven-year-old and a twelve-year-old each have a mental age of ten, they both get the same number of items right, but probably not the same items. They arrived at their scores by different paths. In all likelihood, the bright younger child earned his credits on tasks requiring analysis and judgment, the dull older child on tasks based on factual information that comes from schooling or experience.

1. Ms. Sharp believes that two children with the same mental age do not have the same kind of mind. Underline the explanation for this in the paragraph above.

Other people have argued that I.Q. tests do not measure intelligence at all. The writer of the next selection begins with a question. As you read, decide how he answers the question he poses.

> What then do the tests accomplish? I think we can answer this question best by starting with an illustration. Suppose you wished to judge all the pebbles in a large pile of gravel for the purpose of separating them into three piles, the first to contain the extraordinary pebbles, the second the normal pebbles, the third the insignificant pebbles. You have no scales. You first separate from the pile a much smaller pile and pick out one pebble which you guess is the average. You hold it in your left hand and pick up another pebble in your right hand. The right pebble feels heavier. You pick up another pebble. It feels lighter. You pick up a third. It feels still lighter. A fourth feels heavier than the first. By this method, you can arrange all the pebbles from the smaller pile in a series running from the lightest to the heaviest. You thereupon call the middle pebble the standard pebble, and with it as a measure you determine whether any pebble in the larger pile is a subnormal, a normal, or a supernormal pebble.
>
> This is just about what the intelligence test does. It does not weigh or measure intelligence by any objective standard. It simply arranges a group of people in a series from best to worst by balancing their capacity to do certain arbitrarily selected puzzles, against the capacity of all the others. The intelligence test, in other words, is fundamentally an instrument for classifying a group of people. It may also be an instrument for measuring their intelligence, but of that we cannot be at all sure unless we believe that M. Binet . . . and a few other psychologists

have guessed correctly when they invented their tests. They may have guessed correctly but . . . the proof is not yet at hand.

The intelligence test, then, is an instrument for classifying a group of people, rather than "a measure of intelligence." People are classified within a group according to their success in solving problems which may or may not be tests of intelligence. They are not classified according to their ability in dealing with the problems of real life that call for intelligence.

[Block and Dworkin, *The I.Q. Controversy*]

2. How does the author answer the question, "What then do these tests accomplish?"

_____

_____

_____

_____

[By permission of Johnny Hart and Field Enterprises, Inc.]

HEREDITY–ENVIRONMENT

Ever since I.Q. testing came into being, people have argued over whether one's I.Q. is primarily a product of the environment or heredity.

Environment: All the condition, circumstances, and influences surrounding and affecting the development of an organism.

Heredity: The transmission of characteristics from parent to offspring by means of genes in the chromosomes.

Two other terms often used in place of *environment* and *heredity* are *nature* and *nurture.* Check the meaning of these words in your dictionary and write them in the space that follows.

Nature: _____

_____

Nurture: _____

_____

Within the context of this discussion, *environment* means the same as

_____ . *Heredity* is a synonym for _____ .

One of the most controversial figures in the "nature–nurture" question is Dr. Arthur Jensen, an educational psychologist. The following selection from *The Stranglehold of the I.Q. Score*, by Benjamin Fine, explains the focus of the controversy.

It is [Dr. Jensen's] view that . . . genetics must take precedence over the . . . environment. The genetic factors are formed at conception, when sperm and ovum unite.

[After much testing, Dr. Jensen found that Blacks generally scored about fifteen points lower than whites on I.Q. tests.] . . . Dr. Jensen concluded that blacks had an inferior I.Q., and that nothing could be done, as far as schools or colleges were concerned, to make up the 15-point deficit. If nothing could be done, then why try?

This viewpoint was quickly, almost eagerly, embraced by Dr. Shockley of Stanford University, who went even further. He called for a complete reevaluation of the schooling now being given to blacks or others with low I.Q.s. Much to the . . . dismay of some of his colleagues at Stanford and psychologists elsewhere, Dr. Shockley proposed a "sterilization plan" for parents of low I.Q. children. He would have the state or government pay each person, white or black, who agreed to be sterilized, $1,000 for each I.Q. point they had below 100. Thus, if a person had an I.Q. of 90, he would receive a bonus of $10,000; if it registered 75, the subsidy would rise to $25,000.

Dr. Shockley based his plan on the theory that low I.Q. parents produced low I.Q. children, and that these children then became welfare cases, thus costing the government millions of dollars annually. In the long run, said Dr. Shockley, the nation would save money through his plan because an initial outlay of, say, $15,000 would be less than it would cost to maintain the numerous children of the low I.Q. parent on welfare. No indication was made by Dr. Shockley as to who would give the I.Q. test, what test would be used, which score would be the determinant as to how much money the person would receive if he agreed to be sterilized, or how the damage could be rectified if at a later date the 90 I.Q. had changed to 115.

[Benjamin Fine, *Stranglehold of the I.Q.*]

In Your Opinion

Would you support or oppose Dr. Shockley's proposal? Why?

_____

_____

_____

_____

_____

_____

_____

_____

    It is important to note that few psychologists support Jensen's position and a number of arguments have been advanced against it.

    First, it is no secret that as a group blacks in the United States are more likely than whites to live in environments that are physically, educationally, and intellectually impoverished. Second, even if we assume that the gap in I.Q. between blacks and whites is hereditary, it is small enough to be corrected by environment. Jensen's reply to this claim is that special educational programs like Head Start have proved incapable of narrowing the I.Q. gap. But it is essentially ridiculous to expect that a brief summer program or a few hours a day are enough to counteract the differences in educational and environmental advantages of blacks and whites.

    Third, Jensen confuses racial and hereditary differences. Many blacks in the United States have as few as 10 percent "black genes," and some whites have as many as 75 percent "black genes." "Race" in the United States is a social concept, not a biological reality.

[Dennis Coon, *Introduction to Psychology*]

1. Underline the three arguments presented in opposition to Jensen's claim of genetic heritage.

2. How can race be a social concept, not a biological reality?

_____

_____

_____

_____

_____

Perhaps the most devastating criticism of Jensen is that his logic is faulty. Consider this example: Corn comes in different varieties selectively bred to grow to a certain height. If we plant tall and short varieties side by side in the same field, we will observe a genetically determined difference in their height at maturity. But what if we take corn (all the same variety) and plant half in a fertile field and half in poor soil? Again we observe a difference in maximum height, but this time it is obviously a mistake to assume that it is genetically caused.

[Dennis Coon, *Introduction to Psychology*]

3. In a discussion of intelligence, the author uses corn as a symbol of _____

_____and height as a symbol of_____.

Only when black children are raised in exactly the same surroundings as white children can hereditary factors be clearly assessed. Along this line, a recent study looked at the fate of black children adopted by white families. These children had I.Q. scores averaging 106, which is comparable to the national average for white children. It is not clear if the black children were actually "brighter" as a result of this experience or if they were just better prepared to take a "white" test. The fact remains, however, that when an equal opportunity for intellectual development is capable of closing the I.Q. gap, then the genetic position must be abandoned.

[Dennis Coon, *Introduction to Psychology*]

In the 1930s, Nazi Germany, led by Hitler, showed how dangerous the philosophy of racial superiority could become. Perhaps that is why those psychologists who advocate the principle of inherited intelligence find themselves attacked and ostracized. We are opposed to any suggestion or belief in a "master race," nor do we accept the theory that whites are mentally superior to blacks, Jews to gentiles, Orientals to Indians, middle-class Americans to disadvantaged poor whites.

Most parents want their children to do better, to rise higher in educational, social, economic, or professional status then they have done. That is why so many families do everything possible to enable their children to go to college and to use their education as a ladder that leads from a lower economic level to a higher one.

It is here where environment plays an important role by encouraging children to aim for higher educational goals and improve their economic and social status. Their I.Q.'s can be raised through motivation. It is well to remember that the I.Q. is a label that can be applied at will, and not something that is stapled onto a child at birth.

It is readily apparent, in viewing the literature available, that both heredity and environment play an important role in developing the child's I.Q. The primary argument boils down to whether the ratio is as high as 80–20 as Jensen, . . . Shockley, and others claim it to be. Or is it closer to a chance 50–50? That this is the case seems reasonable and it should make an extremely significant difference in our approach to learning.

[Benjamin Fine, *Stranglehold of the I.Q.*]

4. If one is to believe, as the author does, that heredity and environment have an equal effect on a person's I.Q., in what ways would this make a significant difference in our society's approach to learning.

_____

_____

_____

_____

_____

_____

_____

Recently, in California, a group of people organized a Sperm Bank. The purpose of the bank is to collect sperm from men with high I.Q.s, which will then be used to artificially inseminate women.

5. Those who organized the Sperm Bank believe that I.Q. is determined by

_____ .

Many of the findings concerning heredity, environment, and intelligence can be summarized in these terms: Inherited intellectual potential may be compared to a rubber band that is stretched by outside forces. A longer rubber band may be stretched more easily, but a shorter one can be stretched to the same length if enough force is applied. Of course, a superior genetic "gift" may allow for a higher maximum I.Q. but in the final analysis intelligence reflects development as well as potential, nurture as well as nature.

[Dennis Coon, *Introduction to Psychology*]

The following quotes present two different points of view about the nature–nurture controversy. Choose the one you agree with and explain why.

1. With a good heredity, nature deals you a fine hand at cards; and with a good environment, you learn to play the hand well.
   —Walter C. Alvarez, M.D.
2. We can escape from the level of society, but not from the level of intelligence to which we were born.
   —Randall Jarrell

_____

_____

_____

_____

_____

_____

_____

_____

_____

_____

_____

_____

_____

_____

_____

_____

CULTURAL BIAS IN I.Q. TESTS

The following selection discusses many of the shortcomings of I.Q. tests. As you read the material, write a heading which explains the topic of each section on the lines provided. Then, in your own words, write the main idea(s) below. The first one is done for you.

The WISC norms are based on tests given to children prior to 1955. The test originally was issued in 1949. Are the norms of a generation ago an honest reflection of 1983 or the years beyond? Does Stanford-Binet, with its norms based on standardizations made in the 1930s, cope with the changes that have taken place in the last twenty to forty years?

Examples can be cited of how far off the "norms" are in these outdated tests, still found in every guidance counselor's office in the nation's schools. The *WISC Manual*, which gives the directions for those administering the test to follow, lists the scoring limits for a correct answer to the question, "What is the population of the United States?" as between 130 and 190 million.

That is definitely unrealistic. Our population has already passed the 220-million mark! Yet, if the examiner followed the Manual implicitly, as he has been admonished to do, he would have to mark the answer wrong. This, in turn, would lower the I.Q. score of the child who answered the question correctly, and give credit to the one who may have answered it incorrectly.

Outdated Questions

Many questions on the WISC are outdated.

Some of the items on the various I.Q. tests are unfair to foreign students, recently arrived in this country from Cuba, Puerto Rico, or elsewhere, or children from disadvantaged slums, from the Appalachian Mountains regions, or poorly supported rural schools. Could you reasonably expect these children to identify the poems of Longfellow, distinguish between two abstract concepts, or recall the names of the early Presidents of the United States?

All of the WISC subtests use words, pictures, and materials that are more familiar to middle-class white Americans than to any other social or ethnic group. Three of the eleven subtests require knowledge of factual information—definition of a word, an author, or a socially acceptable rule of behavior. . . . Children who are well read, it is obvious, are most likely to secure higher I.Q. scores on the vocabulary and information sections of the test. Professor Jerome Kagan of Harvard University lists five questions taken from the vocabulary or information subtests found in the WISC and five designed by a psychologist, Adrian Dove. The latter items were chosen as being familiar to urban poor blacks, while the Wechsler questions presumably favored middle-class white Americans.

Wechsler Test
1. Who wrote *Hamlet*?
2. Who wrote the *Iliad*?
3. What is the Koran?
4. What does *audacious* mean?
5. What does *plagiarize* mean?

Dove's Test
1. In C. C. Ryder, what does C. C. stand for?
2. What is a gashead?
3. What is Willis Mays's last name?
4. What does "handkerchief head" mean?
5. Whom did "Stagger Lee" kill in the famous blues legend?

Observes Dr. Kagan: "Is it unreasonable to ask whether high scores on either test measure anything to do with basic mental capacity? A person's score reflects the probability that he has been exposed to the information requested."

We know that the early preschool years give the child from a disadvantaged home too few experiences that produce proper learning attitudes or environment. Since the child cannot, or does not, find success in school, he seeks it in the streets or through his own peer group. Because they must concentrate on bare economic survival, parents in the lowest economic brackets have little time to devote to their children's intellectual growth, nor are they motivated to do so.

It is obvious that children will do poorly on the I.Q. test when they are apathetic, withdrawn, unmotivated, hostile, and in constant conflict with their teachers or supervisors.

As Dr. Martin Deutsch, Director of the New York University Institute for Development Studies, points out, not only do the culturally deprived youngsters fall behind in basic skills, such as reading and arithmetic, they also do not respond to any other aspect of the learning process. Education simply passes them by, and going to school becomes an ever-growing chore to which they respond only in negative terms.

The effect of the I.Q. score can be devastating to the child and to his parents. If a child scores low on an intelligence test because he cannot read, notes Dr. Kenneth B. Clark, nationally known psychologist, and then is not taught to read because he has a low score, the child is imprisoned in an iron circle from which he cannot escape. He becomes the victim of an educational self-fulfilling prophecy. The I.Q. score showed he could not read. Since he is then not taught, the prophecy of the I.Q. is fulfilled—he never learns to read properly.

[Benjamin Fine, *Stranglehold of the I.Q.*]

Recently, Adrian Dove devised the "Chitling Test of Intelligence" as a half-serious idea to demonstrate that if the language and concepts of Blacks in the Watts area of Los Angeles were used in a test, most Whites would perform poorly. Part of the Chitling Test is shown (below). That most (white) college students have difficulty with the questions on this test suggests that common experience is in fact difficult to define. At least some of the differences in intelligence supposed to exist between urban and rural children or Blacks and Whites are due not to genuine differences in ability to profit from the environment, but from cultural biases found in tests, that is, from the choice of test items that occur more frequently in middle-class urban environments.

[Ehrlich and Feldman, *The Race Bomb*]

Dove Counterbalance Intelligence Test

Time limit: 5 minutes

Circle the correct answer.

1. T-bone Walker got famous for playing what?
   a. trombone
   b. piano
   c. T-flute
   d. guitar
   e. "hambone"

2. A "gas head" is a person who has a
   a. fast-moving car
   b. stable of "lace"
   c. "process"
   d. habit of stealing cars
   e. long jail record for arson

3. If you throw the dice and 7 is showing on the top, what is facing down?
   a. 7
   b. snake eyes
   c. boxcars
   d. little joes
   e. 11

4. Cheap chitlings (not the kind you purchase at a frozen-food counter) will taste rubbery unless they are cooked long enough. How soon can you quit cooking them to eat and enjoy them?
   a. 45 minutes
   b. two hours
   c. 24 hours
   d. one week (on a low flame)
   e. one hour

5. Bird or Yardbird was the jacket jazz lovers from coast to coast hung on
   a. Lester Young
   b. Peggy Lee
   c. Benny Goodman
   d. Charlie Parker
   e. Birdman of Alcatraz

6. A "handkerchief head" is:
   a. a cool cat
   b. porter
   c. an Uncle Tom
   d. a hoddi
   e. a preacher

7. Jet is
   a. an East Oakland motorcycle club
   b. one of the gangs in West Side Story
   c. a news and gossip magazine
   d. a way of life for the very rich

8. "Bo Diddly" is a
   a. game for children
   b. down-home cheap wine
   c. down-home singer
   d. new dance
   e. Moejoe call

9. Which word is most out of place here?
   a. splib
   b. blood
   c. gray
   d. spook
   e. black

10. If a pimp is up tight with a woman who gets state aid, what does he mean when he talks about "Mother's Day"?
    a. second Sunday in May
    b. third Sunday in June
    c. first of every month
    d. none of these
    e. first and fifteenth of every month

11. How much does a "short dog" cost?
    a. 15¢
    b. $2
    c. 35¢
    d. 5¢
    e. 86¢ plus tax

12. Many people say that "Juneteenth" (June 10th) should be made a legal holiday because this was the day when:
    a. the slaves were freed in the United States
    b. the slaves were freed in Texas
    c. the slaves were freed in Jamaica
    d. the slaves were freed in California
    e. Martin Luther King was born
    f. Booker T. Washington died

13. If a man is called a "blood," then he is a
    a. fighter
    b. Mexican-American
    c. Negro
    d. hungry hemophile
    e. red man or Indian

14. What are the Dixie Hummingbirds?
    a. a part of the KKK
    b. a swamp disease
    c. a modern gospel group
    d. a Mississippi Negro paramilitary strike force
    e. deacons

15. The opposite of square is
    a. round
    b. up
    c. down
    d. hip
    e. lame

Answers:

11. c	12. b	13. c	14. c	15. d
6. c	7. c	8. c	9. c	10. c
1. d	2. c	3. a	4. c	5. d

If you scored 14 on this exam, your IQ is approximately 100, indicating average intelligence. If you scored 11 or less you are mentally retarded. With luck and the help of a special educational program, we may be able to teach you a few simple skills!

[Dennis Coon, *Introduction to Psychology*]

What does Adrian Dove mean by the last sentence?

_____

_____

_____

_____

_____

_____

Think About This

If you wanted to develop a "culture free" intelligence test—that is, one which would not reflect a person's economic, national, or racial background—which of the following items would you include and which would you omit?

Select the word that has the closest meaning to the first word.
histrionic   A. antiquated B. legendary C. theatrical D. surgical

[Arthur Whimbey, *Intelligence Can Be Taught*]

Select the correct figure from the six numbered ones

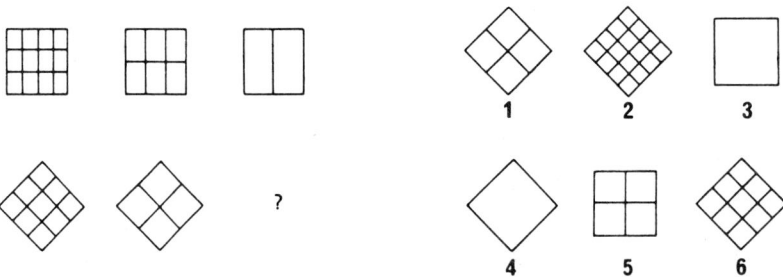

[Eysenck and Kamin, *The Intelligence Controversy*]

Select the word that is different from the other three words.
A. peregrination B. pilgrimage C. outlandish D. promenade

[Arthur Whimbey, *Intelligence Can Be Taught*]

If the circle below is taller than the square and the cross is shorter than the square put a *K* in the circle. However, if this is not the case, put a *C* in the second tallest figure.

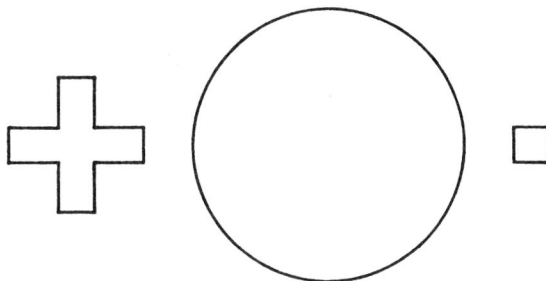

[Arthur Whimbey, *Intelligence Can Be Taught*]

Hospital is to *Sickness* as _____ is to _____ .
A. Patient-Disease   B. Jail-Prisoner   C. Doctor-Patient
D. School-Ignorance   E. Nurse-Illness

[Arthur Whimbey, *Intelligence Can Be Taught*]

Picture completion: What part is missing from this picture?

[Spencer Rathus, *Psychology*]

Picture arrangement: These pictures tell a story, but they are in the wrong order. Put them in the right order so that they tell a story.

[Spencer Rathus, *Psychology*]

Complete:

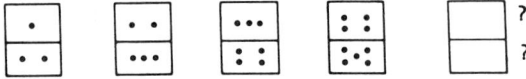

[Eysenck and Kamin, *The Intelligence Controversy*]

Show me the man you honor. I know by that symptom, better than any other, what you are yourself.—Carlyle

Select the alternative that is most nearly equivalent in meaning.
A. The works of great scholars should be read and studied.
B. A man can be judged by his works.
C. A man can be judged by those he emulates.
D. Each human being has his own unique worth.

[Arthur Whimbey, *Intelligence Can Be Taught*]

Which is least like the others?
   a. iron
   b. oxygen
   c. gold
   d. salt
   e. nitrogen

[Gail K. Gaines, *Brain Power*]

WAYS TO INCREASE YOUR I.Q. SCORE

1. Assume for a moment that it is possible to increase a person's I.Q. score. What kinds of activities do you think would help to raise that score?

_____

_____

_____

_____

_____

_____

_____

One experiment divided 40 children from extremely disadvantaged (slum) families into two groups. Children in the control group received no extra attention or training. Beginning shortly after birth, the experimental group was given a wide variety of stimulation to develop perceptual, motor, and language abilities. At age two the children were placed in small classes with other children and several teachers. Each child received lots of teacher attention and exposure to a broad range of topics and thinking exercises. When tested at age $5\frac{1}{2}$ the average IQ for the control group was about 95; the average for the experimentals was 124. . . . These results should be encouraging to everyone interested in the fulfillment of human potentials.

[Dennis Coon, *Introduction to Psychology*]

2. What factors caused the experimental group to achieve a higher I.Q. score at the end of this study?

_____

_____

_____

_____

3. Were there any similarities between your ideas in question 1 about how to increase I.Q. and the experimental techniques described?

_____

HOW TO TAKE TESTS

It has been shown that simply knowing how to take a test will help a student increase his/her score. There are commercial "cram" courses offered throughout the country to help students prepare for such tests as the SAT, the GRE, law exams, and so on. Even the authors of these tests have acknowledged the efficacy of these courses.

When taking a multiple-choice or short-answer test, the following suggestions will prove helpful to you.

1. Be aware of the time alloted for each part of the test.
2. Answer all the questions which are easy for you first.
3. In the time you have left, go back and answer those questions you are unsure of.
4. Eliminate those possibilities which make no sense, and then guess from the remaining choices.

5. Unless you're told that you will lose credit for wrong answers, don't leave any questions unanswered.
6. Statements which use absolute words like *always, never, all,* and *none* are not good choices when you are guessing. A better choice would be statements using such general words as *sometimes, usually, often,* and *most.*

WHAT I.Q. SCORES PREDICT

Schools, the military services, and industry frequently administer I.Q. tests. What might be the reasons why these institutions want to know the I.Q.'s of the people they test?

_____

_____

_____

_____

_____

_____

_____

_____

_____

_____

I.Q. tests have been seen to be pretty good predictors of how well a student will do in school, and how long he or she will stay in school. But one can hardly be surprised since from the very beginning the tests were validated by school success. That is, tests which seemed to pick out good students were considered good tests, and those that did not were dropped. But are I.Q. tests useful for predicting anything else—for example, success in later life?

The answer to that question is apparently not. Christopher Jencks of Harvard and a group of his associates surveyed most of the available information about intelligence testing, education, and social and economic status in America. The results were published in *Inequality: A Reassessment of the Effect of Family and Schooling in America.* Jencks's unexpected conclusion was: "Scores in the tests show remarkably little relation to performance in most adult roles. People with high scores do a little better in most jobs than people with low scores, and they earn somewhat more money, but the differences are surprisingly small." . . .

There have been more than a hundred studies of the relationship between I.Q. and people's performance on different jobs, using a wide variety of techniques for rating performance.

[Daniel Cohen, *Intelligence—What is It?*]

One study conducted by a psychologist to show this relationship follows.

I took the top eight students in a class in the late 1940s at Wesleyan University, where I was teaching—all straight A students—and contrasted what they were doing in the early 1960s with what eight really poor students were doing—all of whom were getting barely passing averages in college (C– or below). To my great surprise, I could not distinguish the two lists of men 15-18 years later. There were lawyers, doctors, research scientists, and college and high school teachers in both groups. The only difference I noted was that those with better grades got into better law or medical schools, but even with this supposed advantage they did not have notably more successful careers as compared with the poorer students who had had to be satisfied with second-rate law and medical schools at the outset. Doubtless the C– students could not get into even second-rate law and medical schools under the stricter admissions testing standards of today. Is that an advantage for society?

[David C. McClelland]

Why, then, do some people succeed and others fail? Jencks and his associates can offer no easy answers to such a question. The social and economic background of an individual seems to count about as much as his I.Q. score. Beyond that, a wide variety of skills exist that have no relationship to I.Q. "The ability to hit a ball thrown at high speed is extremely valuable, if you happen to be a professional baseball player," Jencks notes.

The ability to understand what your boss wants, or to get your subordinates to understand what you want, is an ability that can be at a great premium in a large organization, yet it is not necessarily related to I.Q. Other personal traits, like the ability to inspire trust and confidence, and just plain being likable, are also assets in employment and personal life that have little or nothing to do with I.Q.

Then there is luck. "America," says Jencks, "is full of gamblers, some of whom strike it rich while others lose hard-earned assets. One man's farm has oil on it, while another man's cattle get hoof-and-mouth disease."

There is an old American saying: "If you're so smart why ain't you rich?" The answer seems to be that "smartness," at least as measured by I.Q. tests, has very little to do with getting rich.

[Daniel Cohen, *Intelligence—What is It?*]

1. What is the main idea of the selection you just read?

2. What arguments does Jencks use to support his point of view?

_____

_____

_____

_____

_____

Lewis Terman, of Stanford University, conducted a study similar to the one previously described, with very different results.

> Terman found that for the most part these high-I.Q. children in later adulthood markedly excelled the general population on every indicator of achievement that was examined: a higher level of education completed; more scholastic honors and awards; higher occupational status; higher income; production of more articles, books, patents, and other signs of creativity; more entries in *Who's Who*; a lower mortality rate; better physical and mental health: and a lower divorce rate.... Findings such as these establish beyond a doubt that I.Q. tests measure characteristics that are obviously of considerable importance in our present technological society. To say that the kind of ability measured by intelligence tests is irrelevant or unimportant would be tantamount to repudiating civilization as we know it.

> [David C. McClelland]

3. What is the author's main idea?

_____

_____

_____

In Your Opinion

Do you agree with the position advanced by Christopher Jencks or Lewis Terman? Why?

_____

_____

_____

_____

_____

_____

_____

_____

Following is a list of professions. Check those you think require a high I.Q. score in order to perform that job well.

What Other Factors Are Important in Order to Perform These Jobs Well?

_____ 1. pilot   _____

_____ 2. plumber   _____

_____ 3. cashier   _____

_____ 4. lawyer   _____

_____ 5. policeman   _____

_____ 6. baker   _____

_____ 7. assembly-line worker   _____

_____ 8. computer programmer   _____

_____ 9. elementary
            schoolteacher   _____

_____ 10. engineer   _____

The following excerpt describes one point of view about the use of the I.Q. test as job predictors.

Suppose you are a (black) ghetto resident in the Roxbury section of Boston. To qualify for being a policeman you have to take a three-hour-long general intelligence test in which you must know the meaning of words like "quell," "pyromaniac," and "lexicon." If you do not know enough of those words or cannot play analogy games with them, you do not qualify and must be satisfied with some such job as being a janitor for which an intelligence test is not required yet by the Massachusetts Civil Service Commission. You, not unreasonably, feel angry, upset, and unsuccessful. Because you do not know those words, you are considered to have low intelligence, and since you consequently have to take a low-status job and are unhappy, you contribute to the celebrated correlations of low intelligence with low occupational status and poor adjustment. Psychologists should be ashamed of themselves for promoting a view of general intelligence that has encouraged such a testing program, particularly when there is no solid evidence that significantly relates performance on this type of intelligence test with performance as a policeman.

[David C. McClelland]

Psychologist Michael Lewis commented: "The function of the I.Q. score is and has always been to help stratify society into a heirarchy."

[Dr. Paul Jacobs, *Up the I.Q.*]

1. How does the incident describing the Roxbury policeman contribute to the stratification of society into a hierarchy?

_____

_____

_____

_____

_____

_____

_____

The best testing is criterion sampling. . . . If you want to know how well a person can drive a car (the criterion), sample his ability to do so by giving him a driver's test. Do not give him a paper-and-pencil test for following directions, a general intelligence test, etc. . . . There is ample evidence that tests which sample job skills will predict proficiency on the job.

[David C. McCleland]

2. Using the information in the preceding paragraph, define "criterion."

_____

_____

_____

_____

3. What is the dictionary definition of "criterion"?

_____

_____

_____

Academic skill tests are successful precisely because they involve criterion sampling for the most part. . . . The Scholastic Aptitude Test taps skills that the teacher is looking for and will give high grades for. No one could object if it had been recognized widely that this was *all* that was going on when aptitude tests were used to predict who would do well in school. Trouble started only when people assumed that these skills had some more general validity, as implied in the use of words like "intelligence." Yet even a little criterion analysis would show that there are almost no occupations or life situations that require a person to do word analogies, choose the most correct of four alternative meanings of a word, etc.

[David C. McClelland]

4. According to the author, what was the original purpose of academic skills tests?

_____

_____

_____

5. In what ways are these tests used incorrectly?

_____

_____

_____

Criterion sampling means that testers have got to get out of their offices where they play endless word and paper-and-pencil games and into the field where they actually analyze performance into its components. If you want to test who will be a good policeman, go find out what a policeman does. Follow him around, make a list of his activities, and sample from that list in screening applicants. Some of the job sampling will have to be based on theory as well as practice. If policemen generally discriminate against blacks, that is clearly not part of the criterion because the law says that they must not. So include a test which shows the applicant does not discriminate. Also sample the vocabulary he must use to communicate with the people he serves since his is a position of interpersonal influence—and not the vocabulary that men who have never been on a police beat think it is proper to know. And do not rely on supervisors' judgments of who are the better policemen because that is not, strictly speaking, job analysis but analysis of what people think involves better performance. [Researchers have] found that black policemen in Chicago who were rated high by their superiors scored high on the Deference scale of the Edwards Personal Preference Test. No such relationship appeared for white policemen. In other words, if you wanted to be considered a good cop in Chicago and you were black, you had to at least talk as if you were deferent to the white power system. Any psychologist who used this finding to pick black policemen would be guilty of improper job analysis, to put it as mildly as possible.

[David C. McClelland]

6. Why does the author believe that supervisors' judgments of employees are unreliable?

_____

_____

_____

7. What is the meaning of "deference"?

_____

_____

_____

Criterion sampling, in short, involves both theory and practice. It requires real sophistication. Early testers knew how to do it better than later testers because they had not become so caught up in the ingrown world of intelligence tests that simply were validated against each other. Testers of the future must re-learn how to do criterion sampling. If someone wants to know who will make a good teacher, they will have to get videotapes of classrooms . . . and find out how the behaviors of good and poor teachers differ. To pick future businessmen, research scientists, political leaders, prospects for a happy marriage, they will have to make careful behavioral analyses of these outcomes and then find ways of sampling the adaptive behavior in advance. The task will not be easy. It will require new psychological skills not ordinarily in the repertoire of the traditional tester. What is called for is nothing less than a revision of the role itself—moving it away from word games and statistics toward behavioral analysis.

[David C. McClelland]

In Your Opinion

If you wanted to find out who would make a good teacher, what kinds of behavior would you study? How would you test for those behaviors?

_____

_____

_____

_____

_____

_____

Think about the career you would like to pursue. If you were going to be evaluated as to the qualities necessary for that career, what should you be tested for?

_____

_____

_____

_____

_____

_____

_____

_____

The application of the preceding discussions to your personal understanding of intelligence can be summarized in this way: Intelligence tests are a two-edged sword. We have learned much from their use, yet they have the potential to do great harm. In the final analysis, it is important to remember that creativity, motivation, physical health, mechanical aptitude, artistic ability, and numerous other qualities not measured by intelligence tests contribute to the achievement of life goals. Also remember that *I.Q.* is *not intelligence*. I.Q. is an *index* of intelligence (as defined by a particular test). Change the test and you change the score. An I.Q. is not some permanent number stamped on the forehead of a child that forever determines potential.

[Dennis Coon, *Introduction to Psychology*]

In this chapter you have learned how best to research a topic in the library. You are now familiar with:

1. The card catalog.
2. Various dictionaries.
3. Encyclopedias.
4. The Reader's Guide to Periodical Literature.

If you have made a friend of the librarian, you have a good friend, indeed!

You have also learned some organizational techniques to help you in using the materials found in the library when writing a research paper. These include:

1. The use of 3 X 5 index cards for "chunking" information.
2. Keeping track of sources—author, titles of books, page numbers, and direct quotations.

In addition, you have studied several important test-taking techniques. Use them and watch your test scores improve.

A Further Reading

INTELLIGENCE–WHAT IS IT?

The most important figure in the modern study of the development of thinking is undoubtedly the Swiss psychologist Jean Piaget. Piaget's scientific background is a bit unusual. As a student in Switzerland he did most of his work with snails and other mollusks, but by the time he came to Paris to study at the Sorbonne, he had given up mollusks for child psychology.

Shortly after coming to Paris Piaget began working in a laboratory attached to a public school. His main task was to translate and standardize certain English psychological tests for use in French schools, not a very exciting job. Piaget, however, began to approach the work from a unique angle. Instead of merely tabulating right and wrong answers on the tests, he tried to find out how and why a child arrived at an answer, particularly a wrong answer. Wrote Piaget: "I continued for about two years to analyze verbal reasoning of normal children by presenting them with various questions and exposing them to tasks involving simple concrete relations of cause and effect. . . . At last I had found my field of research."

Piaget's research got him an appointment to the J. J. Rousseau Institute in Geneva, Switzerland. He had originally intended to stay just a few years, but he stayed for more than fifty, until his retirement a few years ago at the age of seventy-five. During that period he acquired a worldwide reputation and is regarded as the founder of an entirely new school of child psychology.

Piaget has often described himself as a compulsive worker. In over half a century he has produced a staggering number of papers, books, and research reports. His students have added their own writings to the already huge body of Piagetian doctrine which grows impressively year after year. It would be a hopeless task to try to summarize all the work and theories here, but we can give a picture of the approach that Piaget and his followers take toward the subject of intelligence and how it should be examined.

Like Binet, Piaget did much of his early work with his own children. When his daughter Jacqueline was seven months old, Piaget watched her play with a toy duck. When the duck slipped under the covers and out of sight, the baby seemed to lose interest in it—she did not try to look for it. If she could not see it, apparently it did not exist for her. Piaget put the duck near his daughter's hand and, when she tried to grab for it, he covered it with a sheet. She took back her hand and immediately gave up looking for the toy. It had ceased to exist.

Piaget's conclusion from repeated observations of this type was that for children only a few months of age objects were not yet permanent. The infant's world consists of things which appear and disappear—but lack an independent existence. Just discovering that objects continue to exist even when out of sight marks an important early stage in the development of thinking, say Piaget.

He recorded a further development when he tested his son Laurent at the age of nine months. Laurent was interested in a watch and the psychologist hid it under a cover on one side of the baby. Laurent watched his father, lifted the cover, and grabbed the watch. The next time Piaget hid the watch on the other side, but Laurent continued to look for it in the place where he had successfully found it the first time, though he had clearly seen his father hide it in a different place. A few months later, however, Laurent would always find the object in the place where he had seen it disappear.

Piaget labels the first two years of a child's life as the sensory-motor phase. The infant develops from living in a world of shifting and impermanent objects into a world where objects persist even when out of sight and where effect follows cause.

During the next period of development the child's world becomes more concrete and less self-centered. This period runs from about the age of two to the age of four or five. In these years the child realizes, for example, that the moon does not really follow him down the street, and that a person who stands on another side of an object from where he is standing may have an entirely different view of that object.

Piaget has charted the development of a child's thinking in a number of different areas. He is best known for his work in the development of the concept of numbers. The fundamental thing that a child must learn about numbers is that the basic amount doesn't change just because its appearance has been altered—something must be added to it or taken away from it This seem obvious to us but it is not at all obvious to a four-year-old child.

One of Piaget's most famous and frequently repeated exercises explores this concept. The child is shown two identical glasses, each filled with the same amount of colored liquid. The contents of one of the glasses is then poured into a thinner but taller glass, where the level of the liquid reaches higher than it did in the original container. When children below the age of about seven or eight were asked which of the two glasses—the short, fat one or the tall, thin one—contained more liquid, they would almost invariably reply that the tall, thin one did. Their reason was that the level of liquid in the glass was higher. The same children also thought that there was more total liquid when the contents of the original container was poured into three smaller containers. But by the time these children reached the age of eight, they gave the correct answer, pointing out that the quantity had not been changed: "It's only been poured out."

As a check on the liquid experiment, Piaget tried a similar one with beads. The experimenter began putting beads into one vessel, and the child put the same number of beads into a different shaped vessel. Despite the fact that the child and the experimenter counted out exactly the same number of beads, when asked which of the containers held more beads, a four- or five-year-old would point to the one with the highest level of beads. Only later does the concept of a stable number exist in the child's mind, even though he may be able to count very well.

The idea of giving "wrong" or "stupid" answers does not exist in Piagetian testing. The aim of the test is not a score, but an understanding of the thinking process. Piaget reported the following encounter with a girl named Ric, who was five years and eleven months old. He showed her a picture of flowers, most of them poppies, but a few bluebells. "Look at these poppies and these bluebells. If I take all the flowers, or if I take the poppies, which will be the biggest bunch?"

"The bunch of poppies, because there are more," she answered. This answer certainly was wrong, and by adult logic quite "stupid." But Piaget wanted to know why this particular kind of answer had been given.

He determined that Ric knew what poppies were and what flowers were. Yet when he asked again: "Then which bunch will be bigger—the one with the flowers or the one with the poppies?" she again answered: "The one with the poppies."

Other children the same age as Ric gave similarly "illogical" answers to the same sort of questions. Piaget believes that at a certain state of development a child cannot think about the whole and the parts at the same time. When Ric thought about one she forgot about the other. Asked to compare the poppies with something, since the whole was gone, she compared them with the only thing left, the bluebells, and obviously there were more poppies.

Very young children, Piaget found, also have no notion of length. He tested them by showing them a straight ruler, and a wavy plastic "snake," the two ends of which were in line with the ends of the ruler. A child would be asked which was longer, and the usual response for a four- or five-year-old would be "the same." Then the child would be asked to trace the straight ruler and the twists and turns of the "snake" with his finger. The snake was even straightened out. But as soon as it was allowed to snap back to its wavy shape and laid out next to the ruler, the child would again assert that the two were the same length, and nothing could shake this belief. By the age of seven, however, the child is able to straighten the snake out in his mind and give the correct answer.

The concept of speed is also different for children under the age of about six than it is for adults. In a test two dolls were passed through two tunnels of different length. They entered the tunnels and arrived at the end at exactly the same moment, but if a five-year-old is asked which is faster, he will reply that their speed is the same because they got out of the tunnels at the same time. Even if he has actually watched one of the dolls moving more quickly through the tunnel that the other, the fact that they both arrived at the end at the same moment is the most important thing to him. As far as he is concerned that means that both of the dolls are moving equally fast.

Piaget himself has never claimed that his methods can be used as an alternative I.Q. test. He used his tests only in order to develop a theory of the various stages in the development of learning. But his admirers (and they are increasing among the ranks of educational psychologists) believe that his methods will ultimately provide an entirely new and more useful form of mental testing and a new mental scale.

[Daniel Cohen]

Suggested Readings

Dale, Arbie M., with Leida Snow, *Twenty Minutes a Day to a More Powerful Intelligence*. New York: A Playboy Press Book, 1976.

An easy to understand program which demonstrates how to improve reading skills, enlarge vocabulary, train memory, solve problems, etc.

Fine, Benjamin. *The Stranglehold of the I.Q.* New York: Doubleday and Co., Inc., 1975.

A critique of the current uses of the I.Q. tests.

Jacobs, Paul I. *Up the I.Q.* New York: Wyden Books, 1977.

How to increase a child's intelligence—not just I.Q. scores.

Jensen, Arthur R. *Straight Talk About Mental Tests*. New York: The Free Press, a division of Macmillan Publishing Co., 1981.

What do mental tests measure? How accurate are they? What do they predict? Are they biased in favor of middle-class whites? This book attempts to answer these and other important questions.

Keyes, Daniel. *Flowers for Algernon*. New York: Harcourt Brace Javonovich, 1966.

A fictional account of the successes and failures of a radical procedure to improve the I.Q. of a mentally retarded man.

Loehlin, John C., et al. *Race Differences in Intelligence*. San Francisco: Freeman, 1975.

A clear discussion of race and class differences in I.Q. The authors reject the view that these differences are genetically determined and present evidence to support their conclusions.

Mayerson, Evelyn. *Sanjo*. New York: Lippincott, 1979.

A psychiatrist has written this story of a 34-year old woman whose mind has remained at child level due to Down's syndrome. She confronts her overly protective family and her ignorant neighbors to eventually discover a life on her own terms.

Montagu, Ashley. *On Being Intelligent*. New York: Henry Schuman, 1951.

Professor Montagu believes that when an individual develops an intelligent approach to others, he acquires the means for an intelligent approach to himself. This book promises to develop skills and help you live intelligently.

Sharp, Evelyn. *The I.Q. Cult*, New York: Coward, McCann and Goeghegan, 1972.

A highly critical look at I.Q. testing and an exciting preview of the alternatives.

VOCABULARY SHEET   Name _____

1. Word _____

   Definition _____

   _____

2. Word _____

   Definition _____

   _____

3. Word _____

   Definition _____

   _____

4. Word _____

   Definition _____

   _____

5. Word _____

   Definition _____

   _____

6. Word _____

   Definition _____

   _____

7. Word _____

   Definition _____

   _____

8. Word _____

   Definition _____

   _____

9. Word _____

   Definition _____

   _____

10. Word _____

    Definition _____

    _____

11. Word _____

    Definition _____

    _____

12. Word _____

    Definition _____

    _____

13. Word _____

    Definition _____

    _____

14. Word _____

    Definition _____

    _____

15. Word _____

    Definition _____

    _____

VOCABULARY SHEET

Name _____

1. Word _____

   Definition _____

   _____

2. Word _____

   Definition _____

   _____

3. Word _____

   Definition _____

   _____

4. Word _____

   Definition _____

   _____

5. Word _____

   Definition _____

   _____

6. Word _____

   Definition _____

   _____

7. Word _____

   Definition _____

   _____

8. Word _____

   Definition _____

   _____

9. Word _____

   Definition _____

   _____

10. Word _____

    Definition _____

    _____

11. Word _____

    Definition _____

    _____

12. Word _____

    Definition _____

    _____

13. Word _____

    Definition _____

    _____

14. Word _____

    Definition _____

    _____

15. Word _____

    Definition _____

    _____

VOCABULARY SHEET   Name _____

1. Word _____

   Definition _____

   _____

2. Word _____

   Definition _____

   _____

3. Word _____

   Definition _____

   _____

4. Word _____

   Definition _____

   _____

5. Word _____

   Definition _____

   _____

6. Word _____

   Definition _____

   _____

7. Word _____

   Definition _____

   _____

8. Word _____

   Definition _____

   _____

9. Word _____

   Definition _____

   _____

10. Word _____

    Definition _____

    _____

11. Word _____

    Definition _____

    _____

12. Word _____

    Definition _____

    _____

13. Word _____

    Definition _____

    _____

14. Word _____

    Definition _____

    _____

15. Word _____

    Definition _____

    _____

VOCABULARY SHEET   Name _____

1. Word _____

   Definition _____

   _____

2. Word _____

   Definition _____

   _____

3. Word _____

   Definition _____

   _____

4. Word _____

   Definition _____

   _____

5. Word _____

   Definition _____

   _____

6. Word _____

   Definition _____

   _____

7. Word _____

   Definition _____

   _____

8. Word _____

   Definition _____

   _____

9. Word _____

   Definition _____

   _____

10. Word _____

    Definition _____

    _____

11. Word _____

    Definition _____

    _____

12. Word _____

    Definition _____

    _____

13. Word _____

    Definition _____

    _____

14. Word _____

    Definition _____

    _____

15. Word _____

    Definition _____

    _____

VOCABULARY SHEET   Name _____

1. Word _____

   Definition _____

   _____

2. Word _____

   Definition _____

   _____

3. Word _____

   Definition _____

   _____

4. Word _____

   Definition _____

   _____

5. Word _____

   Definition _____

   _____

6. Word _____

   Definition _____

   _____

7. Word _____

   Definition _____

   _____

8. Word _____

   Definition _____

   _____

9. Word _____

   Definition _____

   _____

10. Word _____

    Definition _____

    _____

11. Word _____

    Definition _____

    _____

12. Word _____

    Definition _____

    _____

13. Word _____

    Definition _____

    _____

14. Word _____

    Definition _____

    _____

15. Word _____

    Definition _____

    _____

VOCABULARY SHEET

Name _____

1. Word _____

   Definition _____

   _____

2. Word _____

   Definition _____

   _____

3. Word _____

   Definition _____

   _____

4. Word _____

   Definition _____

   _____

5. Word _____

   Definition _____

   _____

6. Word _____

   Definition _____

   _____

7. Word _____

   Definition _____

   _____

8. Word _____

Definition _____

_____

9. Word _____

Definition _____

_____

10. Word _____

Definition _____

_____

11. Word _____

Definition _____

_____

12. Word _____

Definition _____

_____

13. Word _____

Definition _____

_____

14. Word _____

Definition _____

_____

15. Word _____

Definition _____

_____

VOCABULARY SHEET   Name _____

1. Word _____

   Definition _____

   _____

2. Word _____

   Definition _____

   _____

3. Word _____

   Definition _____

   _____

4. Word _____

   Definition _____

   _____

5. Word _____

   Definition _____

   _____

6. Word _____

   Definition _____

   _____

7. Word _____

   Definition _____

   _____

8. Word _____

   Definition _____

   _____

9. Word _____

   Definition _____

   _____

10. Word _____

    Definition _____

    _____

11. Word _____

    Definition _____

    _____

12. Word _____

    Definition _____

    _____

13. Word _____

    Definition _____

    _____

14. Word _____

    Definition _____

    _____

15. Word _____

    Definition _____

    _____

VOCABULARY SHEET   Name _____

1. Word _____

   Definition _____

   _____

2. Word _____

   Definition _____

   _____

3. Word _____

   Definition _____

   _____

4. Word _____

   Definition _____

   _____

5. Word _____

   Definition _____

   _____

6. Word _____

   Definition _____

   _____

7. Word _____

   Definition _____

   _____

8. Word _____

   Definition _____

   _____

9. Word _____

   Definition _____

   _____

10. Word _____

   Definition _____

   _____

11. Word _____

   Definition _____

   _____

12. Word _____

   Definition _____

   _____

13. Word _____

   Definition _____

   _____

14. Word _____

   Definition _____

   _____

15. Word _____

   Definition _____

   _____

VOCABULARY SHEET   Name _____

1. Word _____

   Definition _____

   _____

2. Word _____

   Definition _____

   _____

3. Word _____

   Definition _____

   _____

4. Word _____

   Definition _____

   _____

5. Word _____

   Definition _____

   _____

6. Word _____

   Definition _____

   _____

7. Word _____

   Definition _____

   _____

8. Word _____

   Definition _____

   _____

9. Word _____

   Definition _____

   _____

10. Word _____

    Definition _____

    _____

11. Word _____

    Definition _____

    _____

12. Word _____

    Definition _____

    _____

13. Word _____

    Definition _____

    _____

14. Word _____

    Definition _____

    _____

15. Word _____

    Definition _____

    _____

VOCABULARY SHEET   Name _____

1. Word _____

   Definition _____

   _____

2. Word _____

   Definition _____

   _____

3. Word _____

   Definition _____

   _____

4. Word _____

   Definition _____

   _____

5. Word _____

   Definition _____

   _____

6. Word _____

   Definition _____

   _____

7. Word _____

   Definition _____

   _____

8. Word _____

   Definition _____

   _____

9. Word _____

   Definition _____

   _____

10. Word _____

    Definition _____

    _____

11. Word _____

    Definition _____

    _____

12. Word _____

    Definition _____

    _____

13. Word _____

    Definition _____

    _____

14. Word _____

    Definition _____

    _____

15. Word _____

    Definition _____

    _____

VOCABULARY SHEET

Name _____

1. Word _____

   Definition _____

   _____

2. Word _____

   Definition _____

   _____

3. Word _____

   Definition _____

   _____

4. Word _____

   Definition _____

   _____

5. Word _____

   Definition _____

   _____

6. Word _____

   Definition _____

   _____

7. Word _____

   Definition _____

   _____

8. Word _____

   Definition _____

   _____

9. Word _____

   Definition _____

   _____

10. Word _____

    Definition _____

    _____

11. Word _____

    Definition _____

    _____

12. Word _____

    Definition _____

    _____

13. Word _____

    Definition _____

    _____

14. Word _____

    Definition _____

    _____

15. Word _____

    Definition _____

    _____

VOCABULARY SHEET   Name _____

1. Word _____

   Definition _____

   _____

2. Word _____

   Definition _____

   _____

3. Word _____

   Definition _____

   _____

4. Word _____

   Definition _____

   _____

5. Word _____

   Definition _____

   _____

6. Word _____

   Definition _____

   _____

7. Word _____

   Definition _____

   _____

8. Word _____

   Definition _____

   _____

9. Word _____

   Definition _____

   _____

10. Word _____

    Definition _____

    _____

11. Word _____

    Definition _____

    _____

12. Word _____

    Definition _____

    _____

13. Word _____

    Definition _____

    _____

14. Word _____

    Definition _____

    _____

15. Word _____

    Definition _____

    _____

VOCABULARY SHEET   Name _____

1. Word _____

   Definition _____

   _____

2. Word _____

   Definition _____

   _____

3. Word _____

   Definition _____

   _____

4. Word _____

   Definition _____

   _____

5. Word _____

   Definition _____

   _____

6. Word _____

   Definition _____

   _____

7. Word _____

   Definition _____

   _____

8. Word _____

 Definition _____

 _____

9. Word _____

 Definition _____

 _____

10. Word _____

 Definition _____

 _____

11. Word _____

 Definition _____

 _____

12. Word _____

 Definition _____

 _____

13. Word _____

 Definition _____

 _____

14. Word _____

 Definition _____

 _____

15. Word _____

 Definition _____

 _____

VOCABULARY SHEET   Name _____

1. Word _____

   Definition _____

   _____

2. Word _____

   Definition _____

   _____

3. Word _____

   Definition _____

   _____

4. Word _____

   Definition _____

   _____

5. Word _____

   Definition _____

   _____

6. Word _____

   Definition _____

   _____

7. Word _____

   Definition _____

   _____

8. Word _____

   Definition _____

   _____

9. Word _____

   Definition _____

   _____

10. Word _____

    Definition _____

    _____

11. Word _____

    Definition _____

    _____

12. Word _____

    Definition _____

    _____

13. Word _____

    Definition _____

    _____

14. Word _____

    Definition _____

    _____

15. Word _____

    Definition _____

    _____

VOCABULARY SHEET   Name _____

1. Word _____

   Definition _____

   _____

2. Word _____

   Definition _____

   _____

3. Word _____

   Definition _____

   _____

4. Word _____

   Definition _____

   _____

5. Word _____

   Definition _____

   _____

6. Word _____

   Definition _____

   _____

7. Word _____

   Definition _____

   _____

8. Word _____

   Definition _____

   _____

9. Word _____

   Definition _____

   _____

10. Word _____

    Definition _____

    _____

11. Word _____

    Definition _____

    _____

12. Word _____

    Definition _____

    _____

13. Word _____

    Definition _____

    _____

14. Word _____

    Definition _____

    _____

15. Word _____

    Definition _____

    _____

VOCABULARY SHEET   Name _____

1. Word _____

   Definition _____

   _____

2. Word _____

   Definition _____

   _____

3. Word _____

   Definition _____

   _____

4. Word _____

   Definition _____

   _____

5. Word _____

   Definition _____

   _____

6. Word _____

   Definition _____

   _____

7. Word _____

   Definition _____

   _____

8. Word _____

   Definition _____

   _____

9. Word _____

   Definition _____

   _____

10. Word _____

    Definition _____

    _____

11. Word _____

    Definition _____

    _____

12. Word _____

    Definition _____

    _____

13. Word _____

    Definition _____

    _____

14. Word _____

    Definition _____

    _____

15. Word _____

    Definition _____

    _____